Harry McShane
No Mean Fighter

Harry McShane
and Joan Smith

HARRY McSHANE
No Mean Fighter

Pluto Press

First published 1978 by Pluto Press Limited
Unit 10 Spencer Court, 7 Chalcot Road, London NW1 8LH

Copyright © Pluto Press 1978

ISBN 0 904383 24 5 paper
    0 904383 29 6 cloth

Cover designed by Tom Sullivan
Front cover photograph by Robert Golden

Typeset by Red Lion Setters, Holborn, London
Printed in Great Britain by Robert MacLehose & Co Ltd
Printers to the University of Glasgow

Contents

Acknowledgments

Thanks are due to Paul Foot for first suggesting the idea of putting Harry McShane's life story on tape; to Richard Kuper and the infant Pluto Press for paying out £30 in good money for a cassette tape-recorder and for not hounding me as the two years allowed for writing stretched into five; to Jim Higgins for advising on the narrative form of the final book; to Laurie Flynn for advice in the closing stages of the book, and to Vincent Flynn for its title; to Vaila Wishart for transcribing my poorly recorded tapes and to Robert Barltrop who proved a knowledgeable and sympathetic editor; above all to Alan and Lesley Fowler for reading all three drafts of the book and making invaluable suggestions for each.

It is normal to acknowledge the 'wife's' help in writing a book, if only for her work behind the scenes. For years, countless academics have used their wives and secretaries as unpaid research assistants. As a woman, I have no 'wife'! But encouragement to complete the book came from many people in Glasgow and, in recent years, from the many unemployed workers who met Harry on demonstrations organised by the Right to Work Campaign.

Finally, thanks are due to Jeannie and Willie McShane who welcomed me in their home with great kindness every Tuesday afternoon for two years.

Joan Smith
London, September 1977

Introduction

Harry McShane's story is not an ordinary autobiography. It is history scooped out of the movement by a man who is still fighting to this day for the full-blooded socialism he has always believed in, a man who came through great struggles as well as great setbacks and who wants people to know the truth about them.

Harry was born in 1891. His insights into the working-class struggles of our time challenge many assumptions and arguments found in the histories. For Harry, the vital struggle during the first world war in Glasgow was not the Shop Stewards' Movement but John Maclean's anti-war campaign. For Harry, the tactical and strategic weakness of the early Communist Party in 1920-22 led him to support John Maclean's group, the 'Tramp Trust Unlimited'. For Harry, one of the most important issues facing the British working class has always been the question of Ireland, but it was through the unemployed movement that he joined the early Communist Party in 1922.

His own background marks him off from many of those who have written about this period. He was a skilled engineer like many another; but unlike many he was amongst the first generation of catholics to gain an apprenticeship. Harry's early history - as a catholic boy in Glasgow - is very different from Willie Gallacher's protestant upbringing in Paisley. His view of the Clyde Workers' Committee - the skilled engineers with their bowler hats and rolled umbrellas - is very different from that of Gallacher. But Harry was also a shop steward and extremely proud of his own craft skill.

McShane's training was in debating: catholic versus protestant, arguing with the freethinkers, agonising over the most crucial question of all - could a good catholic be a socialist? This training stood him in good stead during the political battles that lay ahead. It encouraged him to *read* marxism and all his life he could distinguish the real from the phoney: the John Macleans and Wal Hanningtons from the rest.

Above all, the training in street-corner meetings and outdoor agitation meant that Harry's talents were directed towards creating the movement of the unemployed that was so special to the working class of the 1920s and 1930s. In his own words: 'It became my life's work as a revolutionary.' First with John Maclean in the early twenties, then with Wal Hannington in the twenties and thirties, Harry helped to organise the Glasgow unemployed around countless demonstrations, hunger marches and protests against unemployment. This movement - so different from those of 1889 and 1908 - heralded a new step forward: the creation of a permanent organisation of the unemployed themselves, the National Unemployed Workers' Movement.

When the Movement was disbanded on the eve of the second world war Harry McShane went to work on the Scottish edition of the *Daily Worker*. He remained a communist journalist for most of the next ten years. But at the age of sixty his differences with the Communist Party became so great that he resigned, returning to work as an engineer in a Glasgow shipyard. Remaining a marxist, he re-worked his entire political philosophy over the following six years, and now speaks on marxism throughout Britain.

Harry's life story is in very many ways unique in British history. It is not the story of a career in the labour movement - he was a rank-and-file leader who never left the rank and file. It is not the story of a man who remained faithful to one socialist party, so he does not have to protect any reputations. Nor is it the story of the 'perfect' professional revolutionary - when times were hard he travelled England and Canada looking for work. It is the story of a man who did his best political work in his home town, Glasgow, among the unemployed: a Scottish revolutionary with a reputation throughout the socialist movement in Scotland and England; an organiser who could lead masses.

Harry McShane is a man who has always been repelled by the idea of some self-centred 'autobiography'. His lifelong concern has been to make the philosophy of marxism live in the self-activity of the working class. That, really, is what this book is about. And that is why Harry McShane has put so many hours into the making of this book by talking into a tape-recorder over three years.

Joan Smith

1. Glasgow in the 1900s

My father was a catholic and my mother a protestant. They met and married while they were working in a fish-hook factory in Kingston, Glasgow. My father's family were Irish catholics; both his parents came from County Tyrone. My mother's name was Janet Sanson and her family were Scots, obviously of French descent, and originally from Edinburgh. After their marriage my parents lived in a two-roomed house, the top flat of a tenement in Govan Street, Glasgow. I was born there, the eldest of the family, on 7 May 1891.

Mixed marriages were denounced bitterly in those days, by both catholics and protestants. In Glasgow the catholic was looked upon with only a degree less hatred than in Belfast at the present. When I was a few months old my parents separated, and my father took me to live with his family. The differences were over status as well as religion. My father and his father were builders' labourers. My mother's father, Tom Sanson, was a blacksmith and a member of the Church of Scotland. He was fired by John Knox and was very anti-catholic.

It wasn't long before my father and mother got back together - my sister was only a year younger than me - and they never separated again. There were another ten children that came after me, eight boys and two girls. But I didn't go back home with my father; I stayed with my grandparents and I never saw much of my mother, though my father came regularly to the house and I went out with him a lot.

I was named Harry after my grandfather - my father's name was John. My grandfather was a well-respected man. He had a beard and was always decently dressed in a blue suit. He set his watch every Sunday night by the Edwards clock on Buchanan Street so he would rise in good time for work in the morning; he never missed a minute of work and I never remember him being sick. He made me behave myself, but he couldn't have the kind of influence on me that my father had because neither he nor my grandmother could read or write.

Grandfather worked in a local builder's yard, in Gloucester Street, and from there he was sent out on various little jobs. For a while he worked with the mason - in those days the stone-masons worked by hand with a hammer and chisel. I loved to go to the yard and watch the men while I played, and it was there that I got a thirst for work. My father worked with Currie's at a place in Wallace Street. He was a handy-man, a step up from labouring. He did a lot of drainage work and repair work on trams and was in fairly constant employment most of his life, though he had a spell of unemployment in 1908. His only trouble was a fondness for beer.

Both my father and my grandfather were early members of the old 'Workers' Union' that got merged into the Transport and General Workers' Union (TGWU) after the first world war. A man named Finlay used to come and collect my grandfather's dues but my father went into the office in Hope Street to pay. Often I went with him. George Kerr was the organiser of the Workers' Union (although he didn't become a paid full-time organiser until later, 1911) and was one of the early secretaries of the Scottish Trades Union Congress.

At that time there were very few unions for labourers. The Workers' Union tried to recruit the unskilled men in engineering and in the building trades. It was mainly the building workers that George Kerr was trying to get, but it was very difficult and I don't think they were ever fully organised in Glasgow. Craft unions wouldn't accept labourers, and labourers' unions were weak because the type of work they did made them hard to organise. There were a lot of casual labourers in the building trade, going from job to job like navvies. It was hard work with a pick and shovel. A big number of them were Irish, although some were ordinary unskilled workers who had never learned a trade. In jobs where there was constant employment, like those my father and grandfather worked in, the establishments were usually so small that there was no possibility of strike action. Although my father and grandfather were both very strong for the union, I don't think that either of them was ever on strike in his life.

One of the strange things about the Workers' Union was that a lot of people who were not labourers were involved with it. Charlie Duncan, Tom Mann, Neil Maclean all did meetings for them although they were not unskilled workers themselves. It was like that in the early days of a lot of the labourers' unions: the skilled workers, particularly those who were socialists, helped them to get organised.

My father and my grandfather got 24 shillings a week as labourers. They made another 7 shillings a week working at nights in the music-hall as ticket collectors and chuckers-out. Earning 31 shillings a week wasn't so bad because the skilled men, the engineers, were getting only just over 32 shillings; but the two of them worked very long hours for that money. Work started at six in the morning and my grandfather wouldn't get home until six in the evening. Then he had to change and get across to the music-hall for seven o'clock. He never got in before eleven.

On Saturday nights, when they were paid, my grandmother took me to the music-hall. I knew all the music-hall turns before I went to school - part of my education must have been in the Britannia at Trongate and the Tivoli at Anderson's Cross, where they worked later. My grandfather had a reputation for toughness. One night, to get at someone who was making a row in the gallery, he walked right round the *edge* of the gallery. When he reached the man he grabbed him out of his seat by his face and put him out. My father told me he was ashamed of him that night.

Compulsory education started at six years old, but my grand-parents sent me at five and they sent me in shoes - most of the other children had bare feet. My first day, I saw a teacher hitting a boy's bare leg with a cane. It annoyed me very much; then, to make matters worse, I lost my road home. My grandmother decided not to send me back. My grandparents moved from Gorbals to Tradeston so that I could have a room of my own, and from there I went to another school.

St. Margaret's in Kinning Park is still there, although it has been rebuilt. It was there I got my meagre, catholic education. The school was next door to the church and there was, and still is, a little covered passage between them. It was very convenient for the priests to walk in any time they liked. I hated them coming in. They only came to hit some child for not being at mass. 'Were you at mass yesterday?' 'No' - then bang! - they would slap the child's face. Then they looked round and smiled at everybody else. They were not educa-tionalists, they never tried to be, and I never knew them to impart anything worth a damn. But their presence in the school overawed some of the teachers, especially the women.

The headmaster was a terribly cruel person. He never did anything to me, but I got very angry at the atrocious things he did to other kids. He would take a boy into his room, pull down his trousers and cane him, and then make him march around the school with his trousers at his feet. All the teachers had canes and used them. I had the impression that they didn't want to; but the headmaster was a brute, the worst I ever saw. He was highly respected, a great man in the city. Only in recent years have I learned that he actually owned a public house.

We started school at 9.30 and went on until 4.30. We had to learn the catechism; there was reading, writing, arithmetic and grammar, and an awful lot of religion. Two sisters who taught there were very religious. The headmaster was excellent as a teacher. The strictest man apart from him was the one who taught maths: he had to be strict to teach that subject.

Many of the children went to school bare-footed, without boots or socks. I liked my bare feet but my grandparents were strongly against it and I only sometimes got away with it, in summertime. Many of the poor children had no breakfast before they came to school and they were given a cup of coffee if they paid a halfpenny. My grandparents wouldn't let me have that coffee - they insisted it wasn't for me. I loved coffee, so on the way to school I often went to the coffee shop where it cost a penny.

I had no quarrel with schooling, and my father encouraged me to read. When I was very young I used to read 'bloods', stories about Sweeney Todd and Dick Turpin with people cutting throats and trap-doors and stuff like that. My father stopped it. He said: 'Harry, I wouldn't read that kind of stuff.' I never read another one: that was his influence on me. After that I began to pick up better things off the second-hand book stalls.

There was a string of barrows right along the riverside then, past Stockwell Street, with second-hand tools and books - this was before Barrowland grew up in the East End of Glasgow. I remember picking up two volumes of Macaulay's essays for one-and-eight-pence. That was a lot of money at the time, specially as I was still at school, but I wanted to read Macaulay. He was often quoted in support of the Catholic Church, though he hadn't really defended it. At school I was told that for a knowledge of English I had to read Macaulay's essays and the *Glasgow Herald*.

It was not only my grandparents who couldn't read. In the close where we lived nearly all the catholic folk were elderly and illiterate. In 1910 the Oscar Slater trial was on, and all the Irish people came to our house so that I could read the reports to them. It was the murder of a Glasgow woman, and there was doubt whether Slater had done it or not. Eventually he was sentenced to death, then reprieved and given 20 years. In those days the newspapers gave several pages to a murder charge; the trial lasted quite a while and I had to read the papers out every night.

The tenement where I lived had a ground floor and three storeys above that. Each separate entrance, or close as we called it, had several one-and two-room dwellings on each floor. The toilet at the stairhead of each close served the purposes of three or four families. In the back court of each tenement was a washhouse with a boiler and a place for a fire. The women did their washing in these boilers and it was hard, hard work. There were lots of fights about whose turn it was for the washhouse key, and it was a common topic of jokes at the music-hall.

Here and there in some of the back courts were little workshops. There were two where I lived and one in the next block. They were often owned by blacksmiths who got their living from making sparables (nails) for shoes. All the shoes were nailed in those days and the blacksmith simply put a rod in the fire and knocked off sparables galore. One of my relatives, a temperance socialist, worked as a baker in a back court and did well out of making rolls. In later years when some comrades and I were working late for the movement, we would go and get fresh rolls from him at midnight and take them back to the party rooms to have with some tea - others did the same. You can still see remains of these little buildings in some of the back courts of Glasgow.

Old people had a lot of trouble before the first world war. Old-age pensions started in 1908 and even then amounted to only five bob at seventy. Most people didn't reach that age - they were lucky if they got to fifty. If they were too old or too ill to work they had to go to the parish council. It was always difficult to get anything out of them; the Poor Laws were designed to stop people getting anything. At the most they were given two or three shillings. If you were able-bodied and unemployed, you had to go into the workhouse to get even that for your wife and family.

All the old people in our close depended on the few shillings they had from the parish council and on the help their neighbours gave them. They couldn't get much help from their families because their children were mostly married, had big families and had their own problems. There wasn't the same attachment within families as there is now. But many of the neighbours helped out, even with money occasionally, and we lived pretty well together. There wasn't the crime and vandalism that exists today because nobody wanted to get a 'bad name'. We kept each other in good behaviour but there was an awful lot of poverty.

Food was cheap and it was possible to get through with a few shillings a week. Fish and chips cost twopence, rolls were three a penny, and it was quite common for herring to be sold at three for a penny. Rent was three or four shillings a week and coal eightpence a hundredweight. But if anyone was ill the doctor had to be paid: a doctor's visit cost two shillings and sixpence (half a crown).

We ate a lot of fish, brought round on barrows. Sometimes when I was a child a herd of nanny-goats was brought round and we took our tins out to the street for the milk. We also drank sour milk and put it on our porridge because, at 1½d a pint, it was cheaper than fresh milk. Of course for the elderly it was nearly all they could afford. They didn't get much food and one of their biggest problems was clothing: parish clothing was allowed once in years - 'once in a blue moon'!

Prices kept rising before the first world war, and because of the terrible poverty a lot of people died very young. Those who didn't worked for as long as they could. There was no compulsory retirement then, and even skilled men worked until they were well on in years; my wife's father was a cooper and he was in nearly constant employment until he was seventy. Nobody wanted to go to the parish. The parish councils gave as little as they could in order to force people to go to the churches and get alms. The worst people on the parish council were always the clergymen, and especially the catholic priests.

Thousands of people never went outside Glasgow in their lives. Some of the skilled men got away for a holiday now and again; very rarely you heard of somebody going to Blackpool, or occasionally, Ireland. Sometimes you heard of someone spending the night at Millport. Rothesay was a popular cruise for those who could afford it. On Saturday and Sunday nights there would be a crowd of ships facing the Broomielaw that were going to Rothesay. You could get a cup of tea on the boat, go down and look at the engines, or listen to the band playing. There were always a lot of songs about sailing down the Clyde. Occasionally someone in the workshop would organise a trip - I went when I was an apprentice. The socialist movement also organised trips and I went with them later on.

The New Year and the Glasgow Fair in July were the big holidays in Glasgow. Everybody got ten days off work at each, but as they received no wages it was more like ten days' unemployment. Whisky was three shillings and sixpence a bottle, and nearly everybody drank beer and whisky together. Parents would often, if they could, help out the younger people with some money to let them enjoy themselves and this was particularly true of the Fair holidays.

New Year was the really important holiday in Glasgow. Most people worked over Christmas and Christ wasn't much in the picture - about the only people to celebrate Christmas in Glasgow were the catholics, who went to midnight mass. The kids used to hang their stockings up and get some wee present, something like a stick of rock, but that was all. What money there was bought whisky for New Year's Eve, which people celebrated in their own homes singing songs until two or three in the morning. But before the holiday was up, most people were having a real struggle to live. The only ones who managed were those who had been exceptionally careful and saved a little bit all the year. But they were the minority; the ordinary worker was quite glad when the holiday was over even though he had enjoyed himself.

Near to where I lived in Tradeston were the Kingston Docks. As a boy I used to play there. On the side of the docks were revolving capstans; one boy would use his foot to swing a capstan round while another sat on top of it. In those days the Clyde was jammed up with ships on either side and ships waiting in the middle before they got in to unload. We got to know the ships and the railway traffic that came through.

The only men on the docks who had constant work were the ones who worked the salt boat. Otherwise, a particular stevedore would get a contract for loading or unloading a ship and he would pick out the men he wanted to employ for that day. It was all casual labour, a lot of them Irish. The stevedores did well for themselves; they lived in the better tenements and had their offices along the docks. One or two of them became Tory councillors.

Despite a lack of organisation the dockers fought. (I remember seeing a police baton charge against dockers at Springfield Lane, now Shearer Street.) They would strike quite often over the rates they were offered and over the picking of men, when some workers got privileges from some stevedores. There were also cases of blacklegging when Liverpool dockers were sent to Glasgow, or Glasgow dockers to Liverpool. But heaven help them if the other workers knew what they had done! Nobody blacklegged in his own place: to blackleg was a terrible thing.

The Glasgow dockers' lack of organisation was a result of the casual type of employment and the tremendous influx of Irish people who were in competition for the jobs that were available. The dockers used to build the union, let it collapse, build it up again, see it collapse again, and so on. There had been organisation on the Glasgow docks before the London strike of 1889 but it didn't last; and it was not until the seamen's strike of 1911 that the dockers really got organised, long after the London and Liverpool dockers.

At the heart of every organisation of these casual workers there seemed to be skilled workers, socialists who were prepared to help the labourers. In 1911 it was Emmanuel Shinwell of the ILP who helped organise the seamen in a rival union to that of Havelock Wilson, and O'Connor Kessack who brought the Glasgow dockers into the Scottish Dockers' Union. He was one of the earliest Labour Party parliamentary candidates in Glasgow, for the Camlachie Division.

One of the problems for labourers, whether they were dockers or building labourers like my father and grandfather, was that the craft unions wouldn't take them. Engineering labourers couldn't join the Amalgamated Society for Engineers and had to join a general labourers' union. That meant the labourers' unions became spread out with membership in many industries. Because they were like that, and because they were often run by people who were not in the trade, they were much less democratic than the craft unions. It was difficult for the labourers' unions to survive during periods of bad trade. The labourers had no experience of trade unions and of regular payment of dues, and periods of unemployment were much more serious for them. The officials had a terrible job just to keep the offices going and find salaries.

Although a lot of Irish catholics lived where I lived because it was near the docks, I was the only catholic boy in my particular close. The other catholics who lived there were all elderly, and the only boys were protestants of Northern Irish extraction. So I grew up knowing about the Falls Road and the Shankhill in Belfast, and about Derry, long before I ever saw them. I knew the names, the history, and some of the arguments about religion and about Irish politics. All the catholics I knew who had any interest in anything at all made themselves informed about their religion, and since in Scotland the Catholic Church was closely connected with the Irish movement their interest in religion often took them towards politics.

Politics, of course, meant Home Rule for Ireland. Although the leadership of the Irish movement had passed from the insurrectionary Fenians like Michael Davitt and O'Donovan Rossa, to the parliamentarians like Parnell, the Fenian movement was still part of the Irish tradition. As schoolboys we all knew the words of 'God Save Ireland', a song written to commemorate 'The Manchester Martyrs' the Fenians executed in 1867. When O'Donovan Rossa came to Glasgow in 1906 I was one of the many hundreds who went to hear him speak.

The Liberal Party favoured Home Rule for Ireland and thus the large body of Irish Nationalist MPs elected directly from Ireland to the House of Commons always worked with, and voted for, the Liberals. The United Irish League, which organised the Irish vote in Britain, nearly always recommended Liberal parliamentary candidates. But the situation in Ireland meant that the Irish people themselves were amongst the most radical Liberals. During the Boer War there were huge patriotic demonstrations, the Kruger and Ladysmith demonstrations, and I remember knowing very well that all the Irish people were on the side of the Boers and not the British.

The membership of the UIL in Glasgow was mostly middle-class Irishmen: publicans, grocers, iron merchants and suchlike - men who were making their way. I knew of them by repute only; none of my grandfather's friends were in it. But ordinary Irish workers didn't need to be members, because they all voted according to instructions. Some, like my grandfather, were becoming increasingly worried about voting Liberal. The Labour Party, although very small, was also prepared to support Home Rule for Ireland. But it wasn't until the 1906 General Election that the catholic vote went Labour, and that was because the official recommendation of the UIL itself changed.

2. Dying Like Flies of Socialism

Every Sunday, at Glasgow Green, people would gather to hear open-air lectures and debates. Three or four hundred people would listen to a well-known lecturer, and there would be speakers and their audiences all the way along the Green up to Nelson's Monument. Shortly after my father stopped me reading 'bloods' he took me to hear the lecturers and the debates, though I don't think he was very keen on any particular school of thought.

A large number of the debates were between catholic and protestant speakers, and they lectured on their doctrines in a way that they don't do now. Two of the greatest disputes were about papal infallibility and transubstantiation. Were the popes infallible? Was the Pope the real successor to Peter, and did Christ refer to the Catholic Church when he said: "On this rock I'll build my Church'? Was the bread and wine the true body and blood of Christ - during the Last Supper when he passed bread and wine and said 'This is my body, this is my blood' - was that a literal statement? Of course the protestants were refuting all this and arguing for their doctrines: predestination, and whether baptism by immersion was eligible.

The thing that made Glasgow Green different from Hyde Park and other open-air speakers' places was that the speakers could challenge one another to debates. Near the Green, across from Jail Square where the mortuary is now, was the Bird Market, a wooden market where they sold birds and goldfish all week but on Sundays they put down seats and had a platform. Emmanuel Shinwell says in his book *Conflict Without Malice* that a thousand people used to listen to the debates, but from what I can remember only about three hundred people could get in. You had to pay twopence, but you heard a real debate. Both speakers brought their authorities and had piles of books on the table; each of them was given fifteen minutes, then ten minutes, then five.

The popular time for speakers to challenge each other was on

Sunday afternoon at two o'clock; all the lecturers would be speaking and suddenly there would be a challenge from one to another. A debate between James Cotterell, an English catholic lecturer, and Harry Alfred Long, a protestant minister, attracted a tremendous crowd. Long would debate with anybody, atheist or catholic: he debated G.W. Foote, a freethinker and one of the leaders of the Secular Society. Long would say: 'You say we come from monkeys. Speak for yourself.'

Dr Jamieson was another protestant lecturer, and at one time a man called Brennan came over from Belfast and caused a real stir. He set out to prove that St. Patrick was really a protestant. He argued that it was impossible for St. Patrick to have been controlled from Rome, that he wasn't an emissary of the Pope, and the church he was part of didn't have the same Roman influence and hierarchy that later developed. I thought he made out a very good case, and it caused a rumpus amongst some of the catholics. The catholic lecturers apart from Cotterell weren't very good; all they could do was quote 'This is my body, this is my blood' and one or two other phrases that they probably never read in the scriptures but only in some catholic pamphlet. They did it in order to make a few coppers. Only James Cotterell was well-informed, well versed in religion and politics; he used to save the reputation of the catholics in these debates.

Sometimes debates were held on some aspects of Irish history. There was one outstanding lecturer on this subject, a man called James Ward. He was a big hefty fellow, a navvy; I never heard anyone with such a grasp of Irish history. There was also a man called Weir, a very bitter Orangeman who was obsessed by King Billy crossing the Boyne but who could really debate. When he and Weir debated each other they were really informative and worth listening to. Of course the one political question most often raised at Glasgow Green was Irish Home Rule, because it was so closely bound up with religion.

Although protestant v. catholic were the main debates at the Green, they weren't the only ones. Glasgow had a number of very strong temperance organisations whose lecturers would come down and argue that drink was the cause of poverty. The temperance organisations were rivals to the socialist movement in the early days (although many socialists themselves were temperance), and the Catholic Church also preached temperance.

There were Tory and Liberal lecturers, but few who supported Labour. One man who died shortly before my time was remembered as one of the chief speakers in the Labour cause. His name was John Ferguson, a town councillor, an Irish protestant but who had fought for Home Rule for Ireland. He advocated the formation of a Labour Party and regarded himself as belonging to Labour like Michael Davitt did; he earned himself a lot of respect.

There was one town councillor who was an outstanding speaker, Scott Gibson. He attacked the town council fearlessly and criticised all kinds of corrupt practices; he protested and exploded against the people at the top and got himself thrown out of the Corporation on a number of occasions. He was nowhere near the Labour point of view, but he was one of the best speakers I ever heard. I must have been very cheeky in those days because I can remember clashing with him at one of his meetings - a boy opposing Scott Gibson!

The only speaker who was anywhere near the socialist outlook was an Edinburgh anarchist called McAra. He only came occasionally and unlike the other speakers he brought a platform, a little box which contained four legs and his pamphlets. Everyone else spoke from the ground with a wide circle round them. McAra was a very able speaker and could always get an audience, but he had no influence on me.

My father took me once or twice to Glasgow Green and after that I went on my own. I couldn't be kept away from the place, and got into a lot of rows for getting home late. The meetings started about twelve o'clock and went right on until nearly ten o'clock at night. They weren't like Hyde Park: we didn't mock the speakers, we only asked questions and we learnt a lot.

Suddenly, about 1904 or 1905 when I was thirteen or fourteen and still at school, there was a whole crop of 'No-Popery' lecturers. They were really vicious anti-catholic protestants who deliberately said things that would insult the catholics in the audience. They made jokes about the Immaculate Conception and about nuns and priests; and later on one of them, Samuel Boal, trampled rosary beads into the ground. They were a very disturbing element on Glasgow Green and they annoyed me an awful lot.

The proper religious debates did me a lot of good because I followed up the controversy in the Mitchell Library, which was then in Miller Street. I used to get out books on the different questions and work my way through the arguments. I actually owned a Bible -

the other catholic boys never even saw a New Testament - and could recognise all the quotations from the Gospels. Because I was acquainted with these things the priests and the teachers at school began to take an interest in me, and in a boy called Tom O'Halloran who was also outstanding in terms of religious knowledge. When I left school the priest and the O'Halloran family tried to persuade me to go to St. Mungo's Academy and put all kinds of inducements to me concerning the advantages of that kind of education. I flirted with the idea but really I wanted to go to work.

Fortunately my grandparents didn't want me to go to St. Mungo's. It was a good bit away from where we lived and they were worried that I would have to take two trams to get there and to carry food with me. So we had to decide what I was going to do. Both my grandfather and my father were keen that I should not be a labourer or a handy-man as they were. My father had strange ideas: he thought I should get a job where I didn't have to take my jacket off, and wanted me to be a railway clerk. I didn't fancy that. Then he said that the coming thing was to be an electrician; I didn't mind that idea, but I didn't know any electricians and didn't see any possibility of becoming one. Finally it was agreed that I should try for an engineering apprenticeship. As employers didn't take apprentices until they were sixteen, I had to get a job in the meantime.

To fill in the time I went to work as an apprentice in a sail-making firm near Scotland Street. I was paid six shillings for a full working week. In those days everybody started at six in the morning, and nearly everybody walked to work. So from half-past five the streets were very busy but it was dark and all you could see were shadows going past you. There were two breaks during the day - the breakfast break and the lunch break - and you worked until half-past five at night. On Saturday you worked from six to twelve, and then you were paid.

After a year at sail-making I decided to go to a job with more money, in a wire-works for ten shillings a week. There I met a cheery old socialist called Willie Booth, a member of the Independent Labour Party. He never stopped preaching ILPism and he was also an anti-Christian, a secularist. He used to trot out the sayings of Robert Blatchford, one of the great socialist propagandists, in a very humorous way. I was still a catholic and only fifteen, but he and I had some heated discussions. He told the others that one day I would be a socialist; when I heard what he had been saying I got quite indignant about such a ridiculous idea!

Willie Booth was an exceptional man because most workmen were either Liberals or Tories. In Glasgow the majority were Liberal. In Britain the more advanced working men usually voted Liberal; it was the Liberal Party who had fought for the working class to have the vote, and the few working men who were actually MPs were sent to parliament with Liberal support. In 1875 two working-class representatives were elected this way. Alexander MacDonald, an Airdrie man who first got the miners organised, was sent to parliament from Stafford; and Burt, another miners' leader, from Morpeth.

The Liberals fought the 1906 election on the issue of free trade versus protection. They put up a poster with a great big loaf and a small loaf; to vote Tory was to vote for the small loaf, but to vote Liberal was the way to get the big one. But in Gorbals the Liberals didn't win. For a few years the Irish catholics had been worrying about always voting Liberal and never Labour. The Labour Party was for Home Rule, and their policies were obviously better than the Liberals'.

Then, in the 1906 election, the Liberal Party announced that they would not introduce an Irish Home Rule Bill in the coming session even if they won the election. This created quite a disturbance among the Irish people; in Gorbals the local branch of the United Irish League, the William O'Brien Branch, split. The official recommendation of the UIL was to vote Labour. There was a sitting Liberal MP for Gorbals. The Tories put up Bonar Law against him, and Labour put up George Barnes. The Irish voted Labour and Barnes was elected. The only other Labour MP returned in 1906 in Scotland was Alec Wilkie for Dundee.

I was a regular reader of the catholic press at this time and, of course, the question was raised whether a catholic could be a socialist. The catholic press was amazed that catholics could vote for socialism, and the church hierarchy became alarmed. One of the big men in the United Irish League was Charles Diamond. He was also a big capitalist, chairman of the English Sewing Machine Co., and owned a syndicate of local catholic newspapers, one of which was the *Glasgow Observer*. Many priests wrote in his paper and denounced socialism as atheism.

One of the statements made by the priests was that Karl Marx was a German Jew who denied his God. Of course the Labour Party wasn't a socialist party at that time, let alone a marxist party, and the ILP was socialist but repudiated marxism. Then they resurrected a papal encyclical, *Rerum Novarum*, which had been issued by Pope Leo in May 1891 (seven days after I was born), when the German bishops were trying to make catholicism a rival movement to socialism and had started the Catholic Social Movement.

Rerum Novarum put forward the biblical argument that 'Ye have the poor always with you' and that they had to be there in order to give scope for church charity. It argued that the church was in favour of 'social justice', not socialism. They were against the oppression of the poor, against sweated labour, *and* against socialism! I became an expert arguing against *Rerum Novarum* and I still own several editions of it. Even today when I hear the expression 'social justice' it angers me; organisations like the Communist Party use it, yet it is the very antithesis of socialism.

Most of the young catholics who were attracted to socialist ideas joined the Independent Labour Party. Of course, as soon as it became known that they had, the priests would revisit their homes and start hounding them. John Wheatley began to argue with the priests that catholics had a right to be socialists, and a big debate took place in the *Glasgow Observer* between him and Father Puissant.

John Wheatley was a member of the United Irish League. He was born in Waterford and was a miner before he became a draper's assistant. He educated himself at evening classes, set up his own shop and later his own printing business. He was not a member of the ILP at this time - he didn't join until 1908 - but had, with Willie Regan, started a Catholic Socialist Society that later affiliated to the ILP.

I read the debate between John Wheatley and Father Puissant avidly. It went on for months. The letters printed in the *Glasgow Observer* were all against Wheatley and completely misconstrued what he had said. The priest actually wasn't a match for him, but he was a Belgian and claimed that he knew more about continental socialism than Wheatley. Wheatley made mince-meat of him but all the letters said the opposite, and I became very annoyed about it. I had learned to reason and to argue about things at Glasgow Green, and the unfairness of the catholics really angered me. I started being convinced by Wheatley's arguments, even though I wasn't a socialist; when suddenly a catholic lecturer straight from Liverpool appeared in Glasgow - Cornelius Dunne.

Dunne had spoken at Glasgow Green before. When he heard about the catholic-socialist controversy, he came up to trounce the socialists. He was a fine speaker and toured Glasgow. I was at his first meeting and questioned him, and everywhere he went I went. I followed him all round Glasgow, and I'll say this for him - he always insisted that the crowd keep quiet until I had put my question, and then the two of us would have it out. I would ask whether papal encyclicals were infallible documents. Wasn't *Rerum Novarum* just the private opinion of the Pope? Wasn't it a political opinion, and didn't other people have a right to a political opinion as well as the Pope? The whole question allowed tremendous scope for a debate, and I got to know Dunne quite well. We became quite friendly.

I still didn't accept socialism. I believed in catholic doctrine and I was a bit afraid to break with the church. But I also believed that a catholic could be a socialist, and I was enraged by the attitude of the catholic hierarchy. One priest, I think it was Father Thurston, had said young men were 'dying like flies of socialism', and that was their general attitude.

Wheatley made progress with the Catholic Socialist Society despite the hierarchy, so in November 1909 they decided to bring up Hilaire Belloc to debate him. Belloc was a national figure, a very able literary man. He and G.K. Chesterton (a convert) had gained great popularity among catholics because of their fight against Joseph McCabe, an ex-priest who was now a freethinker. But when Wheatley met Belloc, he knocked spots off him.

The catholic hierarchy really hated Wheatley. In 1909, after he had won a municipal election in Shettleston against a sitting catholic member, he was denounced from the pulpit while he sat in the church. The catholics even burnt an effigy of him outside his house. He just stood at the door and watched it burn.

Although I was only fighting for the right of catholics to be socialists, I was coming nearer and nearer to socialism myself. When I began my engineering apprenticeship in 1907 I worked in Howden's where there were three apprentices who were also socialists, which was very unusual. There was Jacky Miller, whose father Willie Miller was a member of the ILP; there was Norman MacKay; and there was Willie Buchanan, brother of a later Labour MP for Gorbals.

There were also quite a few catholic apprentices, which was just as unusual - it was difficult for a catholic to become apprenticed to engineering. When I became a socialist I had the fiercest arguments of all because the other catholics couldn't understand it. Jimmy Breen, Rogan and others became bitter opponents of mine, especially later when I broke with the Catholic Church.

There were about thirty apprentices in all, and our little group of socialists were constantly arguing our propaganda. But it was difficult because, apart from the catholics, a third of the apprentices were middle-class boys who had come into engineering straight from secondary school. They were put in for the experience and to be able to say later that they had served five years in engineering. They had no intention of working at the tools; they wanted supervisory jobs, and some became managers later on. The leader of this group was a boy called Allan Paton who came from Hutchinson School, a real bigoted Tory. Howden's attracted young Tories of that sort because it was dominated by the freemasons; even one of the shop stewards was up to his neck in freemasonry.

Many engineering places had a strong freemason element in them, particularly among the foremen and managers. They were a closed clique with their own code of honour and their own secret meetings; they were all Tories and anti-catholic. Freemasonry was probably stronger in Glasgow than the Orange Order. The Orange Order attracted protestants of Northern Irish extraction, specially in the shipyards; freemasonry was more common among skilled engineers. All the freemasons were Tories because they believed in their right to be privileged workers and had great disdain for the Irish and the labourers. When I worked at Weir's I was approached to become a freemason: I am sure they hadn't realised I was an ex-catholic!

The freemasons were often members of the union, the Amalgamated Society of Engineers, and were among the best payers, but they weren't at all militant. They escaped unemployment because they were in with the management, whereas the socialists were always the first to be paid off. In a place like Howden's there would be six or nine months' work followed by a slack period. The foremen used to go round quietly on a Friday night to the men he was going to pay off. We watched him; each man would keep his back turned, hoping he would pass by, but the men he stopped at were the ILP members and the other socialists. They were good skilled workers and when trade was busy they would be taken on again; but at the next pay-off it would be they who went first again. Willie Miller was an outstanding engineer, but every time trade was slack he was the first man paid off.

As apprentice engineers we had to attend evening lectures twice a week. I went to the Crookston Street School for two years. It meant that I had two very long days each week. I had to get up at half-past five, have a cup of tea and a sandwich or porridge before getting to work at six. I came home for my breakfast break from nine to nine forty-five, when I nearly always had ham and eggs. For lunch I had a sandwich, usually at home because we had from 12.30 to 1.30, and then I worked until half-past five. For tea I had either cooked meat and potatoes, or fish - we never ate meat on Fridays and in Glasgow generally there was a great deal of fish eaten, as well as a lot of mincemeat and corned beef. Of course you only ate like that when you were working! And even when eating well, to do evening classes on top of the day was very tiring. But I kept going to Glasgow Green and reading the debates. And of course, there was a girl I had to see.

John Wheatley's debates in the *Glasgow Observer* lasted more than two years. As well as following them, I began to take an interest in the Free-thought movement. I was still a catholic; and at the time I believed I was learning free-thinkers' arguments in order to refute them!

Many socialists before the 1914-18 war started in the Free-thought movement: John Maclean, Willie Gallacher, Emanuel Shinwell. In Scotland, unlike England, nearly all the ILP members were free-thinkers. Scotland had a tremendous reputation for theological hair-splitting. As well as the catholic v. protestant debates, the argument about church government was very important here. Calvinism was still very strong and to get people away from it, or from catholicism, meant a big fight about secularism.

The free-thought fight was very good for the Scottish socialists. It sharpened them and led them into thinking about socialist principles more deeply, whereas in England some elements of the socialist movement formed a rival faith, more or less, to the Christian

Church. A lot of the socialism of the period was semi-religious; Keir Hardie even wrote hymns that were published in the *Labour Leader*. But although Hardie was a Scot and the leader of the Free-thought movement, Charles Bradlaugh, was English, it was in Scotland that free-thought really took a hold.

Many of the early free-thought leaders were radicals: extreme liberals who identified with republicanism and the labour movement, and people like Dilke, Cunninghame Graham, Edward Aveling and Annie Besant. At that time, and until much later in Scotland, Christians were still denouncing Darwin and arguing against the theory of evolution. At Glasgow Green there would always be a number of ministers attacking evolution. The local evening papers were covered with advertisements for meetings and sermons on this theme. As the socialists began to defend Darwin's theory the sermons shifted to attacking them, Robert Blatchford's *God and my Neighbour* being a favourite target. One of the most vicious of the Christians who spoke on the Green was a man called Cochrane; Willie Gallacher and John Maclean both debated against him.

Now and again lecturers came up to Glasgow from the Secular Society: Chapman Cohen, its secretary; G.W. Foote, who edited *The Freethinker*; and the ex-priest Joseph McCabe. McCabe's exposures and his scientific statements were highly popular. Colonel Ingersoll, an American, was also popular and two volumes of his writings appeared in paperback at sixpence each. Even Darwin's *Origin of Species* came out in paper covers for sixpence, and there were a number of widely-read scientific works, including Ernst Haeckel's *The Riddle of the Universe* and Professor Tyndall on evolution.

There were several local lecturers too, including one known as Scientific Brown. He used to produce a little bottle in which, he said, there was enough poison to kill ten men. Then he would quote the Bible where it says that if you have enough faith you can move mountains, and challenge anyone to test their faith by drinking the contents of the bottle. No one ever tried. There was another man called Ignatius McNulty who had broken with the church. His daughters had gone to the same school as me; he was one of the people I argued with while still a catholic. He was convinced that the priests didn't actually believe a word they said, and he used to attack the Bible as 'a bunch of Jewish tracts' and Christ as a tramp.

Gallacher had been brought up in Paisley and had been a member of the Temperance movement and a lecturer on temperance. From there he also became a free-thinker and debated with Cochrane on the existence of God. The debate was at Glasgow Green in 1908 or 1909. Gallacher was very proud of that part of his background; he and I often used to talk about it. Of course none of us then knew anything about dialectics and Marx's approach to the question. All of us just argued that man's existence was from evolution; we said that spirit was just an emanation of being, and denied the existence of any all-powerful designer of the world. We drew attention to the anomalies that existed in the world, and pointed out that they couldn't be the work of a Great Being, and sneered at the primitive ideas of heaven and hell. The religious people weren't trying to defend the Bible as such but trying to prove that everything was designed.

John Maclean also debated with Cochrane on the same subject. I don't actually remember that debate but John told me about it and so did Gallacher. It was quite common in those days because in Scotland (although not in England) nearly all the socialists were free-thinkers. Cochrane was a religious lecturer who specialised in attacking catholics and atheists. He wasn't well liked by the atheists. The ILP attacked him; they were free-thinkers who based themselves on Blatchford's *God and my Neighbour*.

But it was Emanuel Shinwell who caused the biggest stir on Glasgow Green. He was the first free-thinker to carry with him a small army of young free-thinkers like himself, and they became a formidable crowd. Everyone went to hear the youthful Shinwell; he really took a trick on the Green. He argued mostly on the scientific aspect of free-thought, and he and his followers would stay and put their point of view right on until midnight. I heard him often, then suddenly he disappeared and I remember some of the Christians taunting the free-thinkers: 'Where is your Shinwell now?' Apparently he had joined his trade union and the ILP, and forgot all about the Free-thought movement.

But after Shinwell disappeared and others were no longer as popular, there was one old fellow who sold the free-thought pamphlets round every ring at Glasgow Green. He never annoyed anybody, he never spoke much, he always wore a nice blue suit and had a big grin, selling '*The Mistakes of Moses*, one penny'. It was a reprint of one of Ingersoll's old essays. Davie Baxter was an anarchist and free-thinker. He had his own barber's shop, and it was he who took me in during the first world war after I deserted from the army.

I listened avidly to the free-thought debates - they formed a background to the socialist movement - but I was still a member of the Catholic Church. Then in 1908 the whole character of the socialist movement changed, because 1908 was one of the worst years of unemployment Glasgow had known.

3. My Name is Andrew Finnegan

In those days the unemployed could literally starve to death. There was no social security, and the parish council wouldn't give money to able-bodied men unless they went into the workhouse. Even then, their wives and children would only get a few shillings relief. In 1908 the scale of the unemployment was so terrible that the Corporation of Glasgow started work schemes, something they had always tried to avoid, and on a few occasions they gave out food tickets worth ten shillings each. My uncle worked on one of the schemes; though he was a skilled blacksmith, he built roads in the park for fifteen shillings a week. My father was also unemployed, and for a while he and my uncle went round making sunshades for shops.

It wasn't the first period of bad trade during the 1900s. I lived in Govan, near the shipyards which were always hardest hit during a slump, and I remembered seeing soup kitchens being set up before. But 1908 was the first time there were mass demonstrations about unemployment. Demonstrations took place every week in George Square until the magistrates banned all meetings there. My father used to go with a pal called Smith, and they were quite delighted with the agitation. At that time there was no organisation of the unemployed but the ILP and the Social Democratic Federation, the SDF, worked together to call the meetings to demand more relief.

A large number of socialists became involved in the fight for the unemployed. Tom Kerr of the ILP, a future Lord Provost of Glasgow, was very prominent. He was a very unusual fellow, a piano tuner who had been sacked, and he was one of the outstanding agitators of 1908. He threatened to reveal freemason secret rites if nothing was done for the unemployed, which created a big sensation in the press. In later years others did the same: Willie Gallacher used to tell jokes about the freemasons and an ex-mason in the unemployed movement of the thirties gave us a full performance of baring the left leg, baring the breast, stopping in front of the coffin etc. But in 1908 Tom Kerr's threat caused an uproar.

Cunninghame Graham came to the Glasgow unemployed meetings to speak, and so did a number of others. But the meetings were usually dominated by local men. John Maclean led one demonstration right through the Glasgow Stock Exchange. There were big clashes with the police because so many demonstrators tried to rush the city chambers. This led to the ban on meetings in George Square that stands to this day. The city chambers were the target because the chief demands concerned relief, not the Right to Work Bill which Keir Hardie had introduced in parliament. In fact, there seemed to be a separation between the political question of the Bill, which socialists supported, and the immediate agitation for relief.

The agitation about the 1908 unemployment transformed the labour movement in Glasgow. A number of new people joined the different socialist organisations. Many ILP and SDF members hadn't been unemployed but they had been affected by the agitation.

Finally I resolved to join a socialist organisation. An SDF member came into Howden's, but he annoyed me by spouting marxist phrases which he didn't seem to understand. Willie Buchanan and Jacky Miller's father were in the ILP, so Jacky and I decided to join. We entered the Kingston Branch of the ILP in August 1909.

The Kingston Branch wasn't so bad. There was a regular attendance of about forty and they were all very nice people. It was as much a temperance body as a socialist one; only one man in it drank. Some of its members became very prominent in the Glasgow movement: Pat Dollan, Andrew Hood, Jimmy Welsh, and Tom Kerr, all of whom became Lord Provosts of Glasgow. Jean Roberts, who later took charge of Cumbernauld New Town, was also in it.

The branch was composed mainly of workers, mostly engineers, who were very prominent in the socialist movement before the first world war (and in the communist movement afterwards). It might have been due to the work they did - there was a logic in engineering; yet they were also more slaves to their machines than the other trades, particularly if they worked as machine-turners, hole-borers and shapers. The engineers' trade union was also very democratic.

The ILP wasn't really a socialist party but a party committed to labour representation. At its founding conference in 1893 Bob Smillie moved that the name of the organisation be the Socialist

Labour Party but Ben Tillett opposed him. Tillett said that his socialism was trade unionism, and if they adopted pure socialism as their aim he would oppose the whole party. The ILP gradually came to advocate socialism but it was a mixture of old-fashioned radicalism, the Fabian Society, and Robert Blatchford. Their chief aims were nationalisation and a democratic Britain with Labour in control. They didn't accept marxism; if anything they were anti-marxist. There was a big Methodist influence in the ILP in England, and in Scotland a few churchmen also joined. Jimmy Barr who became the MP for Kinning Park and Campbell Stephen who became the MP for Camlachie were both ministers. In 1904 Jim Larkin moved a resolution for fusion with the other socialist parties and it was rejected.

Still, the Independent Labour Party was closer to the working class than any other labour organisation. They did a great deal of electoral work and knew all the Labour voters; but they were also present in the workshops. They had to be very careful about what they said, but the best of them did a lot of socialist propaganda. They didn't call for strikes; instead, they argued for public ownership in place of private ownership. Willie Miller and the others were always arguing for their socialism, but already the idea of gaining office was becoming an end in itself to some. At Howden's, one ILP member, a shop-steward, was George N. Barnes's election agent - Jock McVey. I tried to get into conversation with him many times but it was impossible; he kept his head down all day at work and never discussed anything. He didn't talk socialism and outside he didn't sell socialist literature - that was beneath him. Ultimately he became a manager in Parkhead Forge.

The ILP fought for the idea of a Labour Party better than anybody else. Although they considered themselves its socialist wing they attached more importance to electoral activity than in changing the Labour Party itself. There was a branch of the ILP in every municipal ward in Glasgow, and every branch had a man looking after the voters' register all year round.

They didn't fight the town council elections only, but also the elections to the school board and the parish council. One of the first victories of the Kingston Branch was when a postman named McDermott was elected to the parish council. He wasn't on it long before he was offered an official's job. We had a tremendous discussion in the branch as to whether he should have taken the job and I was one of those who wanted to condemn him for it. But the majority wouldn't condemn him, and the victory was thrown away.

The school board elections were always very important. The ILP was fighting for free meals for necessitous schoolchildren, for free books and free boots - which the reactionaries were strongly opposed to. At the time there were two school boards in Glasgow: the Glasgow one, and the Govan School Board which covered the south side of the city almost up to Cathcart. William Martin Haddow got elected to the Glasgow one and Harry Hopkins for Govan, and they put up a terrific fight on behalf of the children. Haddow pioneered the whole campaign, and ultimately more ILPers were elected beside him.

There was also a small ILP group on the town council, but they weren't a very vigorous bunch until John Wheatley joined them in 1912. He had been elected to the Lanarkshire County Council from Shettleston and joined the Glasgow Town Council when Glasgow annexed several outer boroughs including Govan and Shettleston. As soon as he got on he shifted the whole attention of the labour group to housing, and the housing agitation built up the group.

At that time there was no housing shortage in Glasgow, but there were thousands of one-room apartments in deplorable condition. Wheatley argued that the council should build working men's cottages with little gardens and proper sanitary facilities for rent at £8 a year. He contended that it could be done by using the profit the corporation made on the trams, taking it out of the common good and not paying interest on it. Wheatley was always arguing against interest payments! Of course the town council was completely opposed, but the proposal caught on and it really built up the ILP.

Wheatley became one of the outstanding ILPers in Glasgow, and certainly he was one of the most courageous. He never let up on his argument with the Catholic Church, he fought hard for the miners, and he was a most honest man. After he got on to the town council the whole Labour group behaved much better, and by the outbreak of the first world war it had 17 members. He never claimed to be a marxist, but I sometimes felt that he was more of a marxist than some who claimed to be. In 1908 he wrote an excellent pamphlet called *Mines, Miners and Misery*; he wrote a lot about the mines as well as on the condition of the catholic working man. I remember a cartoon in his writings which depicted the solution to the Irish problem as a steam roller leaving a trail of dead Irishmen behind it.

B

Wheatley went into publishing and ran *The Eastern Standard* which Willie Regan, the secretary of the Catholic Socialist Society, edited. Wheatley's influence meant that the Glasgow ILP was not like the national body under the leadership of Hardie and MacDonald.

The ILP were particularly anxious to do well in the town council elections. In Britain as a whole their policy was to nationalise, and in every city their policy was to municipalise. In Glasgow where there were already municipal trams, a municipal water supply and (ultimately) municipal electricity, the ILP also wanted a municipal bank and to extend the underground transport system. Since nationalisation and municipalisation was their idea of socialism, their preparations for the town council elections were very thorough.

One municipal election I was sent up to Springburn to help out during polling day. Tom Kerr was organising the fight as soon as I entered the ILP rooms he said: 'Are you going out to vote now?' I pointed out that I didn't have a vote, let alone a vote in Springburn. But Tom Kerr, who had a list of dead voters all of whom were going to vote for the labour candidate, said: 'Your name is Andrew Finnegan and you will have a vote today.' Use of the dead voters' list was a common practice in those days - and not only by the ILP!

The ILP also took a big interest in the ward committees that actually ran the political affairs of the area. In those days the ward committees were elected by ballot, and the ILP wanted to put me up even before I had the vote! I had to go to court to apply for a vote. There were about two hundred others doing the same. When the young fellow before me, who was in the same position, applied for the vote the sheriff said he would make an example of the next case of this kind. So when they called me I just sat there and didn't answer, and that was that!

When I joined the ILP in 1909 the big fight, of course, was with the Liberals, whose secretary at the time was Sir John McTaggart, an ex-ILP member. He was the founder of a firm called Meikle and McTaggart, house-builders. The Liberals held their meetings on Saturday afternoons at the Palace Theatre, and McTaggart used to take the chair. All the socialists - ILPers and SDF members - would go to heckle him. At the time the Liberals were on top of the world because they held most of the Scottish seats and had a big majority; we would go up and argue about unemployment, the budget and so on. The ILP were always promoting people and getting them to do things. They actually sent me to interview Sir John McTaggart in the Liberal Federation premises in Cavendish Street in the Gorbals.

I got more and more involved in the work of the ILP and always attended the branch on a Sunday night. At the branch meeting there was a book-stall, and one night I picked up Robert Blatchford's book *Not Guilty: A Defence of the Bottom Dog*. In it Blatchford argued that man was fashioned by his heredity and environment, that society was to blame for the criminal, and that the idea of punishment after death was just nonsense. He actually put a man in the dock on a charge of having murdered a child and, in the speech for the defence, argued the responsibility of society for this crime. He put forward a marvellous case and completely undermined the Christian argument about sin, heaven and hell. I started to read the book that night, and was still reading it at half-past five in the morning when I should have been getting up. I took it to work and read it at lunch-time, and went on reading as soon as I got home at night. Though I had read much deeper atheistic literature, I was completely carried away by Blatchford. That book broke me from the Catholic Church.

I finished with the church, but it wouldn't finish with me. The O'Halloran family did everything they could to get me to change my mind. All kinds of allurements were placed in front of me: they suggested that I go to sea with one of the brothers, that I get myself some kind of musical training. Then the priest came round and there was a bitter fight. He threatened violence. That was the last straw, and I broke away completely. One or two of the catholic apprentices at Howden's wouldn't speak to me any more, but I just carried on.

I read all the socialist literature I could get, including all the weekly papers. There was an enormous number of them: the *Labour Leader*, the national official ILP paper; *Justice*, the paper of the SDF; *The Socialist*, the paper of the Socialist Labour Party; Robert Blatchford's *The Clarion*; and *Forward*, the paper of the Glasgow ILP. There were others, but those were the ones that I read, in particular *Forward* which was very good because everybody in Glasgow could write for it.

I didn't like the *Labour Leader*. It was too concerned with the ethical approach to socialism, and a dull ethical approach at that; and I never could stand Snowden, MacDonald or Hardie. It was very negative, much more anti-Tory and anti-Liberal than anything else.

But *Forward* was as different from the official paper as the Glasgow ILP members were different from the rest. Tom Johnston ran it; he argued that anyone could contribute to the paper and John Maclean, a member of the Social Democratic Party, often wrote in it. It published debates with other organisations as well. It was a very lively paper with lots of attacks on the landlords - Tom Johnston serialised his book *Our Noble Families* in it - and on the big capitalist propagandists. It carried marvellous exposures all the time.

I also read *Justice* and the *Socialist* because both papers were putting a marxist point of view and I was anxious to understand marxism. In fact the marxism of the SDF and *Justice* was a narrow stupid marxism, and looking back at them now it is possible to see that there wasn't much difference between their leaders and those of the ILP. The *Socialist* was better but I had a terrible struggle trying to understand the paper; it usually published two complete pages of print, with no by-lines, on the materialist conception of history or marxist economics. Reading it now I can see that their marxism was quite crude; but at the time I actually liked the paper and did my best, although I found it very difficult.

The *Clarion*, Blatchford's paper, was very colourful and idealistic and a free-thought paper: it made some swipes at Christianity, not at God. Blatchford's daughter Winifred wrote on literature. A.M. Thompson wrote on the theatre, and a man called Harry Lowrieson wrote a popular column on astronomy. A whole organisation had grown up round the paper; there were 'Clarion' cycling clubs and choirs, and 'Clarion' vans that went out into different districts taking speakers and socialist literature. One of the outstanding 'Clarion Vanners' was Joe Burgess. Tom Groom organised the cycling clubs, and there was another offshoot called the Clarion Scouts. The Scouts could always call very big meetings, and they allowed anyone to speak on their platform.

Glasgow had several socialist choirs. In the main they were under the auspices of the Clarion Scouts, but the ILP also had some organised by Tom Kerr. Music and the arts were important to both the ILP and the Clarion Scouts, both having been greatly influenced by William Morris's dream of socialism. There was a sort of romance about their socialism, and a looking back into the past (you've to to look back if you want to see anything romantic at all). Their idea was that we should municipalise this and nationalise that, and go from stage to stage putting planks down over muddy fields and building bridges, and through planning slowly but surely get into paradise. Blatchford's *Merrie England* painted a beautiful picture of the future Britain.

Before the war this romantic type of socialism almost became a religion in itself. A large number of socialist sunday schools were set up in order to educate children in the ethics of socialism. In Kingston the socialist sunday school was run by Arthur Shelley, a Nottingham man; in his home town he had been victimised for his socialism under his real name Arthur Pinkney, and had used an alias ever since. He made the meetings an elaborate ceremony. Instead of the children being baptized as they were in church, there was a naming ceremony where a big crowd sang socialist songs. When I first saw it I was quite shocked, as I hadn't quite rid myself of catholicism. Four little girls put flowers on the baby for purity, and then a red rose was put on for revolution. Arthur Pinkney, who had a marvellous speaking voice, spoke of the future of the child and the future of all humanity. The singing was the most impressive part of the ceremony, as rich as any religious function I had ever attended; it really stumped me.

The socialist movement was very colourful then. On the May Day demonstration everybody wore red ties and red sashes. It was a socialist demonstration; the trade unions were there but it was the socialist organisations that pulled the crowds. Every organisation had its own lorry which became a speakers' platform at Glasgow Green. At first the meetings would take place in the open space near the museum, but then the demonstration got so big it had to go to Flesher's Hall. By then there were fourteen or fifteen meetings being held at once and all kinds of socialist banners were flying - 'Socialism the only hope for the workers' - and so on. The Social Democratic Federation would usually have some slogan from Marx. The SLP was there, the ILP and the Clarion Scouts; everybody co-operated very well. The children in the socialist sunday schools came from George Square, travelling in seats placed on the lorries; they had their wee banners and sang away. Even the anarchists, led by old Willie McGill, made a splash.

The demonstration was always organised by a voluntary body to which all the trade unions and socialist organisations sent delegates. It met once a month, usually on a Saturday afternoon, to plan the whole thing. Harry Hopkins of the ILP became the secretary and ran it for a number of years, and Geordie Hale of the SDF was the treasurer. I was sent as a delegate by the ILP. The funds to it were all voluntary, but everybody worked together and made it a really spectacular day.

One of the great ways to raise funds for any socialist organisation was a cruise down the Clyde, often as far as Dunoon and back. A man who played an active part in the ILP cruises was Jimmy Allan, owner of the Allan Shipping Line (one of the three shipping lines that ran to Canada on a regular basis). Jimmy Allan was a millionaire. He was a fine old fellow, very modest, with no side to him at all. He ran for the town council in a really middle-class ward and always called himself a socialist candidate, not just Labour. His programme was a milk-and-water municipal socialism, but it was considered very advanced for its day. It was exceptional for a man like him to call himself a socialist when socialism was almost a swear word. Of course, all the folk on the cruises were very pleased to meet this millionaire socialist.

Before the first world war the socialist movement was very broad and socialist speakers could fill halls anywhere. Sunday night was the time for great mass meetings, with the ILP in the Metropole and the Clarion Scouts in the Pavilion Theatre, both packed every week. The ILP confined their meetings largely to their own speakers except for some radical liberals, such as Josiah Wedgwood. MacDonald came up frequently, and Hardie and the others from time to time. Connolly came across from Ireland occasionally, but at these meetings he spoke mostly on Irish history.

The speakers at the Pavilion were from all parties, and they broadened our outlook a lot; the Clarion Scouts invited any notable speaker whether from the SDF or the ILP, a trade unionist, a syndicalist, or a Lib-Lab. Tom Mann was very popular at the Pavilion, and Headingley, who had been in the Paris Commune, spoke there on the anniversary. Madam San Carole of the SDF spoke, and a Russian princess who worked under the stage name of Linda Yvorski. Hyndman and Quelch of the SDF were there, and Victor Grayson the independent socialist MP; and Ben Tillett. Mrs Bridges Adams, the outstanding woman fighter for socialism, also spoke there. Nobody could say that they hadn't heard the different points of view in the movement. Only the SLP didn't speak for the Clarion Scouts, and that was partly because they had no speakers of national standing.

The movement was very diverse. There were some who accepted William Morris's ideal of a future society in which there was plenty of leisure and people sailed up and down streams wearing white clothes. There were those who saw socialism as a more efficient type of society bringing a higher standard of living and shorter working days. Others were so obsessed with the class struggle that all they wanted to do was beat the boss.

All of the organisations, with the exceptions of the SLP and the anarchists, were in favour of winning socialism through parliament, especially after the Social Democrats began to win big electoral victories abroad. They believed that in a democratic country, where everyone had the right to vote, a government by the people could ensure that there was equality and could implement all the reforms in housing, education, health, that were necessary. Outside the SLP there was absolutely no vision of the possibilities of workers' control, let alone workers' power. In those days, the days before the Russian Revolution and before a Labour government, there was a strong belief in socialism without much worry about what it really meant. We knew that Keir Hardie and Ramsay MacDonald weren't the people we wanted, but we had little idea of an alternative. We knew little of the 1905 Russian Revolution and the workers' councils that sprang up then, even though there were a number of Russian refugees in Glasgow.

The socialist movement's concentration on a parliamentary strategy meant that many socialists were prominent in the struggle for women to have the vote. The ILP and the Clarion Scouts took the lead in that sort of fight. But some socialists had doubts about the suffragette movement because it was demanding votes for only some women, a limited franchise. However, the most famous woman socialist in Glasgow, Helen Crawfurd, was also a suffragette.

As well as being the foremost woman in the ILP, Helen Crawfurd went to jail as a suffragette and did a spell in Duke Street Prison. She had been married to a minister and was already a widow when she became active. She was a very courageous, honest woman, and although she was more of a pacifist than a revolutionary she was one of the founder members of the Communist Party, on the Executive of the CP, and actually met Lenin. Her *Memoirs* have never been published because the Communist Party had doubts about what she was writing; a copy does exist and is in the hands of one of the librarians of the Marx Memorial Library.

Nearly all the outstanding women socialists were in the ILP. Pat Dollan's wife Agnes was very active and, I always thought, better than he was; I'm convinced he killed her activity. Mary Barbour, the woman who organised the 1915 rent strike, was an ILP member. Mary Shennan was an ILP schoolteacher. There was also a woman in charge of the Reformers' Bookstall, the ILP bookshop in Gorbals Street. Most of the women in the movement were housewives, some widows, and there were a few teachers. There seemed to be more women in the movement in Lancashire and Scotland than in the south of England, and more in the British Socialist Party and the ILP than in the SLP. The SLP organised very few women because there weren't many women in trade unions and the SLP weren't prepared to do anything about other women's issues.

Most of the socialists were just like other men in their attitudes in the home. Many of them had big families and lived in appalling conditions, and it was the women who carried the burden. Jim MacDonald of the BSP, who later became a close friend of mine and was a good hard worker in the movement, had a big family and his wife was a slave. Seldom did the socialists involve their wives in the movement. When I married my wife came to meetings and joined the Communist Party, although she didn't continue activity after we parted. But most of the wives were no different from other working-class wives - looking after the children and doing hours of housework which was much harder then. They didn't drink, they wouldn't be seen in the pub, they stayed in the home struggling to make ends meet.

The socialist movement's attitude to sex was very bourgeois. Robert Blatchford pioneered a new approach, and my attitude was determined largely by his. He argued that an illegitimate child was no different and maybe better than a child born in wedlock. He contrasted a loving relationship and the child of that love, with a baby produced in a drunken moment on the marriage bed. It was something to argue about before the first world war, but the anarchist movement (particularly Guy Aldred) took it to extremes at the time.

Many socialists were very respectable. John Maclean lived by himself for a time after his wife left him, and he wouldn't let a woman in the house the whole time his wife was away. Although the average socialist looked forward to some vague equality in the new socialist society, on the whole they seemed to think the family would continue. Its abolition never occurred to them, although some did read Engels's *Origin of the Family, Private Property and the State* and Morgan's *Ancient Society* on which it was based. It seems that when they read these books they were more interested in tracing the origins of society from savagery onward, and the other argument passed them by.

Marx mentioned the family in *The Communist Manifesto* but, again, most socialists didn't grasp all that was in it. The ideas they got out of it were about class struggle and international solidarity. Many didn't think about the abolition of the family because looking ahead was frowned on by the marxist movement in those days; the picture of a socialist society had been only hinted at by Marx and Engels.

Because of these attitudes, women's activity in any case was largely confined to the social side of the movement. A lot of women worked around the socialist sunday school; and in the Clarion Scouts they did more of the social type of work than the propaganda. They often looked after the soup-kitchens. They were always prominent in the May Day demonstrations - they seemed to have less hesitation about wearing their colours - and when real street movements grew up they were very active. In the 1915 rent strike and the unemployed movements of the twenties and thirties, women showed just how much they could do.

4. 'The Grand Old Karl Marx'

While I was in the ILP they ran a speakers' class for new members, taken by William Reid, a sub-editor on *The Scottish Co-operator*. He was the only man I ever met in the ILP who had any interest in marxist economics, and the subject he gave me to speak on was: 'How are workers robbed at the point of production?' It was a strange topic to give because it is a marxist one, and the ILP was never marxist. I bought A.P. Hazell's penny pamphlet *A Summary of Marx's 'Capital'* and read it for a whole week trying to grasp the labour theory of value. And then on the Sunday I expounded it from the platform for a quarter of an hour, to William Reid's satisfaction.

I had no intention of leaving the ILP at that stage, but I began to get involved in the controversy over the actions of the Parliamentary Labour Party. At that time the Irish Nationalist Party had over eighty MPs in the House of Commons and they were a very turbulent lot - obstructing the business of the House in order to raise the Irish issue. The Labour Party had only about forty MPs including the Lib-Lab Miners, and many people in the movement thought they should follow the tactics of the Irish Nationalists.

One of the leaders of this viewpoint was Victor Grayson who had fought as an independent socialist against the Liberal in Colne Valley and had won the by-election in 1907. He was determined to raise the issue of unemployment in the House of Commons, created a great stir with his speeches on it and actually got thrown out of the House. The leadership of the Labour Party - especially Hardie and Snowden - attacked him, and a bitter fight began. Grayson attracted the more militant young people. He was without the narrow rigid approach of the revolutionary parties, the SLP and the SDF, but he was also arguing for a perspective wider than just parliament. He believed that parliament should be seen as the camp of the enemy and should be used only as a sounding board. He even refused to speak on the same platform as Keir Hardie, the god of the ILP!

In reply to Grayson's challenge Hardie wrote a pamphlet *My Confession of Faith in the Labour Alliance*, from which it was obvious that the Parliamentary Labour Party had no intention of breaking with the Lib-Lab tradition. Hardie kept his leftist reputation alive with his Right to Work Bill, and the 1907 Labour Conference under him had said it was for 'the socialisation of the means of production, distribution and exchange'; but it was obvious he would never break with the Liberals.

The issue came to a head during the General Election of January 1910. The Liberals had begun to get worried about the Labour threat and introduced a 'radical' budget. They had brought in old-age pensions in 1908, and then in 1909 they decided to do the popular thing and tax land in order to pay for them. The ILP actually claimed that this budget of Lloyd George, the Chancellor of the Exchequer, was a socialist budget stolen from Philip Snowden! Other socialists disagreed.

The first time I ever saw John Maclean was when I heard him speak on the budget. I had walked to Pollokshaws Burgh Hall from Kingston to hear Henry F. Northcote, a London University lecturer, on 'Man's Power over Nature and the Doom of Capitalism'. I didn't know that John Maclean was to be in the chair. I was carried away by the speech he made. He spent half an hour denouncing the Lloyd George budget and ridiculing the idea that it was socialist, and he really caught the crowd. John's speech made my walk worth while.

Although the Liberals fought on what they thought was a popular issue, the budget, they ended up with far fewer seats than before with the Irish and the Labour MPs holding the balance in the House of Commons; in fact the Irish alone could have defeated the Liberal Government. The Liberals then decided to build on the difficulties their budget was having in the House of Lords. They ran a second election in 1910 on the issue 'the peers v. the people'. But they got no more seats than before! Of course on all these kinds of questions, the peers and the landlords, the ILP were very close to the Liberals. But the other socialists weren't, and the conflict between them raised the whole dispute over the tactics of the Labour Party.

Victor Grayson continued his fight with the ILP leadership; Robert Blatchford began to support him, and Grayson started writing in the *Clarion*. Grayson was one of the greatest speakers in the socialist movement and he toured the country arguing his case. He always used simple arguments. At one of his meetings the temperance people turned up to challenge the socialist case about poverty. Grayson asked someone to give him a match. He held it up and said it represented the national income. Then he broke the match in two and said that the bit without the head went in profits, the head went in drink: so what caused the poverty?

On 4 August 1911 an announcement appeared in the *Clarion* of the formation of a new party, the British Socialist Party, by Victor Grayson. I had no hesitation in joining and I went to my branch of the ILP and moved: 'that we sever all connections with the Independent Labour Party and form the Kingston Branch of the British Socialist Party.' I got three votes with fourteen against. The three of us joined the BSP.

The British Socialist Party was formed provisionally. This was because the SDF was to have its annual conference at Easter 1912, and it was agreed to wait until after that for the full foundation. The new party attracted the best elements of the ILP, among them Russell Smart and Leonard Hall who were on the National Advisory Council;they had opposed MacDonald and Hardie and issued 'The Green Manifesto'. Forty-odd branches of the ILP as well as many individual members joined the BSP.

In Glasgow it was mostly unattached socialists who joined, including some ILPers who also retained their membership of the ILP. In other places, apart from the ILP branches, some of the Clarion Fellowships which had a lot of autonomy, and some small socialist groups also joined. In England there were quite a few local socialist bodies that now came together in the new BSP. Its formation seemed to be a fresh beginning for the whole socialist movement in Britain. Although its existence was provisional, we immediately began to hold street-corner meetings in Glasgow and Lanarkshire.

The socialism we preached wasn't the milk-and-water stuff of the ILP or the marxist gibing of the Social Democratic Party (as the SDF now called itself). We began to get in between the two and to preach class struggle, revolution, and extra-parliamentary activity without being anti-parliamentarian. At all our meetings we advocated the Grayson line, that every MP should feel he was in the camp of the enemy and sitting on pins and needles. We weren't big but we were very active.

In Glasgow, before the SDP Easter Conference, the new BSP and the SDP formed a working committee. I was elected to it from the provisional BSP, and John Maclean was an SDP representative. He and I had a difference that night. The SDP were advocating voting Tory when there were only a Tory and a Liberal in the contest - they argued that it was better to vote for the open enemy of the working class than the hidden enemy. There was a by-election in Glasgow at the time, and John Maclean moved that we recommend the electors to vote Tory. I said the move was fantastic and would discredit us completely. I was very diffident, but I was determined to oppose it. Out of the five of us on the committee, I only got my own vote. Fortunately we did nothing about it.

At Easter 1912 the SDP decided to join the new British Socialist Party. The decision disturbed me very much: there was something grey about the socialism of the SDP and something bureaucratic too. I also disliked the domination of the party by Hyndman, and when Hyndman also became chairman of the newly-formed BSP I wondered what role Grayson would play.

My fears were fully justified. Hyndman, Quelch and the old guard of the SDP completely dominated the new party. Russell Smart and Leonard Hall were swallowed up, and Grayson proved no match for their manoeuvrings and trickery. In reality Hyndman and Quelch were the same sort of reformers as the leaders of the ILP, only they used marxist phrases. They had no depth, no philosophy. All they wanted to do was prove Marx's labour theory of value to be right and so show themselves superior to all the bourgeois economists and to the ILP and to everybody.

Hyndman and Quelch were given over absolutely to the idea of a parliamentary revolutionary party. They talked revolution, but believed you could get it by voting! Harry Quelch had made his reputation by using the phrase 'any and every means from the ballot-box to the bomb, from political action to political assassination'. But in my hearing he said: 'if you can't vote right then you can't strike right'. Now what does that mean? For the SDP there was never any way except the purely parliamentary way.

The attitude of Hyndman and Quelch ensured that members who wanted to be real revolutionaries were always splitting off, first from the Social Democratic Federation, and then from the SDP. William Morris split and formed the Socialist League in the 1880s. The Socialist Labour Party was a split from the SDF in 1902. In 1904 another group split off from the SDF and formed the Socialist Party of Great Britain.

Hyndman's parliamentary policy was bankrupt. It created a fragmented socialist movement in Britain. Its credibility derived from the electoral success of the German Social Democratic Party, which impressed all the socialists. We had all joined the BSP because we wanted a different kind of party, a party that was more lively, with less of the old phrases, more active and able to lead struggles. I stayed on in the BSP in spite of Hyndman's influence and even became secretary of the South-Side Branch, but even in 1912 it was obvious that the BSP wasn't going to become the party we had wanted.

The very first strike that I was ever involved in occurred while I was still a member of the ILP. We were still apprentices in Howden's when the management put us on to a piece-rate job. (It must have been the only engineering workshop in Glasgow paying its apprentices piece-rate). The job was to fit a whole furnace front of two or three sliding doors of about twenty pieces, for which we were paid seven shillings per furnace front. We worked on this job for nearly two years and after a while we were taking home thirty shillings a week instead of the engineering apprentice's top rate of fourteen shillings a week in their final year!

The journeymen at Howden's complained because our wage was now very close to theirs. Howden's then cut our rate. We refused to work for less and we all walked out - including even the middle class element. At that time apprentices were not members of the union and we didn't approach anybody in the union - we organised the strike entirely on our own and stayed out for over a fortnight. Some of the other apprentices may have had trouble at home but I had no trouble with my grandfather. We went back after a fortnight, at the standard rate of fourteen shillings a week, but we didn't work the furnace fronts.

At the end of an apprenticeship you were allowed to join the Amalgamated Society of Engineers (ASE). For the first two years after finishing your time you weren't supposed to be paid the full rate of thirty-two shillings but only twenty-five. Very few men I knew were paid only twenty-five, but we were all paid twenty-five shillings at Howden's. Five weeks after my time was up the apprentices went on strike. Three of us were asked to take the apprentices' work and the other two said they would if they got the full rate of thirty-two shillings. I refused to do their work under any circumstances. All three of us were sacked; I took my apprenticeship lines to Butter Brothers and got the full rate, and then went to Fairfield's where I also got it.

Butter Brothers was a very interesting place. There was very little machinery in the works, and the engineers had to do everything by hand. You were given a wheel and the shaft and the keys for the big cranes and they all came still black from the blacksmith's, not even polished; you had to cut the key-way in the shaft and in the barrel by eye, with a candle at the other end. The key had to be tapered to an eighth of an inch so that it wouldn't slip out, and you had to do that without drawings. Butter Brothers did many jobs like that, with no machinery.

One of the things we talked about as apprentices was getting experience of the trade, moving about from place to place. We were especially keen to get some experience in the shipyards or as a ship's engineer. After a month at Butter Brothers I went into Fairfield's, a place which did a great deal of government work. When I went in they were working on a battleship for which the firm received the men's time plus ten per cent; which meant that the management didn't bother themselves and neither did the men.

For instance, the only overtime I ever worked before the first world war was at Fairfield's. Nobody in engineering wanted to work overtime, and there was hardly any demand for it except when some piece of machinery broke down. But all the Fairfield engineers worked on Friday nights, all night. Being a government contract, nobody came round to see whether we were working or not. There were men all over the ship but you couldn't hear a sound.

My job was in the engine-room overhauling the engine. The ship had just been for trials and we had to pull all the machinery to pieces, examine everything, sort out anything that had gone wrong, and put it all back again. One Friday night I was sitting on top of the turbine with a hammer in my hand. Everything was quiet, everyone was asleep, and as I fell asleep the hammer slipped, creating an awful row. Everyone woke up cursing and then went back to sleep again.

I stayed at Fairfield's for about three months before going on to Bobbie the Rogue's, the only place I worked where there was no trade-union organisation. Most of the men there were in with the bricks, and all they talked about was this 'Russian'. They kept saying: 'I hope the Russian doesn't come back. I hope he doesn't come back.' In fact the Russian wasn't a Russian, his name was McElroy. He was a wild reckless man, a big hefty fellow who could rush a job up and only worked for a few weeks at a time. After a spell at Bobbie the Rogue's he would go off and have a booze-up and live with women, mostly prostitutes. Then he would work night and day for a fortnight at Duncan Stewart's and then go off for another debauch at Cavendish Street, not far from Bobbie the Rogue's.

The other engineers were scared to work with him on the cranes, partly because he would curse and swear, attacking God and Christ in what they thought was blasphemy. And when I first went on a job with him I took a hammer up in case he should start any trouble, but it was all nonsense. He was quite harmless, just a wild-living man. Years later I used to see him in my audiences at Gorbals when I was organising the unemployed.

After Bobbie the Rogue's I moved to Mirrlees Watson, the best organised job I worked in before going to Weir's. There was a Tory shop-steward there called Young, a likeable old fellow with a beard (which was rare then). He saw to it that everyone was a member of the ASE and that the rules were carried out, but he was well-in with the management. The foremen were also members of the ASE and liked to see that the union was being organised properly; the ASE was a sort of religion to them. All the shop-stewards did was to check the cards.

Every member of the ASE was a time-served man, and in the union there was a stand-offish attitude: a sort of pride of craft, and a pride of union. The members really believed themselves to be the aristocrats of labour, and they dressed differently and better than other workers. Like all craftsmen they wore blue suits and bowler hats on week-ends but during the week they wore a deep-sea cap, like the ones they wore at sea. They all thought they were marine engineers!

They weren't the highest paid men. The joiners, masons and bricklayers were better paid than we were, but we had much greater security of work. The engineering trade could have slack times but it was never like the building trade that just went up and down. By tradition it was the engineers who 'tossed the brick' at the end of the Fair Holiday and the New Year. On the first day after the ten-day holidays, two or three hundred workers would meet outside the factory gate. One of them, one of the best known, even a freemason, would toss a brick in the air. If the brick didn't come down we would start work, but if it did we would take another day's holiday. Everyone would come to the gate just in case there was a start, and then we would go home. It wasn't a one-day strike - we just weren't very keen on working. Tossing the brick was a common practice in the engineering shops until the war broke out.

Before the first world war I was in the Glasgow South branch of the ASE. The branch officials were all members of the ILP sporting the little party badge. The branch was a very respectable body. It was very well attended, with about fifty or sixty there. We discussed all kinds of problems, but almost everything was referred to the district committee and then to national headquarters. There was a sort of orthodoxy about what trade unions were and what they were supposed to do, and there was never any controversy. Although you had to go to the branch in order to pay your union dues - the shop stewards didn't collect them then - I didn't attend very regularly. I was always more interested in the socialist side of the movement, a political weakness I kept throughout my life. I was interested in industry only if we could get a struggle going in the factories and never worried about the apparatus of the trade union, except to support the syndicalist view that we should organise workers on an industrial basis rather than by craft.

As a skilled engineer I was earning good money. The basic wage was thirty-two shillings a week, but in Fairfield's I earned up to forty-six shillings. No one else in the street was paid as much as that. Even as an apprentice of seventeen or eighteen when I first started going out with a girl from the close next to me - Jeannie Johnstone, the best-looking girl in the whole place - I was making good money. The two of us went out more than anyone else in the locality. Every Saturday night we went to the music-halls and the theatres where we saw all the good artistes - George Lashwood, Florrie Forde and Hetty King. The plays were mostly sob-stuff - 'the girl who took a wrong turning', 'the girl who lost her character', 'the girl who went astray'. For a period there was a revival of semi-religious plays like Wilson Barrett's *The Sign of the Cross* and we went to those, and to the pantomimes. Occasionally we even took a meal in a restaurant, which very few working-class people did then. We courted like this for six years and finally got married in 1915. Jeannie was considered to be rebellious in those days because she wore short skirts before anyone else! It was called the milkmaid style.

Most of my time was spent on behalf of the BSP. A South-Side branch was formed and I was the secretary of that; then we started a Tradeston branch and we even had our own bookshop. I never had any difficulty with my family over my socialist activities. One day a big Russian came to the door looking for me because he wanted to be put in touch with other Russian refugees in Glasgow. My old grandmother and grandfather were quite delighted to meet this man before I took him off to the Gorbals to meet the other political refugees.

The South-Side, Govan and Gorbals, was a very lively place for socialist propaganda. We sold literature, we held meetings, and for a big event we bill-posted everywhere. You couldn't walk through without seeing the pavements chalked with socialist slogans. Most of our work was done outside the factory; there was a danger that you would be sacked straight away if it were known that you were a socialist. You weren't sacked because of your activities but because socialists were looked upon as criminals and cranks.

One of the old SDP members who came into the South-Side branch was a barber, John McAteer, who had been prominent in the 1908 unemployed agitation. I was always in his shop. I used to go there any day that I wasn't working, and most evenings. John used to tell me about the old-timers in the movement and I loved to listen. He had a collection of socialist songs, parodies of old patriotic songs that I have never heard since. To the 'By Jingo' song of the Boer War he would sing:

> We don't want to fight,
> But by the Red Flag if we do,
> Our foes shall be the Master Class,
> The Landlords and the crew.
> We'll need no soldiers on the land,
> No battleships at sea;
> In the good days that are coming
> The Nation shall be free!

Through John McAteer I got to know Tom Anderson, who established the socialist sunday schools in Glasgow and wrote a number of songs and poems for them. The kids learned songs like

'The Grand Old Karl Marx' and the William Morris and Edward Carpenter songs, and sang them in the May Day Parade. They got so popular that the shop-stewards sang them at the anti-Lloyd George demonstration during the war. One of their favourites was:

> O beautiful, my country!
> Be thine a nobler care
> Than all thy wealth of commerce,
> Thy harvests waving fair;
> Be it thy pride to lift up
> The manhood of the poor;
> Be thou to the oppressed
> Fair Freedom's open door!

One song that wasn't particularly appropriate to Glasgow went: 'From each wretched slum, let the loud cry come, England has risen and the day is here.'

Tom Anderson was a fine man; he had a little printing press and was fleeced by everybody in the socialist movement. He once said to me that he was the most milked cow in the movement. He wasn't nine months in the SDF when he ran for the executive and argued for a new socialist password. The Clarion Scouts had a password: when one said 'Boots' the other replied 'Spurs'. In Tom Anderson's version, one said 'Class' and the answer was 'Conscious'.

A lot of us met in John McAteer's barber shop and we had quite heated discussions. One of the fellows was Davie Gilmour, a manager of a chemical establishment in Govanhill. He was a very big fellow and he covered the floor of the shop in three great strides. He used to stride up and down denouncing the latest iniquity of John Burns, whom he hated. The whole socialist movement hated John Burns. After being elected to parliament as a Labour man he had taken a job in the Liberal Cabinet. Joe Burgess, a Glasgow councillor who had been one of the Clarion Vanners and had edited the *Workmen's Times* in Huddersfield, actually wrote a book attacking John Burns called *The Rise and Progress of a Right Honourable*. The campaign against Burns died at the outbreak of the war because Burns didn't agree with the war and left the Cabinet.

There was a large shopkeeper element in the Social Democratic Party. Tom Nolan and my friend-to-be James MacDonald had little shops, and Dan Crerar had a decent-sized grocer's shop in Rutherglen Road. J.W.Mclean had his own leather business and the Cater brothers in the East End were shoemakers. There were also one or two trade-union officials: John F. Armour of the stone-masons, and Laurie Anderson of the toolmakers.

Having shop premises, John McAteer told me that during the 1905 revolution he had guns stacked on the shelves of his shop. The two Cater brothers also hoarded guns for Russia which were handed over to the Russian refugees in Glasgow, who sent them on. It was quite common in the socialist movement. I attended an AEU conference when Little, who was the national president of the engineers' union in the thirties, said that when he was young and daft he had helped get guns for the 1905 revolution.

I didn't have much time for the old leadership of the SDP when I joined the socialist movement, and later I had none at all. McAteer knew Hyndman and Quelch and he hated their bureaucratic, bullying ways. One day he went to meet the pair of them at the station to take them to the hotel where they were staying. When they got there, they called for two whiskys for themselves and didn't even ask him if he would take a drink. Hyndman was looked upon as a great intellectual who debated marxist economics with the Webbs, but really he came from a Tory background and his socialism had elements of Toryism in it; he had actually made money on the Stock Exchange.

In 1912 we had an aggregate meeting of the BSP in the Templars' Halls in Ingram Street, and H.M.Hyndman came up to speak. It was a warm day and Laurie Anderson and I were standing outside when we saw Hyndman's tall hat in the distance. Anderson looked up and said: 'Here is the old bastard coming now.' I didn't like him saying that. Then Hyndman got up on the platform with his top hat and frock coat still on and just looked down on us. He said nothing worth a damn, and by the time the meeting finished I agreed with Laurie Anderson.

Because Hyndman owned the BSP paper *Justice* and Quelch was its editor, they had the match of any opposition inside the SDF or the BSP, and they just ate Victor Grayson. He was at a disadvantage against Hyndman and he took to drink, and eventually he began to disappoint audiences. Before that, he was one of the most popular orators the movement ever produced; he would sketch the tragedy of the poor, told jokes about himself failing as a divinity student, and always ended his speech with a rousing statement about the beauty of socialism.

Grayson last spoke in Glasgow before the war and the Pavilion

Theatre was packed even though he had failed to turn up several times previously. They only just managed to get him to the meeting and he started speaking like his old self. After ten minutes, however, he started repeating himself and the audience tumbled, and he had to be got off the platform. Then Tom Kerr took over the stage. He told the audience about all the men of genius who had taken to drink, and he did a whole programme of songs and poems: he really made his reputation that night.

The new BSP became pretty much like the old SDP. Many of the people left, and it wasn't long before the rest of us found ourselves in struggle against the leaders' policy. Hyndman, and Robert Blatchford of the *Clarion*, began to argue that the Germans were making war preparations and so should Britain. They called for the building of more dreadnoughts and a bigger navy - at a time when the Liberals were refusing to build as many ships as the Tories demanded! A big debate started within the BSP. Theodore Rothstein replied to Hyndman, arguing that international working-class solidarity would prevent war, not the British navy. Rothstein was a Russian refugee, the father of the present Andrew Rothstein, and really dedicated to the socialist movement. He led the opposition to Hyndman in *Justice* and at the conferences of the SDP and the BSP, along with Zelda Kahan.

The Scottish representative on the BSP Executive was Alexander Anderson from Stonehouse, a schoolteacher who supported Hyndman. The Cater brothers and J.W.Mclean also supported him, but the majority in Glasgow were against. John McAteer took a strong stand against the policy; John Maclean led the fight in Glasgow, and our branch agreed with him. Prior to one conference when we couldn't send a delegate I had to send a telegraph of support from the branch to Zelda Kahan and Joe Fineberg in their opposition to Hyndman's policy.

The anti-militarist wing of the socialist movement was strong at the time. Gustave Hervé, a French radical, wrote a book called *My Country Right or Wrong*; I was captivated by it and so were countless others. Phrases from it were repeated by all of us, like 'insurrection rather than war' and 'take the flag to the dunghill'. Our faith in the power of international class action to stop a war was based on the might of the Second International. Kautsky and the German Social Democratic Party had supported the decisions of the International against war. Kautsky wasn't an active politician but he

was looked upon as the theoretician of the movement. Even the SLP
sometimes quoted him: Kautsky was marxism to us. John Maclean
and all of us were very influenced by him and we used his arguments
against Hyndman. We didn't know anything about Lenin, Trotsky
and the workers' councils that had appeared in 1905 in Russia.

The fight about the big navy went on for a long time and was still
going on when the war broke out. But it became overshadowed by
other questions. A great upsurge of working-class militancy had
developed from 1910 and the chief question of the socialist
movement became that of strategy - industrial or political action to
achieve socialism.

5. 'Dirty Scotch Pigs Are Looking for Hough's Digs'

The 1908 unemployed agitation had transformed the socialist movement, but it was transformed again in the strike wave which began in 1910. One of the earliest strikes of the period, in June 1910, was a strike of girls; and that was very rare.

People still spoke of the match-girls' strike of 1889 because it was such a rare event. There was a great deal of sweated work amongst women in those days, small local factories paying the women as little as ten shillings a week. Of course the craft unions wouldn't take women, but the Glasgow Trades Council put a great deal of effort into trying to organise the women and encouraging their trade union, the National Federation of Women Workers. But in June 1910 the girls at Neilston Mill, a little village outside of Glasgow, went on strike and the whole Glasgow movement rallied to their support.

The strike was a present to the socialist movement because one of the directors of the English Sewing Cotton Co. that owned the mill was Charles Diamond, of the United Irish League and owner of the catholic papers. We really went after him and the whole movement turned out to support the girls. A man named Hough, of the English Sewing Cotton Co., had referred to the girls as 'dirty Scotch pigs', and we all marched to his house in Pollokshields shouting: 'dirty Scotch pigs are looking for Hough's digs.' Jock Smith, my father's pal, was on the demonstration and I remember him speaking of 'that old bastard Keir Hardie'. I was quite shocked at that language being used in the socialist movement in those days.

In 1911 seamen, then dockers, then railwaymen were all on strike. The transport workers' strikes of 1911 were a turning point in the struggle before the war, just as the strikes of 1889 had been. Tom Mann was chairman of the Liverpool Strike Committee in 1911 and the most developed movement was to be found there. The strike committee organised all the strikers in all the unions and issued passes for the shifting of goods: nothing moved without the strike committee's authority. The government got very worried. Troops were sent into Liverpool and two gunboats were stationed in the Mersey. The troops were ordered to open fire and this order was also made to soldiers sent to confront strikers in South Wales, where two men were killed. A Liverpool worker wrote an article called an 'Open Letter to Soldiers', calling on them not to shoot.

The 'Don't Shoot' leaflet was reprinted in Larkin's paper the *Irish Worker* and in the *Syndicalist*. People who distributed the leaflet were imprisoned and Tom Mann and others involved in the *Syndicalist* were tried and sent to prison for six months in 1912. Immediately Victor Grayson toured the country repeating all the statements that had landed Tom in jail. We were still waiting for the full formation of the BSP but our provisional committee organised a meeting for Grayson in Glasgow; we planned to smuggle him from Clydebank in case a warrant should be issued for his arrest. In the end the agitation grew so great that Tom served only seven weeks of his sentence.

During the seamen's strike in Glasgow the trades council loaned Emanuel Shinwell to the Seamen's Union to help with the dispute. The national leaders of the Seamen's Union (The National Sailors' and Firemen's Union) were men like Havelock Wilson and Captain Tupper, corrupt reactionary officials. After the strike was over Shinwell formed a rival union, the British Seafarers' Union, and set up premises not far from those of the NSFU. Each union kept breaking into the other's premises, but Shinwell was a very good organiser and they couldn't beat him. But when the British Seafarers' Union went on strike, the NSFU blacklegged on them. Albert Wade French, an official of the NSFU, actually came down with a mob and fired at Shinwell - he missed and killed another man instead! He was charged but got off!

Also in 1911 the London printers went on strike and began to produce their own strike sheet, the *Daily Herald*. After the strike was over it was decided to transform the paper into a daily paper of the whole labour movement and from 1912 the paper appeared regularly. I got the paper every morning and read it avidly. In 1912 the London transport workers were back on strike and every day there were reports of the strike and Ben Tillett's speeches at Tower Hill. Lord Devenport was the chairman of the London Port Authority and Ben Tillett kept calling upon him to come out and fight. It was fortunate that Devenport didn't reply because Ben Tillett was a wee, wee, fellow. Then Tillett decided to call upon a higher power and said: 'Oh God: strike Lord Devenport dead', and he had all the workers chanting - 'He shall die, he shall die.'

George Lansbury became the editor of the *Daily Herald* and the paper became a focus for the movement. Almost anyone who wasn't a Tory could get space in the *Daily Herald*, and the more left you were the better chance you had of getting space. Anarchists, syndicalists, fabians and then G.D.H.Cole and the Guild Socialists, all wrote for it. It carried full reports of the national strikes as well as all the other issues.

In Glasgow Willie McGill, an old anarchist who was very vocal and had great integrity, became the agent for the *Daily Herald*. He had a newspaper shop which became the centre for the Daily Herald League, and all kinds of meetings were held there - years later the Minority Movement met there. He stuck with the paper all the way through, even when in the thirties it became a quite different sort of paper and infamous for the things it said. Because of the *Daily Herald*, the ILP and the Labour Party decided to bring out their own daily paper, the *Daily Citizen*, but that soon died.

The wave of strikes, the huge meetings at Nelson's Monument, and the influence of the *Daily Herald* all contributed to the growing debate on industrial versus parliamentary action. 'Taking and holding' became one of the new slogans: taking control of industry and holding on to it. It was Tom Mann who introduced syndicalist ideas in Glasgow at his meetings in the Pavilion Theatre. He had been to France a number of times and learned about French syndicalism, and had also been influenced by syndicalist ideas in Australia before he returned to Liverpool in 1911. He actually led a strike in Australia, at a place called Broken Hill. Mann was arguing for industry-wide unions, instead of craft unions, which would organise all the workers and be able to take control of an entire industry.

Willie Gallacher was another one who brought syndicalist ideas to Glasgow. He hadn't been to France or Australia, but to America. Before he went there he was quite well known in SDF circles; he was one of three socialist lecturers from Paisley - Johnny Campbell was another. But in America he was influenced by the 'Wobblies', the Industrial Workers of the World, and when he came back he put all his emphasis on industrial action. Strangely enough he remained attached to the BSP, flitting in and out of it, but was contemptuous of parliamentary activity.

In Glasgow the syndicalist agitation centred on one organisation above all, the Socialist Labour Party. But the SLP were not for Tom Mann's type of syndicalism. They believed in a revolutionary party which organised workers on a workshop basis, and they had the idea that you could 'lock the boss out'. The SLP created an industrial wing called 'The Industrial Workers of Great Britain', patterned on the American IWW. They wouldn't allow their members to stand for posts as union officials, and although they wanted a revolutionary party they didn't approve of any electoral strategy.

The SLP was founded in Scotland in 1902 out of a split in the SDF. Three of its most important members were James Connolly, Carstairs Matheson, and Neil Maclean who became the MP for Govan. Because of the importance they attached to workshop organisation, their paper the *Socialist* always concentrated on the issue of how workers were robbed at the point of production - the labour theory of value. They insisted on all their members having some knowledge of economics before they were allowed to join, and they were very sectarian in their attitude to other socialists.

The first SLPer I met was when I was still a member of the ILP. He was a moulder who had walked from Edinburgh that day looking for work. Having found it, he stopped me in the street to ask if I knew where he could get a copy of the *Socialist*. I walked with him to where I thought he could get one and told him that I was a socialist too. He asked me what party, and when I told him the ILP he said: 'You're not a socialist.'

When SLP members found any other socialist speaking at a street corner they always questioned him on marxist economics. They did it to me many times. I remember them doing it to Jimmy Johnstone, an old rigger in the BSP who never wore a collar and tie in his life. He was rough-and-ready and drank an awful lot, but he did socialist propaganda night and day. The SLPer said to him: 'What is surplus value?' Jimmy replied: 'That you don't get. Next question.' They were still doing it after the first world war; they did it to Frank Duffy, who said 'I'll let Harry McShane answer that question' and jumped down.

Their emphasis on workshop organisation led them into the first attempt in the West of Scotland to organise a major factory dispute, in the Singer factory at Kilbowie, near Clydebank. Trade unions were not allowed there, but the SLP got the employees into the Industrial Workers of Great Britain and then called them out on strike. After a bitter dispute they lost; the management went after the workers individually to get them back to work. A lot of workers were victimised, including Scientific Brown the atheist lecturer, and at the end of the srike there was no trade-union organisation at all.

Despite their belief in industrial unionism the SLP, unlike the syndicalists, were marxists who attempted to reach some understanding of the role of the state. One of their members, Willie Paul, wrote a book called *The State, its Origin and Function*, based on the arguments of Engels and Morgan. The BSP was always indifferent to the question of the state, whilst the ILP accepted the capitalist state believing that it was possible to get control and change its character. Only the SLP replied to ILPers like Ramsay MacDonald.

Willie Paul was one of the most prominent SLPers; Tom Bell didn't carry the weight that some have attributed to him. He was a moulder (a lot of the SLPers seemed to be moulders), but he was a very academic man. I was once in the same workshop as he was in a foundry in Anderston, and when we had a clash with the management I couldn't get him to move. He seemed to me to be more interested in getting to grips with marxist definitions. Years later, when we were both in the Communist Party, he wrote a book about John Maclean and asked me to write the introduction. I did; but the introduction that was printed over my name was different from the one I wrote. The Communist Party often did things like that.

Apart from Paul's book most of the SLP literature was reprints of Marx and the pamphlets of Daniel De Leon. I got several of the latter including *What Means This Strike?* and *Two Pages of Roman History*. Some of it was valuable, but my own attitude differed from that of the SLP. I agreed with Willie Paul in his book that all the state forces would be used against the workers in a crisis. But what should we do about it? I was in favour of industrial organisation, but was also in favour of sending people to parliament to represent the mass action of the workers outside. That was John Maclean's attitude also. At that time none of us knew about workers' councils and the possibility of a completely different workers' state.

Before the Russian Revolution transformed him, John Maclean was a Kautskian and gave great weight to the educational and organisational aspects of the socialist movement. He believed that the Labour Party, the trade unions and the co-operative movement together, as the organised forces of the working class, would beat the organised force of the capitalist class. The problem of the seizure of power didn't arise - somehow or other the class struggle was going to bring about socialism and that was that. With this perspective, it was always very important to John that the entire working-class movement had a grasp of marxist economics and he put a large part of his energies into teaching them.

He joined the socialist movement about 1903, through the writings of Robert Blatchford and the secularist debate. Although Blatchford wasn't a marxist, John joined the Social Democratic Federation because he decided that marxism had to be accepted as the only way to look at socialism. One of the best-known SDF members in Glasgow was Willie Nairn, a propagandist who taught Marx's economics on the street corners and in public lectures. John took up Willie Nairn's work, but began to organise it in regular classes. They became so popular that by 1911 and 1912 all the socialist organisations were trying to run similar classes. Unless there was a great struggle on, the most attractive feature of the Glasgow movement before the first world war was John Maclean's economics classes.

They were held every Sunday afternoon at the Central Halls. Several hundreds attended every week - they became even bigger during the war. All the best elements of the working-class movement, particularly the younger people, went to them enthusiastically; countless workers were indebted to them. John packed a lot of advanced material into his lectures but at the same time he never missed what had happened yesterday or the day before. He issued notes of the lectures at a halfpenny a time, and you could buy the whole lot for sixpence. His work seemed to grow by leaps and bounds. He lectured all over Lanarkshire and Fife as well as in Glasgow, and he was tireless. He loved every aspect of socialist work: education, agitation, meetings.

It wasn't just his oratory that influenced people but the feeling that he was a man who could be trusted, a man of integrity. There was no show about John Maclean. He always wore a grey or brown suit and a hat, and his white hair was always in place. He spoke with very few gestures; his two hands stuck out with the palms facing each other level with his sight. It was an explanatory pose, as he was expounding his point. He was always deadly serious, but he could cause excitement by the things he said. He was a schoolteacher and he loved teaching.

John's forebears were poor crofters and his father was a potter. He was very proud of his highland blood. Many other socialists in Glasgow were of highland origin, and many of them knew personally of the terrible suffering the crofters endured when they were driven off their land to provide grazing for the landlord's sheep or deer. Hatred of the landlord and the Tories was very strong in Glasgow, and amongst the highlanders as well as the Irish, even though many highland men became policemen. (By this time the immigration of the highlanders had almost finished but they still used to gather together on Saturday and Sunday nights underneath the railway bridge at Argyle Street and it was known as 'the highlander's umbrella').

John attended Glasgow University while he was a pupil-teacher at Shawlands Academy, and after he got his degree he became a full-time teacher in Kinning Park at Lambhill Street School. In Kinning Park he was known to everybody as 'Daddy Maclean', and he had a very soft side to all children. He was a man who suffered when anybody else was suffering. W. Martin Haddow who organised a campaign for the feeding of necessitous children, wrote that if ever his movement was short of material he would turn to John Maclean and always get a favourable response.

John was a member of the teachers' union and also of the Teachers' Socialist Society. The Socialist Teachers met to discuss all kinds of teaching problems, including the kind of education that was given - school history was purely the history of kings and queens. Some teachers were in the BSP and the ILP, and mostly they were asking for better conditons for the children who were too hungry to learn.

John Maclean never changed his arguments to suit his audience. In 1912 he was invited to speak to the Catholic Socialist Society; I went along to see what would happen. After he started expounding Marx's historical materialism, Wheatley tapped him and explained that this was a catholic audience. John said that he had given this talk to protestant audiences, and if they didn't want it he would go away. The audience agreed to hear him out. At the end he said that Britain was the only country with a socialist organisation which didn't believe in the class struggle - 'I refer to the Independent Labour Party'. The Catholic Socialist Society was affiliated to the ILP and everybody rose to attack him from the floor. There was a very high level of debate that afternoon; but John wasn't invited back until

after the war broke out, and that time he charged the Catholic
Socialist Society a £2 fee which he gave to the BSP. He was opposed
to the Catholic Church in a calvinist way as well as a marxist way,
and he never got on with Wheatley.

In 1912 the whole question of Ireland re-erupted. The Liberals had
a narrow majority in the House of Commons, and in order to
maintain their alliance with the Irish MPs they introduced a Home
Rule for Ireland bill. The Protestant Orangemen of Northern
Ireland immediately organised. Their revolt was led by Sir Edward
Carson, later Lord Carson, and F.E.Smith, later Lord Birkenhead.
With the support of the Tory Party they arranged a mutiny among
the officers of the British army and organised a volunteer force to
defend protestant Ulster against Home Rule.

The mutineers won; mutinies led by the Tories and army officers
often do. The Liberals withdrew on Home Rule and compromised.
An enormous storm broke out as James Connolly denounced the
Irish Nationalist Party for accepting the compromise, and the
socialists denounced the Liberal Party for giving way to Tory
threats. In Glasgow the argument was particularly fierce. There was
a strong Orange group in the shipyard areas. Many of the skilled
boilermakers of the shipyards had originally come from Belfast in
the 1860s; not only the platers and riveters were Orangemen but
often their labourers, and there were twenty-three shipyards on the
Lower Clyde alone. The Glasgow shipyards had strong links with the
Belfast ones - in Harland and Woolf's in Glasgow no catholic was
ever employed.

Other skilled trades supported Home Rule for Ireland. The
engineers had some freemasonry in them but were largely Liberals.
The socialists were strongly in favour of the Irish struggle and had a
lot of links with the Irish movement. James Connolly had been a
member of the SLP in Edinburgh and still wrote a regular column in
Forward. He was well known in Glasgow also, for his fight with the
Irish bishops and his argument that catholics could be socialists. His
book *Labour, Nationality and Religion* was widely read, although I
always thought that Wheatley's attitude on this was more uncompromising. Connolly's *Labour in Irish History* threw a new light on
Irish struggles and had a great influence on me and many others.

The socialist interest in Ireland was intensified by the Belfast strike of 1907 when protestant and catholic workers came together. The leader of that strike was Jim Larkin, the Liverpool socialist trade-union organiser. The whole movement hoped that it would be possible to cut through the catholic-protestant division by militant action of all workers. I heard Larkin speak in Glasgow in 1910, but when I heard him in 1913 during the Dublin lock-out he was a changed man, a great leader.

In 1913 the agitation over the collapse of Home Rule was still going on alongside the industrial agitation, although strikes were no longer as long or as fierce as they had been in 1910-12. But in 1913 Larkin and Connolly worked together in the Irish Transport and General Workers' Union to fight the 'boss' of Dublin, William Martin Murphy. Murphy was the chairman of the Tramway Company in Dublin, and the director of an Irish nationalist paper. On his side he had the backing of all the big capitalists, including Jacobs of Jacobs' biscuit factory, as well as the British government; the only strength that the Dublin workers had was in the support of the rest of the British labour movement.

The tramways strike lasted for four months and affected all the transport workers. Larkin toured Britain to get support for the strikers; he and Connolly tried through the *Irish Worker* to reach both British and Irish workers. One of his usual statements in his speeches was: 'I will break Murphy's heart or die.' But although the great syndicalist strikes had won elsewhere, in Dublin the strikers lost. Larkin didn't get the support of the British trade-union leadership although the rank and file and the socialist movement were behind him.

The Irish clergy also rallied to support Murphy. After the strike had gone on for some time, socialists in Britain offered to care for the strikers' children. Pethick Lawrence and others organised the scheme. But catholic priests went down to the docks to prevent the children leaving Dublin. They told the women that the children were going to protestant homes where their religion would be destroyed and that no good catholic mother should agree. Very few children left Dublin and after four months of the strike the children, women and men were in desperate straits.

Everybody gave money to the Dublin strike. Workers all over Britain and elsewhere collected every week to support the Dublin transport workers. The *Daily Herald* played an active part, and in Glasgow so did *Forward*. The only time I ever remember street collections for strikers was in 1913. During the Dublin strike I ran into old Willie McGill taking a strike collection using a barrel-organ which was covered with Will Dyson cartoons. (Will Dyson was the official cartoonist of the *Daily Herald*.) I offered to help Willie; we went out with the barrel-organ every Saturday night, collecting money in the streets and round all the theatre queues, and every night we collected at least a couple of pounds.

Jim Larkin was a bold, spectacular orator. He rallied great support for the strike, and of course the government decided to arrest him. He disguised himself to get to a meeting in O'Connell Street, and after he had spoken he was immediately taken by the police. His arrest enabled the entire socialist movement to draw the contrast between the government treatment of Larkin, who was fighting for better wages for starving workers, and the position of Sir Edward Carson, who had organised a military force to resist the Government. Larkin was in jail, Carson was free.

There was a meeting with about four hundred present to hear one of the local MPs. Some of us moved a resolution protesting at the imprisonment of Larkin whilst Carson went free. The MP tried to put it off; he was sympathetic, he was friendly, but he thought we should leave it. I insisted on putting the resolution and I carried it in the meeting. No one at all spoke against it - the feeling on the Dublin strike was so strong. That was typical of what was happening up and down the country. At the same meeting we also sold over a hundred copies of a pamphlet called *The Murdering of British Seamen by Mr Lloyd George, the Liberal Cabinet and the Board of Trade*; it was a reprint of a speech by H.M. Hyndman about the raising of the load-line in British ships, which had caused lives to be lost. It was published by the BSP.

Despite the immense sympathy for the Dublin strikers, they were beaten. The British workers were not brought out on strike in their support, and all the force of the military and the police was used against them. It was during the Dublin strike that Captain Jack White organised the Irish Citizen Army to defend the strikers from attack - White was the son of General Sir George White, the hero of Ladysmith, and he used his military knowledge to good effect. The Irish Citizen Army did stop the worst of the police attacks, and it later formed the nucleus of Connolly's Citizen Army.

The Dublin strike was a high point of struggle before the 1914-18 war. The whole movement came together in those years and seemed to undergo a transformation. By the outbreak of war the majority of the BSP were industrial workers and the old shopkeeper element seemed to disappear. We had a number of labourers, several engineers who came in after 1911, and some joiners who had been in the SDP. In the rank and file there was a strong syndicalist influence and by this time the socialist propaganda was very, very good. The socialists were not so shy about their socialism as they had been. The stronger the movement grew, the bolder the individuals became, selling their literature everywhere and doing open-air meetings.

Just before the war broke out I went to work in Weir's of Cathcart. All the factories I had worked in, apart from Bobbie the Rogue's had shop-stewards but sometimes you couldn't tell who they were because they were so quiet. The SLP had talked about factory committees, and George Buchanan's brother Willie had attempted to form one in the Dalmuir shipyard. But in Weir's, in 1914, there was a real factory committee in operation.

The secretary of the committee was James Messer, a member of the ILP, and every week all the shop stewards met and discussed the affairs of the factory. Jock Smith, also of the ILP, was instrumental in it as well. Neither of these men is given enough credit for the formation of the Shop Stewards' Movement on the Clyde; despite being ILP members, it was they who organised the first successful committee.

I have often thought about why there was a factory committee in Weir's and nowhere else. I think there were three reasons. When pay-offs came in engineering it was always the socialists who were paid off; but in Weir's pay-offs seldom happened - there was a constant personnel and therefore more confidence amongst the workers. Apart from that, Weir's was a modern factory with men working in their own bays at their own benches and not moving around; every morning each man knew what job he was going to do during the day. The jobs were so ridiculously simple that anyone could do them; fortunately I worked in the cleaning department which meant that I had a little more to do. The organisation of the factory meant that it was much easier to organise the trade union.

Also, Weir's had the most developed bonus system that I ever worked in before the war. There had been piece-rate in Howden's and Mirrlees Watson's but nothing like the system in Weir's. When

C

the rest of engineering was almost all time-work, everything in Weir's was on bonus. It meant that we got £1 a week more, but I don't remember anyone having to rush for it. It was an easy gong place and we did the same jobs from day to day.

I joined the committee when the shop steward in my section got the sack and I was appointed in his place. Although he had been sacked for a misdemeanour - he was operating as a bookie's runner in the works - we still objected to his dismissal. We were fighting for the rights of shop-stewards, and my first instruction was to bring out my squad in order to get my predecessor reinstated. To discuss the whole issue we booked the local hall for 5.30, and at half-past four I got all my men ready and we walked out through the works. The men at the benches rattled their hammers all the way along as a way of applauding. They all came out on strike that evening.

We were out for a fortnight. During the strike we went to the factory every morning and the officials kept trying to get us back to work, but we wouldn't go back. Finally they insisted on a vote. They wouldn't take a show of hands, but instead lined us all up in a big field and put all those in favour of the strike continuing on one side and all those against on the other. It was remarkable: they only won by four votes, even though we had been out for a fortnight and the Fair Holiday was coming. We returned to work on the promise of negotiations. I went on the deputation to meet the management, although only the officials were supposed to speak.

The meeting was on the day that war was declared. Brody, the organiser, and the Employers' Federation representatives immediately started talking about extending overtime now that war had broken out! I butted in - I protested that we had come to discuss the reinstatement of a shop steward. In my eyes war was wrong anyway, and I objected to them discussing war preparations. I was more or less brushed aside, although they stopped talking about it then and there. We didn't get the shop steward reinstated; but the world war changed the whole picture for the shop stewards movement.

6. The Coming of the First World War

In 1914 there was a general indifference to the danger of war amongst the mass of the working people. There had been the Boer War and one or two crises, but nothing on a big scale, and people were expecting peace to continue. Only Tories and socialists were interested in the question of war preparations: the Tories demanding more armaments, and most socialists supporting the Liberals' stand against the Tories' demands. Hyndman and his followers were supporting the Tories' policy, and our opposition to them led us to believe they were exaggerating the possibility of war. This meant that the anti-war socialists did not attach sufficient importance to the matter.

The socialist movement had been engaged in great industrial struggles and national strikes; we were looking forward to building bigger unions, amalgamating craft unions into industrial unions, and developing the workshop rank-and-file committees. For us, war did not appear to be imminent until a few days before it broke out; we were suddenly roused to the danger by the speeches of Sir Edward Grey and others in the House of Commons, and from the day the Archduke Franz-Ferdinand was shot in Serbia we could see that the danger was acute. The socialist movement tried to keep Britain out of the war, and we were relying on the Social Democratic Party in Germany to do the same. We expected the Second International to call for international working-class action.

We felt that we were speaking for the masses in our opposition to the war. Just prior to the outbreak there was a music-hall song which really caught on - you could hear it sung everywhere, in the workshops and on the streets. It went:

Little man, little man,
You want to be a soldier, little man;
You are mother's only son -
Never mind about the gun,
Stay at home,
Fight for her all you can.

In the socialist movement we were surprised and delighted by the song's popularity. But the day war was declared that song just died; it was amazing the way that *nobody* was whistling it. Instead another music-hall song, 'It's a Long Way to Tipperary', was being whistled and sung everywhere.

'It's a Long Way to Tipperary' wasn't a war song but it was a good marching tune, and that was what everybody thought they would soon be doing - marching straight to Berlin! It was believed that the war would last six weeks, six months at the most, and then the British army would march past the Kaiser in Berlin to celebrate the British victory. Nobody even thought about removing the Kaiser; he was just going to be there to see the Germans defeated. Britain and Russia were fighting together and there was an idea that Russia would send millions of men and overwhelm Germany - Russia was a huge country and 'the Russian steam-roller' would carry all before it.

A terrible war fever developed. Men rushed to join the army hoping that the war wouldn't be all over by the time they got to the front; they had to march in civilian clothes because there weren't enough uniforms to go round. Many young people, particularly those who were unemployed, were caught up in the adventure of the thing. On every hoarding there was a picture of Kitchener, the Secretary for War, pointing his finger and saying 'Your Country Needs You'. There he was, and then along came daft middle-class women with white feathers trying to drive young men into the army.

Quite a few of the men who worked in Weir's were in the territorial army and were expecting to be called up, but they didn't understand the situation. There were a lot of jokes about the war and about Willie Weir who was a territorial officer. He was so proud of his position that he had territorial parades at Weir's. On one occasion the horses were tied so close together that they kicked one another to death; there were jokes about what would happen when he was at the battlefront.

The works committee at Weir's were anti-war, but they had a big influence in the factory so that while most of the men there were against the Kaiser they weren't antagonistic to the socialists who opposed the war. It was a help to us that Russia was fighting on the side of Britain because everybody, Liberals and socialists, hated Tsarist Russia.

Some of the Weir's engineers simply went to sea and that was their war effort - most Glasgow engineers had worked at some point in workshops where they made sea-going equipment. Willie Taylor, a man in the factory I was friendly with, went to sea and was drowned.

As well as believing the war would be short, everyone, including the socialists, thought it would be fought by professional armies and volunteers. But even though we didn't suspect how terrible the war was going to be, we knew that it was a political disaster. Our hopes for an international general strike to stop the war were unfounded. Every section of the Second International supported its own country's war effort. Even Gustave Hervé became a patriot along with the rest. Only a few revolutionaries stood out: Lenin's Bolsheviks in Russia, and Rosa Luxemburg and Karl Liebknecht in Germany.

In Britain the socialist movement was split over the war. Many socialists were also pacifists, and John Burns resigned from the cabinet. In the ILP there was a good deal of anti-war feeling, but the leaders of the ILP took a very weak stand. Ramsay MacDonald and Keir Hardie appeared to be opposed to the war, but actually their speeches were largely against the secret diplomacy that preceded it: they blamed Sir Edward Grey, the Foreign Secretary, and argued that the war might have been avoided. When Ramsay MacDonald came to Glasgow he gave fine pacifist speeches, condemning the government and calling for peace negotiations, and the average ILPer was convinced of MacDonald's opposition to the war. But in their parliamentary constituencies both MacDonald and Hardie said and wrote differently, and the national policy of the ILP was not clear. In February 1915 Keir Hardie presided over a meeting in London of socialists from the allied countries that actually declared in favour of an allied victory.

MacDonald was depicted nationally as an anti-war socialist - the capitalist press ran a virulent campaign against him. They needed someone to whip up feeling against and they picked on him, and later he lost his parliamentary seat in Leicester. But even when the ILP developed a real opposition to the war, when conscription was introduced, MacDonald was never in favour of taking action. In 1918 he claimed that the way to defeat the Manpower Bill which conscripted even skilled married men was to 'create a political atmosphere'.

Before conscription, the ILP case against the war was really no different from that of the advanced Liberals who were opposing

Grey and Asquith in the Liberal Party. Josiah Wedgwood, C.P. Trevelyan and other radicals were also attacking the secret diplomacy that led up to the war and calling for peace negotiations. Many Liberals and ILPers supported E.D.Morel's 'Union for Democratic Control'. Even Lenin praised Morel's opposition to the war although it was not a revolutionary opposition.

The ILP was confused over the war because some of its most notable leaders went pro-war. Blatchford had supported a 'big navy' policy in 1910, but the ILP had not opposed him the way we fought Hyndman; and when he supported the war in 1914 it was a tremendous disappointment to them. Blatchford's pro-war attitude killed the Clarion Scouts completely. Many ILP members didn't know where they were, and concentrated on the issue of secret diplomacy until conscription gave them something they could really fight on.

Of the 17 ILP town councillors in Glasgow only two came out against the war, John Wheatley and John S. Taylor. A.R.Turner, a councillor who was an official of the Gas Workers' Union, went in the army. O'Connor Kessack, the docker's leader who was the labour parliamentary candidate for Camlachie, got a commission and was killed. Emanuel Shinwell didn't become a town councillor until John S. Taylor died, when he was co-opted to his seat, but he was prominent in the trades council and would have been an asset if he had opposed the war. But Shinwell never committed himself at all. He was the organiser of the British Seafarers' Union and involved in manning merchant ships, and that exempted him from the call-up when it came. Once in a while he took part in meetings about the erosion of civil liberties during the war, but we heard much less of him for a time.

Hyndman and the leadership of the BSP were organising war propaganda. Hyndman used *Justice* to put forward his pro-war policies, and helped to spread the illusion that the war would only last six months by claiming that Germany was now an industrial country unable to feed herself and would speedily collapse. It was when we finally defeated the pro-war elements in the BSP in 1916 that we found out he actually owned *Justice*, and when he and the others left they took the paper with them. Our papers became the *Call*, which was already published, and the *Vanguard*, John Maclean's paper in Glasgow.

In Glasgow we completely beat the pro-war faction and several members left. There were the Cater brothers, Bob Blair of Thornlie-bank, an old man called J.W.McLean, and Anderson; they all worshipped Hyndman. Only Anderson, who was on the executive of the BSP when the war broke out, returned to the movement: he eventually joined the Communist Party in 1930, as a very old man.

A lot of the Labour leaders were worse than Hyndman. Ben Tillett toured the country telling how he had seen a greasy spot on a wall where a German had bashed a baby's brains out. He poured out atrocity stories against the Germans and he became hateful, really damn well hateful; and there were others who did the same. The Labour Party itself was not solid on the issue of the war. John Burns had resigned from the cabinet, but Arthur Henderson joined it.

Everyone became war-crazy. Harry Lauder, the popular music-hall star, went to all the halls with pro-war songs and lectures; he brought out 'Keep Right On to the End of the Road' - a very nice song, but a war song. Horatio Bottomley, the editor of *John Bull* who was later jailed for fraud, also toured Britain giving patriotic lectures at £50-60 a time.

One of the most notorious Glasgow regiments was the Highland Light Infantry. It had headquarters in Greenhead Street, next to Glasgow Green, and it recruited a lot of men from the Gallowgate. They were a real lumpen crowd and the HLI always had a terrible reputation. But during the war everything was done to present these fellows as heroes and they were praised to the skies. Early in 1915 a book came out about a soldier called *Spud Tamson*. It was a story about a Glasgow down-and-out who joined the HLI and it played up his Glasgow slang, all the things he did, and how he became a big hero in the army. It became a popular novel all over Glasgow, and of course he didn't die in the war. But the men of the Gallowgate did; most of them had been unemployed, they enrolled in their thousands and they were slaughtered.

It wasn't only novelists who wrote nonsense about the war. The other *Clarion* writers became as war-mad as Robert Blatchford. One of them, Julia Dawson, wrote outrageous articles in favour of 'war babies'. A number of girls who lived near army camps had become pregnant, and Julia Dawson was defending this on the grounds that the girls were comforting 'our' soldiers.

Victor Grayson, who had so strongly influenced me and

thousands like me, also went pro-war. He wrote an article in Horatio Bottomley's *John Bull* on what a young man had to fight for. Disregarding the fact that for a working-class boy the answer was 'nothing', Grayson said every young man had a girl back home - and that was what he was fighting for.

The war hysteria enraged us revolutionary socialists in Glasgow. We were not campaigning about 'secret diplomacy': our stand was on the failure of the Second International to mobilize against the war. We had put our faith in the German Social Democratic Party, and we were nearly shedding tears because they had betrayed us all. Just as in Britain the Liberals had forgotten their hatred of Tsarist Russia and were talking about the Russian steam-roller, the German Social Democrats were using the fact that Germany was fighting Tsarist Russia to justify the war.

The anti-militarist position had become important to us through out fight with Hyndman. We had read Hervé and Liebknecht's *Militarism and Anti-Militarism*, and we had supported Tom Mann and Victor Grayson in their appeal to soldiers not to shoot the miners. John Maclean was on holiday in Tarbert with his family when war was declared, and he went round chalking in the streets of Tarbert: 'Grey is a liar.' Then he came straight back to Glasgow. He held a big meeting at Nelson's Monument to state his revolutionary anti-war position. The meeting was notable also because Arthur MacManus spoke alongside John against the war. Arthur was in the SLP, and until then it had been almost impossible to get anyone from the SLP on a platform with a member of any other socialist organisation.

John Maclean held Sunday afternoon meetings at Nelson's Monument throughout the war. He also started them on Sunday evenings at Bath Street, where the transport offices had been turned into an army recruiting centre. These were supposed to be general socialist propaganda meetings, but John always brought them round to discussing the war and they became very big and stormy. At the beginning a couple of hundred attended every Sunday; then supporters of the war began disrupting them, and the entire socialist movement rallied to defend the Bath Street meetings.

One of the most vehement of the pro-war faction was a house-factor's clerk called Jamieson who later joined the British Workers' League. He started holding meetings next to ours in Bath Street. The crowds at the two meetings jammed the street from side to side.

Jamieson's supporters tried to threaten us, but the large number of socialists present held them off. Although the ILP wasn't doing much about the war their best elements were coming to our meetings; so were the SLPers, who were openly opposed to the war.

John Maclean held the anti-war propaganda together, but the other really outstanding speaker at Bath Street and elsewhere was Jimmy MacDougall. He was a young BSP member, already well known as a great propagandist. He took terrible risks at meetings with the things he said to the patriots who were heckling him. He was actually of middle-class origin. His father had been the Provost of Pollokshaws before its annexation to Glasgow in 1912, and Jimmy was a bank clerk. He had joined Pollokshaws branch of the BSP when Maclean founded it, and was dismissed from the bank for his socialist opinions. He did tireless work for the movement before his arrest in 1916 on a charge of sedition.

In Govan a joint committee of ILP and BSP members was formed to do propaganda opposing the war. The two outstanding personalities were Harry Hopkins of the ILP and Geordie Hale of the BSP. There was also a bunch of young people who had been in the SLP and formed a left break-away group in Govan, calling themselves the British Section of the International Socialist Labour Party. They did a lot of good work, but unfortunately they never joined any other organisation.

The idea grew among some members of the BSP that our propaganda should be directed at the military themselves. With my closest friends, Jim MacDonald and Malcolm MacFarland, I discussed the question of one of us going into the Army to agitate among the soldiers. Obviously I would have to be the one to go; I was single, and the others' wives would never have let them volunteer. We did not discuss it with the district committee, and I'm sure that they would have opposed the daft idea - but a month after the war started I volunteered for the Royal Engineers. I didn't tell anybody what I was doing and my grandparents couldn't believe that *I* was joining the Army.

I went up to Maryhill Barracks and found another forty gathered there; they had, like me, volunteered for the Royal Engineers, but the officer intended us for the HLI and other infantry regiments. I got the others to take a firm stand, and we all refused to go to any other regiment. After a week we were sent to the HLI at Hamilton Barracks. The barracks were lousy: that convinced everybody, and we went to the commanding officer. He decided that I and three others should go to the Engineers, and found some reason why the rest weren't suitable.

The four of us were sent to Chatham. Everybody there was war-mad. We had to march round without uniforms because so many had been recruited, and everybody sang 'It's a Long Way to Tipperary' all the time. We all had to take a trade test in the Royal Engineers: those who passed were sappers, skilled men, and those who didn't were pioneers, unskilled. I became a sapper and learned to handle explosives - digging, under-mining, sapping, making tunnels and laying charges - and to build all kinds of bridges and pontoons. I knew something about explosives by the time we finished.

After a short time we were shifted to Dorset, where all the different regiments were camped in miles and miles of fields. There were two companies of Engineers, the 78th and 79th; I was in the 78th, and I told everybody in my company that I wasn't going to kill any Germans. They all knew where I stood. I was told there was a corporal in one of the other companies who was arguing that Keir Hardie was right (he thought Hardie was opposed to the war). He was the only one that I ever heard of besides myself.

It soon became plain that we were being prepared to go to France. Every soldier had to be inoculated before going, and I used this to create a dispute over pay. Most of the men were married and there had been a delay in their wives being paid the soldier's allowance. On this ground I got them to refuse to be inoculated, which meant that they couldn't go to the front. The entire unit agreed, and on marches everybody was shouting: 'Shall we be inoculated? No!' It was a very opportunist dispute, and of course as soon as the wives got their allowances all the men were inoculated, except three of us. The other two wanted extended leave in order to see their families, and I stood out on principle.

My stand led to a lot of battles with the patriots. There were two very staunch catholics from Manchester; each of them would shout 'No red flag for me' - I ended up in a fight with one of them and came out with a black eye. The Manchester men were antagonistic anyway because they were pioneers and I was a sapper. The pioneers did all the hard work with pick and shovel for the basic army pay of seven shillings, of which half was deducted to send to their wives, while the sappers got fifteen shillings. All the pioneers hated the sappers. But I got some support from Labour men in the company, particularly a big fellow named Tucky who had been a member of the Rugby Trades Council.

After I had been in the army nine months I was still refusing to be inoculated. Everyone else was going to the front. I was put in the reserve section, where I was offered stripes because I was the only one who knew how to splice and knot ropes (from my short apprenticeship in sail-making). I refused the stripes, and I had made my decision about what I was going to do. I agreed to have the first of my two inoculations, and applied for leave before getting the second. I went back to Glasgow and deserted.

Much later I learned what had happened to the men I had known. A sapper named Bogie had told the whole company that when the police caught me he personally would go to Glasgow and bring me back. He was wounded in France, refused to go to the dressing centre and was killed by a bullet in the head. The lieutenant of our section also was killed - a pig of a fellow who wanted to distinguish himself. He wanted some of the men to go out and repair barbed wire while bullets were coming in thousands; a shovel which was held up was peppered with bullets. The lieutenant decided to show the men the way, and was instantly killed.

Going into the army was certainly a silly thing to have done, but I got some satisfaction out of it. It might have been possible to get further with socialist propaganda in the conscripted army of 1916; but among the volunteers of 1914 it was impossible to persuade any of them that the war was wrong.

My army uniform was ditched in the Clyde by a pal from the ILP, and we decided that I ought to get out of Glasgow for a while as the police were looking for me. I was prepared to go to Ireland; John Maclean and Jimmy MacDougall wrote me a letter of recommendation to James Connolly in Dublin. While I was waiting to get away the old anarchist barber from Glasgow Green, David Baxter, took me in. He had his shop in Brunswick Street and had a six-roomed house in Grafton Square. I was glad to live with David to keep out of the road of the police and in his shop I met one of the old Glasgow propagandists, Laurie Anderson. He advised me to go not to Ireland but to Ameria. I waited and waited for him to help me get there; eventually I had no money and decided to get a job under an assumed name.

I went to work under the name of Kellaway, but each place I settled I had to leave because somebody recognised me. I worked in a couple of little places before I was introduced to Archie Henry of the SLP, who got me a place in Dalmuir Shipyard. Before long it became dangerous there; finally I decided to go to sea, and I signed on with the Eagle Oil Transport Company.

I did three voyages as an engineer. On one of them I went to Texas: it was a real lesson to me. Coloured people couldn't drink in the same bar as white people, there were different toilets for whites and coloureds, different seating compartments on the train. I got into an awful row for walking on the coloured side of the street. I wasn't happy. One big white I met told me he had just shot a Negro for rape: I was glad I had refused a drink from him.

The voyage from Glasgow to Texas took three weeks and was very dangerous. Our ship had been repaired in Glasgow and the nut on the piston of the HP cylinder hadn't been properly tightened down; it worked loose and smashed the cylinder cover, in mid-ocean. I had to reassemble the cover. It was like a jig-saw, and the cylinder was red-hot - I burnt a pair of boots right through, working on top of it. We held the cover together with a large plate fastened over it with joints and nuts, and managed to get across patched up like that.

A week out from Texas we had more problems when all the fires went out. Water had got into the oil and from there into the fires; we had to take off all the brass pipes, drain them and put them back again. It was a tremendous experience, made more exciting because we were in waters full of submarines and raiding schooners which were out to rob ships. Every captain was wary of the 'Emden', a notorious German raiding ship, and when a schooner signalled us for its course we signalled back and zigzagged away as quickly as possible.

The engineers were labour aristocrats on board ship. We ranked as officers, had our own galley and ate separately from the crew, and we each had a separate room and could bath in the engine-room. We were paid £13 a month with full board. I actually went to sea under my own name - the company was so short of men that when I showed my apprenticeship lines they just grabbed me. Any Glasgow engineer was welcome because Glasgow was a centre for marine engineering:

a spell at sea was the thing to do for all of us.

The Eagle Oil Transport Company wasn't bad. I would have stayed with them, but when I came home from my third trip I found that my grandfather was dying. I let the ship go and stayed in Glasgow.

7. 'Tuppence or Nothing'

Living conditions in Glasgow were terrible before the war broke out and another depression was about to start - but the war changed all that. Some Glasgow men were fully employed for the first time in their lives; so many had rushed to join the army that you could go anywhere and get a job. The government had to pass the Munitions Amendment Act, 1915, making a 'leaving certificate' compulsory: that was to stop men leaving one job and going to another with more money. Munitions tribunals were set up for workmen to attempt to get leaving certificates and employers to have workmen disciplined over them.

Although men in work were better off than they had ever been, others were suffering. The soldiers' wives, shop assistants who didn't get wage increases, the elderly, labourers who were too old to go in the army, were all suffering from price increases. With the coming of the war food prices and rents immediately rose, and the parish allowances the poor got were no use at all. An examination by the Scottish Poor Law was a terrible fearsome thing. They always paid cash in Scotland, never in kind as they sometimes did in England, but they paid very little.

Prices had been rising from 1900 on, but with the war they rose much more steeply and there were also shortages; rationing was introduced to control the shortages, but there was very little control over prices. The price rises and shortages affected skilled workers as well as the poor. In engineering there had been a national agreement over wages before the war, which kept the engineers out of all the big strikes. But in 1914 this agreement came to an end and the ASE branches in Glasgow demanded an increase of twopence an hour. This was unprecedented - an engineer's wage increase was normally a farthing! Usually the workmen demanded a halfpenny expecting to get a farthing, just as the employers sometimes demanded a half-penny reduction and expected to get a farthing. But nobody had ever heard of twopence; the officials were horrified.

The issue came to a head at Weir's. To help the war effort the management had introduced American engineers who were being paid £6 a week, to the Clyde workers' 38s.4d. Of course the older hands in Weir's demanded the same as the Americans, and when they struck work the whole of the Clyde engineers came out in their support and demanded twopence an hour on the rate. The men remained out for several weeks, against their official trade-union leadership, and finally won a penny an hour and 10 per cent on the piece-rate. They actually rejected an offer of three-farthings an hour by 10 to 1 in a ballot.

It was a solid rank-and-file strike which stayed firm despite the most awful onslaught on them by the newspapers. I was in the army then, in February 1915, and I remember the articles about the Clyde shirkers, the Clyde slackers, the Clyde traitors. Workers on Clydeside took a drink after work, and as far as the press were concerned that made them all drunkards. Lloyd George came out with the statement that strong drink was one of the enemies Britain had to fight. The *Daily Record* carried a photograph of a public house near the Fairfield Shipyard called Number One, which is still there, with all the 'half and halfs' - whisky and a half-pint - lined up along the counter waiting for the yard gates to open at the end of the shift. Some papers even suggested that the strikers were in the pay of the Germans!

It was a shipyard manager who attacked the shipyard workers as drunkards, though he had to withdraw it. The shipbuilding employers were a despicable lot. I'll never forget the sanitary conditions in the shipyards where I worked; they were truly awful. Yet they were among the most arrogant of all employers. The engineering employers were somehow more respectable - although equally vicious in their attitude to the workers.

The 'tuppence or nothing' strike brought the shop-stewards' movement into prominence for the first time, and created the Clyde Labour With-holding Committee. It started the organisation of workshop committees in factories which had never had them. Most of the old shop-stewards, whose only job had been to check the ASE cards, disappeared. Many of the younger ones who led the struggle during the war were socialists from the BSP, ILP and the SLP. Jim Messer of the ILP, who had helped make Weir's the best organised factory in Glasgow, was a fine secretary for the Labour With-holding

Committee and later when it changed its name to the Clyde Workers' Committee.

Willie Gallacher of the BSP and the Albion Works became the chairman of the committee. I never thought much of Gallacher as a political thinker but as an industrial leader there was no one better. He could get action; his arguments were simple, he had a tremendous sense of humour and he could rouse workers. It wasn't easy to rouse up engineers; they were very respectable with their blue suits and bowler hats, and used to come to mass meetings with their umbrellas. Gallacher dressed like that as well.

The engineers' victory helped other struggles, particularly the one over rents. Agitation against rent increases and evictions for non-payment of rent developed all through 1915; it led first to a rent strike and then an industrial strike in November of that year.

In Clydeside there was more discontent about rents than elsewhere because the housing conditions were so much worse. There were streets and streets of one-room apartments, with whole families living in the one room and four or five families sharing one toilet on the stair. The tenement houses were all privately owned and there was a lot of opposition from the landlords to corporation housing. Rents were low because wages were low, but still they were difficult to collect. Rent arrears led to frequent moonlight flittings, which were possible because there was no shortage of dwellings in Glasgow before the war. The builders had even stopped building houses for rent because there was no profit in them.

But when the war started all the unoccupied houses were taken up by workers drafted into the workshops and shipyards for war production. The landlords immediately started to raise the rents and to apply for eviction orders against the old tenants who couldn't pay. The hardest hit were the unemployed and the elderly, and the soldiers' wives; but it even became difficult for the employed workers, despite increased wages, to meet the demands of the house-factors.

The struggle against rent increases and evictions became keenest in Govan and Partick, where most of the skilled workers in engineering and shipbuilding lived. New workers were moving into these areas all the time; everyone was looking for a house near his work because of the long hours of overtime. Mrs Mary Barbour organised the women in Govan to resist the rent increases. They got together to resist the sheriff officer when he came to evict anybody, and had processions two hundred strong against the house-factors. Mrs Barbour became a Govan legend; even now her name is still used by the Labour Party at election times and mentioned in the local press.

Most of the women who led the fight on rents were in the ILP. Andrew McBride was in the thick of it with them. Andrew was a little fellow, modest and not much of a speaker, but he was the secretary of the Glasgow Labour Housing Association from before the war and really built it up. He had a small grocer's business in the Gorbals and spent an enormous amount of time organising. In Partick, Andrew Hood played a big part. He was the editor of the *Partick Gazette* and used it to publicise the rent strike - later he became a Labour Lord Provost.

By October 1915 there were about 25,000 tenants on rent strike. The strikes were all against private landlords, as was always the case in Glasgow, and were helped by the fact that people had to take their rent to the house-factor (the solicitor who managed the rents for the landlord). They could see who was going into the house-factor's office and knew who was paying and who wasn't.

By the end of the year strong feeling had built up about evictions of soldiers' wives and widows and their children. The people's attitude to the war had changed; the stories were coming back from the trenches, it was plain that the war was lasting much more than six months, and they just weren't prepared to go on suffering. The support for rent strikes and the rise in discontent and ill-feeling were so great that the government began to consider whether or not to bring in legislation on rents - althought many in the government were completely opposed to limitation. Then, in November 1915, an industrial strike against the rent increases finished all the discussion.

In November 18 tenants were taken to court in an attempt by the factors to get rent deducted from their wages at source. One of them was an engineer in the Dalmuir shipyard called James Reid and all the shipyard workers from Dalmuir, Fairfield, Stephens and other yards and factories downed tools and marched to the court in support. On the way one contingent stopped at Lorne Street School for John Maclean and took him down to the court with them.

It was John's last day as a schoolteacher; he had been sacked for his anti-war propaganda, and the very next day he was due to go to prison. In September 1915 he had been arrested under the Defence of the Realm Act at a meeting at Shawlands. He had called the war a 'murder business' and got into an argument with a soldier, and the police twisted it and said that John had called the soldier a murderer. Sheriff Lee was the magistrate and John only got a £5 fine or five days' imprisonment; he refused to pay the fine on principle and went to prison, which gave the Govan School Board the chance to sack him. *Forward* campaigned for his reinstatement and there were large demonstrations of workers outside the Govan School Board meetings. Harry Hopkins, secretary of the Govan Trades Council, was the only socialist on the school board and put up a terrific fight; but John was dismissed.

At the court-house there was a mass meeting in the street. Maclean, Gallacher, McBride and others spoke; the police pulled the platforms from under them but they continued speaking, and the meeting demanded that the sheriff receive a deputation. To discuss a case with a deputation of workers before the proceedings opened was against all the court rules, but once again Sheriff Lee was in charge and he agreed. After he had met the deputation he phoned Whitehall, who assured him that the rent restrictions legislation would be introduced in the next month. The house-factors still wouldn't agree to an adjournment of the case, and Sheriff Lee then delayed it on his own responsibility.

When the Act came into force it pegged rents to the level they were before the war broke out, and only allowed a 40 per cent increase if repairs were carried out. In the 1930s it was possible for the socialist movement to use that act and encourage tenants to with-hold rents until they got their repairs done: I used it myself. Even past the second world war there were some tenants in houses that had been rent-controlled in 1915.

John Maclean had great hopes that the Glasgow rent strike heralded the development of political strikes in Britain. We had read about the mass political strikes in Germany and Russia before the war and we knew of Rosa Luxemburg's book *The Mass Strike*. But in Britain the next struggle was by the engineers against 'dilution', the introduction of unskilled men and women into skilled work - a very difficult fight for socialists who had always been opposed to the craft trade unions and advocated industrial unions. The Clyde Workers' Committee led the struggle against dilution, and John Maclean fell out with its leaders.

Wages agitation in engineering died down because managements were introducing bonus schemes such as we had never had before and there was a great deal of overtime working. The agitation over the Munitions Act also died down: managements had to stop using it so viciously against workmen because of the trouble it caused, and the government was forced to amend it. But dilution of labour was seen as a very serious threat. Even before the war some skilled jobs in engineering were so simplified by new machinery that the engineer had to fight to maintain his position. It was a different situation from that of the other skilled crafts: for the boilermakers the question of dilution didn't arise, a riveter's job was one which no plater's helper could do.

Gallacher and others made their reputations in the 'tuppence or nothing' strike, but they failed to keep the movement together during the dilution struggle. John Maclean was opposed to the way the Clyde Workers' Committee and the socialists on it were behaving, and I agreed with him. John argued that the main struggle was against the war. Most of the shop stewards were socialists and anti-war, but they had submerged their politics in workshop struggles and were not even mentioning the war inside the factories. Willie Gallacher's conduct in particular angered John Maclean.

Willie had a peculiar relationship with the BSP, you never knew whether he was in or out, and after he became chairman of the CWC he was impatient with the political side of the movement. Although at the beginning of the war he spoke at an anti-war meeting held jointly by the ILP and the BSP in Govan, after the engineers' strike he concentrated merely on industrial demands. At the end of 1915 he came to speak at Bath Street, where the meetings were at the centre of our anti-war struggle. He did not mention the war at all, and the next Sunday at Bath Street John Maclean criticised him openly. He asked: 'How could any man calling himself a socialist come to speak at a meeting at this time and *not* refer to the war that is raging in Europe!'

The breach between Maclean and Gallacher widened further when Jimmy MacDougall and Peter Petroff were thrown out of one of the CWC meetings. Petroff was a Russian refugee who had come to Britain in 1907 and lived at John's house before he went to London. When the war broke out John proposed to the BSP that we bring him up to Glasgow, and he and his wife Imra came up and lived on £1 a week and joined the anti-war propaganda. Petroff not only spoke at our indoor meetings at the Templar's Hall in Ingram Street but also at the outdoor meetings we started at Brunswick Street.

He was an exceptionally good speaker and he wrote for John's paper the *Vanguard*. He acquainted us with details of the Russian socialist movement, and from him we learned about Lenin and Trotsky and others. Imra was in my branch of the BSP. Both of them were very brave in their anti-war work, particularly in view of their status as aliens: he was a Russian, but she was a German socialist.

Normally only shop-stewards were present at the CWC meetings, but Peter Petroff and Jimmy MacDougall were allowed to attend. It wasn't a delegate body, the shop-stewards who spoke merely said where they were from and I went a few times when I was a shop-steward at Parkhead Forge. There were usually two or three hundred there on Saturday afternoons; any one of them could speak, and they had allowed Petroff to speak. But on this occasion he and MacDougall had been sent by the BSP to raise the question of the CWC officially coming out against the war. Gallacher immediately ordered Petroff out of the hall on the grounds that he wasn't a shop-steward. When MacDougall objected that he was doing this because Petroff was a foreigner, Gallacher said he would prove that wasn't so by throwing MacDougall out as well.

Although the leadership of the CWC were supposed to be revolutionary socialists, they actually came under the influence of other ideas. Gallacher had the usual syndicalist cry - too much education and not enough action; theory wasn't a strong point with him. Johnny Muir was the 'intellectual' of the CWC. Muir was a member of the SLP who worked in Barr and Stroud's, the scientific instrument makers. He argued that the CWC should accept the war as a fact and work for what they could get in the circumstances. Davie Kirkwood was a member of the SLP when the war broke out and because of Muir's attitude he left and joined the ILP. Most other SLP members were anti-war like Arthur MacManus, but didn't oppose Muir in the CWC; neither did the BSP members. This meant that no anti-war fight developed inside the factories; the men were making guns, shells and all kinds of munitions, but the all-important question was never raised. Johnny Muir, of the SLP and the Clyde Workers' Committee, later actually joined the Labour Party and became a parliamentary candidate for the same consti-tuency which had John S. Clarke as its MP for a short time.

John Wheatley of the ILP also had a big influence on the

leadership of the CWC. He wasn't in the workshop, he was in business, but he supported the CWC and advised them more than they were prepared to admit; Gallacher himself told me about their meetings with Wheatley. None of the shop-stewards ever criticised him - he was the only man in the ILP who was never attacked by the revolutionary left - because he did a lot of work behind the scenes for them. But he used his influence to bring Davie Kirkwood to the fore in the CWC and the ILP, and it was Kirkwood who broke up the CWC's united policy against dilution. Although I usually supported Wheatley, I appreciated John Maclean's suspiciousness of him and the ILP. The ILP were so taken up with state and municipal control that they had a very dubious attitude to state-owned munitions factories: Kirkwood later became a foreman in one.

The Clyde engineers' refusal to accept dilution meant that Lloyd George, the Minister of Munitions, decided to visit Glasgow at Christmas 1915. The government had come to an agreement with the trade-union leaders, and Lloyd George was accompanied by Arthur Henderson, a Labour member of the cabinet. They intended to meet the CWC. At first the leadership were determined against a meeting with Lloyd George; but he went to Parkhead Forge and Kirkwood met him and made a long speech - which probably had been discussed with Wheatley - outlining his policy on dilution. The speech was printed in *Forward*, and it made Kirkwood's reputation.

The Clyde Workers' Committee were therefore obliged to meet Lloyd George in order to put forward their policy on dilution. He visited Weir's and then agreed to a meeting in St. Andrew's Halls where he would speak to the shop-stewards. John Maclean couldn't get in because he wasn't a shop-steward, but he stood outside handing out leaflets about the pantomime that was going on. Inside the hall, Lloyd George got a terrible reception and could barely be heard. He had thought that his great oratory and prestige would sway the Clude, but he got no satisfaction at all.

An official account of the meeting was published. It was complete lies; and when *Forward* published the true account it was immediately suppressed. John Maclean's *Vanguard* was found at the same printing press and was also suppressed. With no socialist paper on the Clyde now, the CWC decided to issue their own paper, the *Worker*. It reproduced the *Forward* account of the Lloyd George meeting, and it too was suppressed. All the papers re-started after a month or two, but the government was looking for an excuse to move against the shop-stewards. A national shop-stewards' movement was developing, and the Glasgow organisation was the most prominent.

The government therefore began to move against key individuals. First Peter Petroff was arrested, on the charge that as an alien he should have informed the authorities when he moved from London to Glasgow. Sheriff Thompson tried the case and sentenced Petroff to two months. It was a scandalous decision, and the people in the court stood up and sang 'The Internationale'. After his release he was interned in Edinburgh until the Russian Revolution. His German wife Imra was arrested as an enemy alien because they were not legally married. She was fined £10 or ten days and I did my best to persuade her to let us pay the fine; but she refused, was arrested, and then interned.

The following month, February, Maclean was arrested on a charge of sedition - making speeches to rouse the workers against the war itself. Then Gallacher, Muir, and Walter Bell who printed the *Worker* were arrested. They were charged with publishing an article called 'Should the Workers Arm?' In fact the unsigned article was written by Willie Reagan of the Catholic Socialist Society, and it was against insurrection and argued that the workers should not arm. But, for the government, the title was enough!

A further opportunity to move against the shop-stewards' movement was provided by the split between Davie Kirkwood and the rest of the CWC, over dilution. Once the new policy was established - the workers themselves attempting to control the conditions under which dilution took place - the fight began to be on the *rights* of shop-stewards. During the whole process of the introduction of new labour - women, soldiers, unskilled men - it was important for the stewards to have the right to call meetings and unionise the new workers, and to be able to move freely round the factories. The struggle over these matters came to a head at Parkhead Forge.

This factory was completely different from Weir's, where the whole works was under one roof: it was broken up into different buildings separated by different main gates. As convenor of shop-stewards, Kirkwood had to be able to go from one part to another. Suddenly, in March 1916, this right was challenged. Parkhead Forge struck work; but the other major CWC factories were unwilling to support Kirkwood because he had broken the agreement on dilution, and they did not strike. The government took the opportunity to seize Kirkwood and other shop-stewards (whose factories were *not* on strike), and deport them from Glasgow. Of course underlying this was the CWC's failure to face up to the issue of the war - it provided the government with a strategy for splitting the rank and file.

Nine shop-stewards were deported; then Smith, a shop-steward at Weir's, was arrested on a sedition charge. At the same time, James Maxton and Jimmy MacDougall were also arrested for sedition. Both were conscientious objectors and were refusing to go into the army. At that time conscientious objectors got a terrible time of it in prison - some were actually driven mad. Maclean advised the two of them to be arrested on a political charge. At a Sunday meeting over the deportations, at Nelson's Monument, they both made speeches with that in view.

Jimmy Maxton said: 'Strike and down tools! In case there are any plain-clothes policemen present I will repeat that for their benefit - 'strike and down tools!' MacDougall followed and said: 'Strike, strike, strike and to hell with them.' In April John Maclean was sentenced to three years' hard labour; Gallacher, Muir and Bell were sentenced to a year; Smith, eighteen months; and finally Maxton and MacDougall were sentenced to one year each.

The CWC suffered as a result of the *Worker* article and the dispute about dilution. It was understandable that Davie Kirkwood should have broken the ranks on the latter question. As well as being under Wheatley's influence he was an old-time labour aristocrat. He was a typical engineer, proud of his skill and status, well groomed; he always boasted that he neither smoked nor drank, and that he had been brought up in Parkhead and all his family were buried in the local cemetery. He was very proud of his 'personal influence' with Sir William Beardmore, the owner of Parkhead Forge - he usually negotiated directly with Beardmore. Beardmore, of course, took advantage of Kirkwood's attitude. After the dilution agreement was signed he introduced both women and soldiers into the workshops, and then refused Kirkwood the right to organise them! This time, the other shop-stewards in Glasgow wouldn't support *him*.

After imposing the deportations and jail sentences the government was able to become much more open in its repression, and there were raids on socialist meetings to arrest absentees from the army. Fred Shaw, a BSP member from Huddersfield, was brought up to keep John Maclean's marxist lectures going, and the military raided a meeting in the International Halls when he was speaking. George Pettigrew was in the chair and he made them wait until Shaw finished his lecture; then they rounded up all the absentees.

I had to be careful not to work in the centre of Glasgow on this account. When I returned from sea I worked first in a small manufacturers', A & W Smith's, then a railway workshop, and then a small ironworks in Bridgeton. I didn't like the railway engineering because it was all piece-work and I had never worked where there was no basic rate. I didn't like the Bridgeton Ironworks either because I actually did no work. The company was on government contracts and, like Fairfield before the war, they received so much for every man they employed: so I was on the payroll with nothing to do and being paid £5 a week for doing it. I got so fed up with hanging about that I went to the munitions tribunal to try for a leaving certificate. I was taking a chance doing that; but there were so many chances for the military to pick me up that I thought I might as well.

Of course I didn't get a leaving certificate. I was so bored that I offered to rebuild an old engine, a complete wreck, that lay in the company's yard. They thought I was joking until I rebuilt it from scratch. Then, fortunately, they got a contract to put in some plant at a works in Stevenson, and I agreed to go and do it if they increased my wages. I got on quite well there and enjoyed the work. The foreman of the mechanic squad and I made a deal - I helped him finish his work, then he and his squad worked on mine.

For the six months I worked in Stevenson, I lived in Saltcoats. There was no ILP or BSP branch, but there was a socialist club founded by Willie Kerr who later became Provost of Saltcoats. It was while I was there that John Maclean was jailed; and the same April the Irish Rising took place, and Connolly was murdered by the army.

The Irish Rising of Easter 1916 came like a bolt from the blue. No one who knew Connolly in Glasgow had an idea that he would be leading the citizen army against the British army. In *Forward* he had attacked the Irish Nationalist MPs for supporting the war, particularly John Redmond and his brother Willie (who actually took a commission). The whole of Ireland was angry with the MPs who obviously thought of themselves as British and not Irish, who were not fighting for Home Rule - and were now supporting a British army alongside Carson and the Ulster Volunteers who had prevented Irish Home Rule before the war. But although the majority of the

Irish people were against the war and the government didn't dare to try and introduce conscription in Ireland, we had no idea of a rising. Connolly had hoped to inspire the rest of Ireland, but the Dubliners were left to fight alone. A week after the rising, the news came that he was wounded. Willie Kerr in the Socialist Club actually blamed the rebels - he said there had been enough bloodshed in the world! I had a terrible battle that night; but Willie wasn't the only one. MacDonald and others condemned the rising as another form of militarism. Forward was against it, the pacifist ILP didn't support Connolly. The BSP in Glasgow were united for him, but the SLP he had helped to found were completely split: their best comrades supported the rising, but others opposed it because it wasn't based on industry the way they liked things to be. The Glasgow Irish, who were then much closer to Irish happenings than they are now, began to collect guns for the next time, and all of them came closer to the socialist movement.

Although the Irish Rising and the subsequent murder of Connolly strengthened the best of the revolutionary elements, the ILP was growing much faster. The start of conscription, the call-up of single men that began in April 1916, strengthened pacifist feeling enormously. Liberals and ILPers opposed the call-up bitterly: conscription into an army went against all their feelings about state interference with the freedom of the citizen. At the beginning of the war some of the ILP leaders had decided in support of it, at a secret meeting in Glasgow; but because some of their most prominent people - like Wheatley, John S. Taylor and George Buchanan - were opposed, they had done nothing about it. Conscription changed most of their minds, and of course quite a number of other people suddenly discovered they had consciences.

There was also a growing weariness with the war. The old assertions about it lasting six months now looked ridiculous. So did the phrase 'Russian steam-roller'; the Tsarist army had thrown nearly weaponless men at the Germans and they had been mown down in their millions. The reports of the British casualties were also coming back. The number of people in Glasgow who had lost husbands and sons was enormous. The Highland Light Infantry had been cut to pieces. Every night, trains full of wounded came into Central Station and the ambulances went rushing up to Bellahouston Hospital: we could all hear them. For years after the war men lay in Bellahouston with no arms and no legs.

The papers carried horrific pictures of the war - men hung over barbed wire, men with their faces blown away. The patriots said these men were making sacrifices for all of us, but to most of the people the war became an atrocious thing. John S. Clarke, a member of the SLP, wrote poems. One, called 'A bundle of bloody rags', was about the remains of a man hanging on barbed wire and the bullets going through him. Clarke also wrote doggerel verses against the war. One, about Lloyd George, had the line 'still-born kids kicked the coffin-lids'. Another was on the occasion the king went to review the troops at the front and fell off his horse. Clarke wrote, to the refrain of 'Pull for the Shore':

> Follow your Martial Monarch, see how he goes
> Mounted on gallant charger, facing his foes.
> Far from the distant foeman bravely he fell —
> Follow his example, and all will be well.

Clarke wrote for the *Socialist* and for the *Worker* and published some of his poems in a book called *Satires, Lyrics and Verses*.

As the war-weariness spread, the patriots became even more active. A 'British Workers' League' was organised by people who were too old for the army themselves but wanted (far away from the front, of course) to back their sons. I think it was affiliated nationally, but all we saw was the Glasgow membership who were mostly middle-class. Some of the employers, like Beardmore and Yarrow, were connected with it in some way; Scott, the biggest hatter in Glasgow, took an active part. A man called M'Glashan was in it and he and I had a set-to when we broke up one of their outdoor meetings one night; he always wore a tall top hat and a frock coat at the meetings.

We went to make a stand against their pro-war propaganda. I couldn't keep away; I used to go to their indoor and outdoor meetings. I was now married, and one night I took my wife to one of the British Workers' League meetings in City Hall. The speaker was a French officer. It was a Saturday, and the meeting was packed. As the chairman sat down I asked if there would be questions, and would they be moving a resolution and would they allow amendments to it? The chairman was Scott the hatter, and he replied in a threatening manner that an amendment would be allowed. I sat trying to anticipate their resolution and to phrase an amendment, when someone behind me said that he and his friend were going to move one.

The resolution was real pro-war, and then the man behind me was called on the platform to move his amendment. He had to give his name: he was Willie Reid, who later went to parliament. He didn't get very far before he was pushed off the platform, and the chairman asked for the seconder. Reid's friend turned and asked me if I would second: he couldn't because his foreman was on the platform. I went up and gave my name and address - and, of course, after the Easter Rising with a name like McShane there were shouts of 'Sinn Feiner!' and I was pushed off the platform. The City Hall holds 1,300, and to my surprise when they called for votes for the amendment 83 stood up. Apparently Jamieson, the pro-war factor's clerk, stood up to see what was going on and when we went out all the pro-war women were battering him; and the man who wouldn't second the amendment was John McGovern, the future MP for Shettleston.

The meeting where I clashed with M'Glashan was an open-air one, and that time I didn't get away. He was saying that the Clyde workers were paid 'German gold' to disrupt industry. I walked into the ring and wouldn't let him go on speaking: I demanded that he produce one shred of proof of any worker receiving a farthing of German gold. They tried to stop me, and when a soldier walked into the ring they started shouting 'Let the soldier speak!' As soon as he got on the platform I recognised him as a man called Livingstone who had been deported from South Africa. He said 'Not a soldier, only wearing soldier's clothes'; a navy man knocked him off the platform and the police arrested him.

My wife and I went to Central Police Station, and there was a large pro-war crowd outside arguing with a young couple. The couple had to be got away; we went with them up to Argyle Street, stopped a policeman and got him to put them on a tram. The crowd chased the tram, then gave up and came back for me. I had my wife with me still, and we had to get back across the river to Tradeston where we lived. We worked our way down Argyle Street, over Jamaica Bridge and down Norfolk Street. Any time one of them came near me I batted out; they started to use their feet, and when we were across the river I grabbed my wife's hand and we ran for it.

Then, at Nelson Street, some girls joined in the chase shouting 'A socialist, a socialist'! They tried to grab my wife's hat. I dared not let that happen - the hat was held on with many hatpins. I reached over and hit the girl who was going for my wife. That was it! In those days to hit a girl was unthinkable, and the crowd came straight for me. My wife ran round the corner, and I ran to a close where they got me. I was beaten unconscious - but I went to their meeting again the next Saturday.

To me the anti-war fight was the most important one of all for socialists. I supported the industrial movement, but the horror of the war had to be fought first: we were praying and hoping to build a campaign that would put an end to it. John Maclean's struggle had given us heart; and when the Zimmerwald document, where Lenin and others came out against the war, was reprinted in Britain it renewed our hopes. But we were only thinking of stopping the war. We never thought of building a revolution *out of* the war. The Russian Revolution changed our world.

8. The Accuser of Capitalism

During my stay at Saltcoats I was arrested. I had got the Socialist Club to hold open-air propaganda meetings on the foreshore on the question of the war. Nothing came of my arrest at the time, but later the police came looking for me in Glasgow. Malcolm MacFarlane advised me to bluff it out. My wife had received a letter from the army telling her that I was off the strength and she would receive no more money. Carrying this, we went out and found a policeman and asked if he was looking for Harry McShane. He started to read out a description; we told him there was no point, as I was Harry McShane.

The police-station was a little sub-station where Kingston Library now stands and the superintendent was quite old. When the policeman said he had arrested me I pointed out that I had found him, and showed the superintendent the letter. He took my address, asked if I could always be found there, and sent me off. As I left, the young policeman asked if they should not check in the *Police Gazette*, which had all the 'wanted' notices in it. The old man replied: 'We'll do nothing of the kind, we'll take the man's word for it.' The next day I met two policemen who accused me of bluffing the superintendent. I told them to tell him that; they shut up, and I went off laughing.

After the war the police came to me again after being tipped off by someone who knew that I had been in the army. This time I produced my engineer's exemption card as a skilled craftsman, and they went away. Finally, in 1922 when I was arrested over an eviction fight and held on a charge of sedition, the chief constable told me he could get me on desertion but wasn't going to bother because they already had enough. The police thought I was going to get two years, and so did I, but I got off on a technicality.

When I came back from Saltcoats to Bridgeton I wanted to pick up my books because once again I was on the payroll doing nothing. But the company wanted to keep me because there was one job that only I could do. There were some ships on the dock bound for France, and the inspectors insisted that the engines be tested to 2,000 pounds hydraulic pressure. The engines ran perfectly, but the screws in the valves wouldn't hold under that pressure and quite a few engineers left it. When I was put on it I took the valves to pieces, ground down the bronze plate between them in about five minutes, trimmed the stems, and put them back. When the inspectors tried again, the screws held. I was the only person who could ever do it. I did it at night and I never told them how, because so many other engineers had failed. The result was that if I wasn't in the works at difficult points the manager would send for me.

When I finally left the Bridgeton firm I went down the road to Parkhead Forge and started there. I was still taking the chair at anti-war meetings, and Parkhead was a good place for me; it was a wee bit out of the centre and I wasn't known. Although my predominant interest was in the anti-war fight, I ended up as shop-steward of the howitzer shop. It was a newly set-up shop where guns and shells were built, and there was constant employment and overtime. The men and the shop-stewards there were among the most militant in Parkhead Forge. You could always rely on them to back you up; in fact it was difficult to keep them in sometimes because they stopped work for the most trivial reasons.

The war effort made the engineers' hours longer than ever before. We were working twelve-hour shifts from six to six, five days a week, with a fortnight on day shift and a fortnight on night shift. We also worked six to twelve in the mornings on Saturday and Sunday. I was earning about £6 a week including overtime, but I didn't work Sundays if I could avoid it. My wages had gone up - but so had prices and the rent. My wife and I had moved from Kingston to Gorbals, and our rent was 25s. a week; before the war, that was nearly two-thirds of my weekly earnings.

We had girls and soldiers working in the howitzer shop. It had about two thousand workers represented by twenty shop stewards, and our job was to see that everyone was in the union. The soldiers were actually skilled engineers who had been brought back from the front, and they all joined the union except one. There were no meetings of all the shop-stewards in Parkhead Forge, as there had been at Weir's when I was there. Bob Blair, an ex-member of the SDF, was the convenor and he never called a meeting; but he was quite amenable in other ways. Although he was initially pro-war he didn't oppose the anti-war people inside the factory. Like many others, he was getting increasingly disillusioned with the war after the reports of the Battle of the Somme in July 1916, and after the beginning of conscription.

As a shop-steward I used to attend the Clyde Workers' Committee meetings which were held in the Templars' Halls in Ingram Street. It was a very open meeting all about industrial questions and action in the workshops, and everyone put forth their own point of view. It was a strange looking meeting, too - a couple of hundred engineering shop-stewards, all with their bowler hats, blue suits and rolled umbrellas, discussing the next policy to pursue.

The news of the first Russian Revolution of February 1917 came while I was working at Parkhead Forge. We all studied every report. The best were those written by Phillips Price in the *Manchester Guardian*; he was their Russian correspondent, very sympathetic to the Revolution, and from his articles we could work out what was going on. Everybody except the worst Tories welcomed the Russian Revolution, but the reasons varied. The average Liberal had always hated the Tsarist tyranny as much as socialists did and was overjoyed that the Tsar had been brought down. But for the Liberal Government the Revolution meant new hope for the war effort. The 'Russian steamroller' had collapsed and the soldiers were completely demoralised; for our Government, the real issue was to get new leaders at the head of things in Russia to keep them in the war.

But for the mass of the people the Revolution meant hope that the war would end. It wasn't only revolutionary socialists who saw it in that way. Even the right wing of the Labour Party understood that it was part of a whole movement of social change which could bring about different relations between states and a negotiated peace. But the revolutionaries had a special interest: we were watching a man called Lenin.

Lloyd George made speeches about the 'wonderful young man Kerensky'. That gave us the clue to see Kerensky as another Lloyd George, a real hypocrite, and to keep watching the struggle for someone else. We had heard of Lenin during the Zimmerwald Conference, although we didn't know who he was until Petroff had explained something of the Russian movement, and now in some of the reports on the Revolution Lenin's figure began to emerge. I remember turning to Tommy Linden, who worked alongside me in Parkhead Forge, and saying: 'That's the man we've got to watch.' A lot of revolutionary socialists were saying the same. We knew the Revolution wasn't over. We had our own doubts about parliamentary 'democracy', and we were looking forward to the overthrow of Kerensky as well.

The agitation for John Maclean's release from prison was renewed. A tremendous mass campaign developed. In June 1917, the month of the Leeds Convention of Workers' and Soldiers' Councils, John was released after serving half of his three-year sentence. In the same month the Clyde deportees also returned; Gallacher had got out of jail in February; and the reappearance of all of them brought new life to the movement.

The CWC, which had become small and sectarian after the arrests in 1916, was reconstituted. As a shop-steward in Parkhead Forge I sometimes attended. The meetings were held in the Templars' Halls, where John Maclean's economics classes had started; Gallacher was in the chair and James Messer was the secretary once again. They were very open meetings, with everybody putting his own point of view about industrial questions and action in the workshop. We were all facing different problems over the introduction of dilution schemes and bonuses.

The management of Parkhead Forge wanted to impose a collective bonus while I was there. Our shift was completely opposed to it: a collective bonus meant that all the men on the shift watched one another and every man was your boss. The shop-steward on the opposite night shift to us was Bob Smillie, the famous miners' leader's son. Although we had agreed that both shifts would take the full time to the job and not collect the bonus, Smillie's shift were working hard and putting their bonus lines on the wall in order to collect it later. There was trouble over this, and we decided that the two shifts should meet.

The night shift started work at 6.30 and we stopped at 6.00. It was decided that in order to meet our shift would stop at 5.30 and theirs would start at 7.00, and that we would meet in the ILP Halls in Parkhead. The management came to me and said that if I spoke to any man in our department I would be dealt with. In order to watch me the manager and the foreman entered the glass box in the middle of the shop, where they could see right down the bay.

My assistant shop-steward, Tommy Linden, had stood by me on the issue of the petition. Tommy was quite fearless; he had a brother who died quite young who had been very prominent in the SLP, and Tommy seemed to get inspiration from that. At 5.30 he and I, without speaking to a soul, took off our overalls. Every man in the place followed suit, and we all walked out of the gate.

The meeting got nowhere. We couldn't win the fight over the collective bonus because of the split between the two shifts. Smillie was up in the office suggesting alternative bonus schemes which I wouldn't have anything to do with. I would accept nothing but the time rate, but he was ready to compromise (later on he became an official of another union). Most of the other engineers in Parkhead Forge were also hostile to the bonus, but after they got the extra money under the new system they were broken in to it. The system of bonus payments in general entered engineering during the first world war, with the demands of the government for extra effort. It meant that you were really kept at it in Parkhead Forge.

After the bonus dispute I was shifted to another section of the same bay and the management made life difficult for me. In my new place I could be seen whenever I moved from the vice to talk to any man, and I was in trouble time and again for moving. Finally they decided to sack me for bad workmanship. In that section we made hundreds of levers for guns, and all the levers were piled in one corner. A bad one was picked out, they said it was mine, and I was sacked. Of course it was impossible to identify who had made the lever and I objected.

Tommy Linden had noticed how I made the levers; I always took away the sharp champers of every lever before I started doing anything at all. No other workman did this, so the lever they had picked out couldn't possibly be mine. They still.sacked me - just before lunch time, which meant that we didn't have time to arrange a normal meeting (usually we advertised our meetings in the breakfast break and then held them at lunch time). But Tommy ran round the whole shop; everybody agreed that the thing was a fake, and nobody restarted after lunch. The men sat at their benches playing cards and the girls sat singing songs. I had never had any contact with the girls in the shell department, never spoken to them; but this was the sort of spirit there was. Everybody just sat there enjoying themselves.

We sent a deputation to the management who said they would settle the dispute when work was resumed. We then sent another

D

deputation who were instructed to use a famous four-letter word. They did - at that time it was a very shocking thing. The management decided to reinstate me, but after that I never got any peace. They put me right next to the foreman's box and he watched everything I did: I just couldn't move. I stuck it out for another couple of months but then I left.

Shortly before I left Parkhead Forge the shop-stewards were invited to attend a meeting at which Flora Drummond, the militant suffragette, was to speak. When we got there we found that it was organised by the British Workers' League and they had packed the hall with their supporters. Like many of the middle-class suffragettes, Flora Drummond was now a pro-war speaker, and she and the other speakers attacked the shop-stewards who were hindering the war effort. But at the meeting there were two courageous women socialists, Helen Crawfurd and Agnes Dollan, and they made a great fight of it.

It was Helen Crawfurd, who had herself been a suffragette as well as a socialist, who replied. She was a very dignified widow, always dressed in black, and she walked right up the hall to the reporters' table and gave Flora Drummond a real dressing-down. I thought the crowd would murder her, and we had a difficult job to get her clear of them. They threw us out one by one and some of us were hurt. (Jamieson, the pro-war speaker, was also hurt: when we were under attack there always seemed to be someone who mistook him for one of us.) Eventually we managed to get together and start fighting in a bunch; that quietened them, and we were able to get away. We were led into a trap that night, but I'm sure that it actually stiffened our anti-war work.

In September the Stockholm Peace Conference took place. The calling of the conference and the attempt by leading Labour Party members to attend it actually led to the sacking of Arthur Henderson from the war cabinet. A petition began to be circulated, demanding an immediate peace without annexations and indemnification. I think it was even supported by the district committee of the ASE. I took the petition into Parkhead Forge and immediately ran into trouble. The soldiers who were working there came after me, demanded to know if I was responsible, and threatened me with the Defence of the Realm Act and they got the backing of the management. We had to hold a meeting of the whole shop, and when it was made clear that everyone would stop work if I was sacked the management climbed down. I collected a large number of names, but I never heard of any other shop-steward who brought the petition in and the whole idea seemed to fizzle out. After that my situation at Parkhead Forge became even more impossible.

From Parkhead Forge I went straight back to A & W Smith's, and they opened the doors for me. They were already off war work and back on sugar machinery, and were having real trouble with one job. The foreman saw me at the door and said 'Come in. You'll do the job while he's still getting his tools ready' - the fellow who was doing it was shifted to another job. The welcome didn't last very long, though I stayed there for the next two and a half years. I became the shop-steward, and the foreman and I had a lot of battles.

Smith's was a difficult place to organise. The foremen were members of the union and the workers were very orthodox engineers, mostly church-goers. It was a small workshop and there were no real issues to organise round. Everybody was paid the proper time rate for doing jobs they had all done before and knew; we all earned £4.8s. and there was no bonus. It was only when a special job came in that there was any difficulty at all, but I had already worked on all kinds of sugar machinery at Mirrlees Watson's and I had no trouble.

I was in A & W Smith's when the Russian Revolution of November 1917 occurred and the Bolsheviks took power through the Soviets, the new form of workers' government in Russia. The Liberals went stone mad. Winston Churchill toured the country speaking against the Bolshevik 'beasts' and lost any popularity he had ever had among the working class. The Labour Party wouldn't support the Bolsheviks either. Like the liberals, Ramsay MacDonald and his colleagues had been for Kerensky, the leader of the Menshevik faction of Russian socialists who wanted a parliamentary 'Duma' and not Soviets.

When the Labour Party called the Leeds Conference of 'Workers' and Soldiers' Councils' in June 1917 the object had been not to bring about a revolution in Britain or support further change in Russia, but social change without revolution. They had seen the first Russian Revolution as a democratic movement from below that would establish a socialist parliament, not one which would challenge bourgeois parliaments. The ILP itself nearly split over the second Revolution that brought the Bolsheviks to power, not knowing whether to support the Soviets or not. Many ILPers saw that the second Revolution was completely different, that it was destroying Liberalism, destroying the old type of democracy.

The revolutionary element, including some of the ILP, began to understand workers' democracy for the first time. For the Glasgow socialist movement the new Soviet system was a revelation. From Phillips Price's reports we got to know the slogan 'All power to the Soviets' and to get some idea of what they were. We had realised that they were workers' and soldiers' councils, a new kind of rank-and-file organisation, and everybody had welcomed the Leeds Conference in June. But what some there had not understood was that this organisation was the form of government of the future. When Lenin called for 'All power to the Soviets' it meant that they had discovered a system of working-class self-government through which the old crowd could be completely destroyed. We began now to realise what was meant by revolution. We had only known working-class revolt: now we could talk about working-class power.

Of course the mass of the workers didn't support the Bolsheviks. Many were still Liberals, and the Liberals were campaigning for the overthrow of the Bolsheviks and the return of Kerensky. But for the first time ordinary workers saw the possibility of something being gained by revolution - and the kind of fight we had conducted in Glasgow for workshop organisation made it easier for them to understand what was happening in Russia. We seized the ideas of the Russian Revolution and spread them, and found sympathy which had not existed before. Lenin's *State and Revolution* helped enormously towards understanding. Before, the SLP idea of workshop organisation had been counterposed to the idea of parliamentary action; now we saw the unity of all types of action.

After the Bolsheviks took power in Russia they named John Maclean Russian Consul in Glasgow, the first Bolshevik consul to be appointed. Already, in October 1917, Lenin had declared John Maclean of Britain to be one of the handful of real revolutionary socialists in Europe who had taken a principled stand during the war. While the British government were forced to concede something to the Russians - they released Petroff and Tchternine from internment after Maclean's long campaign to free them - they put every possible impediment in the way of his work as consul. But by now the whole movement on the Clyde was drawing together again. In January 1918 the shop-stewards' movement officially declared opposition to the war and John Maclean and Willie Gallacher became much closer. Maclean was inspired by the shop-stewards' decision; that and the Russian Revolution transformed his work.

The decision to oppose the war was taken at a meeting of the Clyde Workers' Committee at which Sir Auckland Geddes spoke. Geddes had steered the new Military Service Bill through the House of Commons; the bill extended conscription to skilled men, with the single men to be called up first. This repeated what had been done with unskilled workers in 1916. The government was running short of cannon-fodder, and every engineer in the Clyde expected it would be their turn next; already their skilled labour had been replaced by the labour of women and they were no longer essential workers.

At the Geddes meeting in St. Andrew's Halls a trade-union official named Lawston was in the chair, but it was Gallacher who took charge of the meeting. He brought a young boy on to the platform, an eighteen-year-old apprentice - led him right up to Auckland Geddes and said: 'Do you want this boy to go and fight for you?' There is no reply to that kind of question. Arthur MacManus proposed the resolution against the war and he was seconded by James Maxton, both from the floor. There were only six dissentients - six blacksmiths too old for the army! Geddes got less satisfaction than Lloyd George had at Christmas 1915; for the Government, it was very serious.

The Geddes meeting marked the return of the influence of the shop-stewards who had been deported and jailed: except one, Davie Kirkwood. Jimmy Maxton of the ILP was there because after his imprisonment, having lost his job as a schoolteacher, he became a plater's helper for a few months; it was a bit of a show really, because very quickly he got a job as secretary of the ILP in the West of Scotland. But Kirkwood of the ILP wasn't there because he had become a foreman in a munitions factory on his return and was now becoing more notable inside the orthodox labour movement, thanks to the help of John Wheatley.

On their return some of the deported shop-stewards had been sent to work in a government shell factory. Davie Kirkwood became the foreman in charge, and actually boasted about his output of shells. Of course this was the same attitude he had shown in Parkhead Forge. He had even once held up a bowler hat and said it had been presented to him by Sir William Beardmore for his output of shells. It was because of his zeal for increased war production that when

John Maclean was arrested again in April 1918 he not only attacked capitalism from the dock - he attacked Davie Kirkwood as well.

By 1917 living conditions for the workers were becoming more and more difficult. Not only were they working fantastically long hours, but the money they earned bought very little. Prices had reached an impossible level. In Glasgow the Lord Provost, Thomas Dunlop, urged the workers to follow his example and eat only half a potato with each meal - he became known in the city as 'half-a-potato Dunlop'. Rent increases had stopped, but bad housing and shortages were everywhere. Everyone was getting sick of the war. The government tried all manner of tricks to counter the anti-war feeling. Victor Grayson had joined the New Zealand Expeditionary Force while he was abroad, and he was actually brought up to Glasgow to speak in his uniform. He was faced by a hostile audience and couldn't finish his speech, though Glasgow had always been a centre of support for him.

By 1917 civil rights meetings were being organised to support those in opposition to the war - particularly conscientious objectors. Emanuel Shinwell never came out openly against the war but he did support the rights of those who did. At one large meeting the stewards carried lead piping in order to protect the crowd from the pro-war forces but the meeting went off quietly. The BSP, on the other hand, organised meetings in the Central Halls that were openly against the war and for the Russian Revolution. It was the Central Halls meetings that led to John Maclean's arrest. The charge was his anti-war speeches, though the real reason was his support for the Bolsheviks and the inspiration he gave to thousands of workers not only on the Clyde but throughout Britain. He was also raising money for the Russian refugees; when the Bolsheviks sent Kamenev across with a cheque for £1,000 the authorities seized Kamenev in Aberdeen and took the money.

Shortly before Maclean was arrested he made a speech at Central Halls in defence of the Russian Revolution. He was answering Ramsay MacDonald, who had spoken for the ILP at the Metropole. MacDonald had said he wasn't a Leninist but the Bolsheviks were making great sacrifices and were honest men though he didn't agree with them - the usual MacDonald speech that anyone could read anything into. John Maclean replied by saying that he was a Leninist and advocated a British revolution along Russian lines. He spoke of the buildings that could be taken over, various other measures, how society could be run. Then he ended by saying we would not necessarily do those things: we would do what was right for Britain, but the Russian Revolution was a guide to our action.

He was arrested in April and tried in May. He missed the May Day demonstration in Glasgow - the first one that had been held on the first of May, a work day, instead of a Sunday, and it was massive. In his famous speech from the dock John Maclean addressed the masses who had been there, and turned his trial into a political forum.

He conducted his own defence and spoke for over an hour in his final summing-up. He said: 'I am not here as the accused. I am here as the accuser of capitalism dripping with blood from head to foot.' He indicted international capitalism for what it had done in the war and was preparing to do against the Russian Revolution. But he also attacked those workers who had been prepared to give record output for the war. Maclean said he had always supported the policy of 'ca'canny', of the workers giving as little output as they could to the bosses; he was against them working long hard hours of overtime and giving up their holidays for the capitalists. Then he said:

'Now David Kirkwood, representing the Parkhead Forge workers, at the end of 1915, when the dilution of labour began, put forward a printed statement for the benefit of Mr Lloyd George and his colleagues, the first sentence of which in big type was - "What you wish is greater output". He said that the Parkhead Forge workers were then prepared to give greater output and accept dilution if they, the workers, had control over the conditions under which the greater output would accrue. That was his contention. Since he has got into position he seems to have boasted that he has got a record output. The question was put to me. Was this consistent with the position and with the attitudes of the working class? I said it was not consistent with the attitude and position of the working class, that his business was to get right back down to the normal, to "ca'canny" as far as general output was concerned.'

His criticism of Kirkwood was true. Kirkwood had no basic principles.

The speech had a tremendous impact. At first we had only edited press reports, but later the Glasgow Trades Council reprinted it in full with a photograph of John Maclean standing in the dock between two policemen. But his political act brought him a sentence of five years. The authorities had to treat him as a political prisoner: he was allowed to have food brought in from outside and got various other privileges for the first time. The sentence was regarded by everybody as savage, and a great agitation grew up in all sections of the movement to get him released.

As well as the inspiration John Maclean's stand gave us, the socialists in Glasgow were encouraged by the reports of trouble at the front. There were stories of threatened insurrection in the German army, mutiny in the French and disaffection in the British. It was everything we had been hoping for. Before the war we had always believed that the German workers would lead the fight, and now our hopes were rebuilt by the German soldiers' revolt. The anti-war movement grew, and although we never got a majority in Glasgow we could get two to three hundred on an anti-war demonstration and nobody attempted to interfere with it.

In November 1918 the war ended. It had become obvious that the armies were breaking up and it couldn't be continued. When the end came there were spontaneous demonstrations all over the streets. I was in A & W Smith's when the news came. I threw down my hammer, everybody looked at the others, nobody said anything, and we all walked out. We went and joined the celebrations in the streets. Everybody was carried away; for some it might mean the end of their jobs, but all the pent-up feelings for peace found expression at once. We socialists were delighted - we hoped that this peace jubilation would find a political expression.

One of the things I still regret about the first world war is that we socialists never got a true picture of what happened at the Western Front: a picture of what a ruling class is really like when it gets popular support for a war like that. Millions of men were sent to their deaths with the utmost callousness and brutality. All we knew was that the British army was breaking down, that the Russian soldiers had already helped create a successful revolution, and it was just fortunate for the British that the German army collapsed first.

The feelings of revenge against the German people disappeared quickly among the ordinary workers. The politicians were talking about making Germany pay for the war, but when that was imposed later on it put the shipyard workers out of work. We were more affected by the stories of distress in Germany, when we heard that thousands of women were being forced to sell themselves on the street in order to live. Because we supported the German people's struggles, socialists were pleased at the downfall of the Kaiser. But when the Social-Democrats of Germany began to save German capitalism in the name of German socialism, we looked to Rosa Luxemburg and Karl Liebknecht and hoped that they could pull the German revolution through to a Soviet-type victory.

It was much easier for socialists in Britain once peace was announced. We weren't hated in 1918 the way we had been a year or two earlier, and after the Armistice the patriotic movement against us was finished. The government realised this, and called an immediate general election while people were still happy about the end of the war. It was for December 1918 and was a 'coupon' election in which the wartime coalition government sanctioned the candidatures of its supporters, both Liberal and Tory. Some Liberals didn't receive the coupon, neither did the official Labour candidates.

Because George N. Barnes had stayed in the war cabinet he was no longer accepted as the official Labour candidate for Gorbals, although he was still standing with the government coupon. John Maclean, in prison, was the official candidate: he was eligible because the BSP had affiliated to the Labour Party in 1916, when Hyndman and the others were driven out. We used the election as a means to campaign for John's release. Willie Gallacher stood in for him, gave his speeches, and held tremendous meetings all over the Gorbals. He came straight from work in his overalls to speak every night, and St. Mungo's Halls were booked time and time again to rally John's support. There was great Irish support for him too. At the end of a meeting we usually sang 'The Internationale', but one night the entire hall rose and sang 'God Save Ireland', the song of the Manchester martyrs.

In the whole election no parliamentary candidate could speak at any meeting without answering the question whether or not he was in favour of the release of John Maclean. It was raised at *every* meeting and a week before the poll the government were compelled to release him. He had served eight months of his five-year sentence. A huge crowd waited for hours outside Buchanan Street Station, where the train was coming in from Peterhead prison in Aberdeen. As we waited Jimmy Johnstone, the old rigger, took the platform. He had great style; he wasn't a deep thinker but he spoke real working-class language. Near the station were some tenement houses, and Jimmy pointed to these 'birdcages' and started talking to the crowd about what they should fight for. Suddenly he grabbed a child out of its mother's arms and shouted: 'Will you fight for this?' It had a great emotional effect on the whole crowd.

John's train came in hours late and he was so weak and worn-out he couldn't speak. The crowd got a lorry and pulled it themselves down Renfield Street, down to Carlton Place where the ASE rooms were, and John insisted on waving the red flag all the way. He spoke a week later but he was very erratic, and it was obvious that he wasn't yet well. But when the poll came out he had got over 7,000 votes against Barnes - even though he had declared that, like the Irish MPs, he wouldn't take his seat in the House of Commons.

Despite great hopes, the only Clydesider to be elected was Neil Maclean, who had helped James Connolly form the SLP and was one of the better parliamentarians. But really the election was a fake. Half the men weren't back from the army, men in work had moved, and the dominant feeling was relief that the war was over.

In Tradeston we ran Jimmy MacDougall against a Tory and a Liberal. The Tory got in - he was an officer: not for nothing was it called the Khaki election. But Jimmy beat the Liberal. From 1918, the Liberal Party lost support as the Labour Party gained. There could be no return to the pre-war days.

9. The Strike for the Forty Hour Week

In 1919 the atmosphere in the whole labour movement was one of change. There was talk of forming a communist party; there were unofficial movements in the trade unions, and amalgamations of unions; talk of the nationalisation of the mines; rumours of a miners' strike and other discontent - in London and Liverpool even the police went on strike. Above all there was the influence of the Russian Revolution which had shown us what working-class power meant. The 'Hands off Russia' movement and the decision of the Labour Party over nationalisation reflected the new feeling in the movement which was inspired by Russia.

The thing on everybody's mind was unemployment. Before the war it had gone up and down but always existed, and after the 1911 National Insurance Act we could see from the figures that this was the case nationally and not just for Glasgow. Now, after the Armistice and the songs about 'when the boys come home', everybody was thinking about what would happen when they did. Where would they find work? Although relatively few skilled men had gone in the army, apart from volunteers, it was the engineers who decided to strike for a 40-hour week in order to ensure work for all.

Up to 1914 our week was 54 hours. All working people, including boys and girls, started at 6 a.m. and finished at 5.30 p.m., and worked until noon on Saturdays. During the war it had been extended to a 12-hour day and Saturday and Sunday working. The six- o'clock start was miserable: you had to get up at five, and you couldn't go out or do anything at night because you would tire yourself for the morning. When I worked at Dalmuir during the war I had to get out of the house before five to get the ferry to Anderston Cross and the train to Dalmuir; there were no lights on the train, nobody spoke, and the only sign of life was the spark from somebody's pipe. To get the hours reduced would be a victory for us all as well as helping unemployment.

The ASE nationally decided to open negotiations for a 47-hour week with men starting at 8 and working until 5 on weekdays and noon on Saturdays. On the Clyde we wanted a shorter week than that - though the employers were trying to hang on to the old 54 hours, or to reduce wages. The CWC was already less strong than it had been: the national leadership of the ASE and the other engineering unions were now negotiating for the workers. Nevertheless, the CWC was one of the bodies which formed a joint committee to launch the campaign for 40 hours. The Scottish Trades Union Congress, the district committee of the ASE and the Glasgow Trades Council were others. This co-operation was possible because Labour men had got positions on all these bodies; George Kerr of the Workers' Union was now secretary of the Scottish TUC, Harry Hopkins of the ILP was district secretary of the ASE, Emanuel Shinwell was the chairman of the trades council.

The Glasgow Trades Council had much more standing in the movement then. It was a trades and labour council, with Labour Party delegates on it, and its backbone was made up of locally controlled unions like the Municipal Employees. As today, it was controlled by the Scottish TUC but it had a good deal of influence in that body. The STUC also was very different then. At that time there were many local Scottish unions, and the Scottish sections of national unions had more autonomy than today. Neither the Glasgow Trades Council nor the Scottish TUC led strikes during the war, but the trades council had been prominent in raising the questions of rents and prices and was well respected throughout the movement.

It was Shinwell who took charge of the 40-hour strike and made the most outstanding speeches in connection with it. The Scottish TUC delegation on the joint committee were prepared to call for a 30-hour week, and the CWC was inclined to support them, but Shinwell persuaded them to accept the demand for 40 hours as more realistic. The joint committee proposed that the strike start at the end of January, and made efforts to contact the other engineering centres: Belfast and Newcastle did come out on strike, along with the rest of Scotland.

John Maclean disagreed with the timing of the strike. He thought it should be postponed until March, when the engineers' demand could be linked with an expected national strike of the miners. John saw the miners as the political wing of the movement and was always trying to break down the divisions between them and the engineers. He had encouraged Jimmy MacDougall, who had a nervous breakdown after he got out of jail, to go to work at a pit in Blantyre; Jimmy got a job as a labourer above ground and did a lot of educational work among the miners and they always supported John Maclean.

When there was a strike of the whole coalfield Jimmy flew round encouraging and organising the miners, and marched them into Glasgow on a Sunday to publicise their case. They had a big meeting at Nelson's Monument, and thousands of engineers and shipyard workers were there as well. Jimmy MacDougall got up and said to them: 'You say you support these miners. You haven't the so-and-so guts to support them.' That broke up the meeting; everybody huddled in groups discussing the terrible, impossible language Jimmy had used. But he was always eloquent, even with that kind of language, and he came down from the platform and said 'You never heard these words before, did you?' and walked away. He was right to be angry. The engineers did say they supported the miners but they weren't doing anything.

John Maclean's strategy was to encourage the building up of all the big industrial battalions so that they would ultimately take power in the country. He saw the 1919 strike as an opportunity to line up those battalions against the capitalists. He didn't see himself as building an alternative party. He supported the co-operative movement, the Labour Party, and all movements of industrial workers. And he had most faith in the miners. He had more confidence in Bob Smillie, the miners' leader, than I ever had! I thought that John's confidence in the miners was out of all proportion. The first workers to go to parliament were miners but they were Lib-Labs and were not among the early supporters of the Labour Party. Their terrible conditions of work meant that they always got the support of the rest of the labour movement but that they themselves did not do as much in terms of class solidarity with other workers.

While John could lead masses he couldn't organise workers as Gallacher, who wasn't a political animal, could. Gallacher was concentrating on getting the engineers out, and he backed the Scottish TUC and Shinwell. John could have no direct influence on the movement because he was not an industrial worker and the BSP didn't impose one policy on all its members. The miners' strike he expected didn't take place because the government recognised the danger and offered them large wage increases and a royal commission to investigate the possibility of nationalising the mines! At the time of the 40-hour strike John Maclean was actually on a tour speaking for the BSP in Liverpool, Manchester and London; but even if he had been in Glasgow his opinions would have had no effect against the joint efforts of the new combination in the trade-union field.

The 40-hour strike began on Monday, 27 January 1919, with a meeting which was announced through the trades council and by the shop-stewards in the workshops. Throughout Glasgow the coming strike had been common talk for weeks, and some workshops were already out on strike that Monday before the meeting. A & W Smith's wasn't, but I took the day off and went to the meeting.

St. Andrew's Hall was jammed to the door with well over three thousand workers. I never remember a meeting where there was such an emotional feeling. The platform party were slow coming down, and somebody in the hall started singing. It wasn't a socialist song he sang but a sentimental little song popular at the time that went: 'My ain wee house, my ain wee house, there's nae place in a' the world like my ain wee house.' It was a nice-sounding, easy-sung song, and the whole hall took it up. We sang it over and over again. The atmosphere created by an army of men singing an easy slow-going song again and again was terrific: the entire audience was tied up with it. When the platform party came on, the result was a foregone conclusion. There were only a few speakers - Willie Gallacher, Emmanuel Shinwell, George Kerr.

From the floor someone moved that we have a mass picket throughout Glasgow to bring out all the workshops. That was something new, and it was adopted. During a strike we always went to the factory gate for information, but this time men from one factory gate marched to the next and built up a mass picket heading for all the engineering workshops and all the shipyards. On the south side it went from Govan through Kinning Park, along Scotland Street past McNeil's Foundry, Howden's, Mirrlees Watson's, A & W Smith's. The same sort of thing happened in Bridgeton and from Clydebank down to Partick. We could always rely on the leading workshops - Albion, the shipyards, Howden's, Weir's - to come out, and the mass picket was used to spread the strike from these places to the others.

In many workshops it wasn't necessary; the 40-hour strike was very solid and the men came out spontaneously. Workshops came out that had never been on strike, including A & W Smith's: I went in on Tuesday and told them that if they didn't come out the mass picket would be there to get them out. There was no trouble about it at all, and they were among the last workers to go back. There wasn't the fear that developed later among engineering workers - they weren't facing unemployment then because peace-time contracts from before the war still had to be finished.

There were meetings of the strikers in George Square on Monday, Wednesday and Friday, and we met in local halls. In my own area there was the Gordon Halls, where the Rolls Royce Club now stands, and the engineers from all round met there every afternoon except when we went to George Square, all through the strike. We had speeches from leaders of the joint committee; the strike bulletins were on sale at these local meetings, and some of us took copies of it to sell round the doors. It sold for a penny. I used to take it to the Paisley Road area where I was brought up and where I worked, and all kinds of workers bought it off me at their doors and in the streets. I'm sure that the same thing happened in Partick, Govan and the other areas. The selling of the bulletin wasn't organised, but socialists were used to selling papers - we had always sold the CWC's paper the *Worker* without being organised to do so.

The week-ends were always the most active time for socialist propaganda, and during the 40-hour strike we organised all we could. Most of the shop-stewards were men who knew something about socialism and the working-class movement, and they could discuss tactics and policies; many of them had been street-corner propagandists for socialism. It isn't true that workers are better educated now than they were then: we had our own socialist education and we knew how to spread it. We also knew how to organise processions. On the days we went to George Square we met at the established local meeting-place - everybody knew what time through word of mouth - and the shop-stewards lined everybody up and marched them in. In my area all the engineers met in Scotland Street and marched right across the river to George Square.

When we got to the Square we took possession of it. The speakers spoke from the windows of the city chambers, climbing up the outside of the building to them, or from Gladstone's statue. Besides being rallies, these meetings and the strike bulletins provided all the information on the strike. Of course, meetings in George Square had been banned since the 1908 unemployment agitation. At first, because there were so many of us, the authorities didn't do anything; but trouble started on Friday 31 January.

The Friday before the strike, the joint committee had warned the magistrates that the trams must be got off the road while the 40-hour strike was on. Though a week was given to stop them, by 31 January the trams were still on the road and were running through George Square; and that started the riot. The trams were of the trolley type attached by ropes to the overhead lines. One of the strikers pulled a rope down and cut it, and a soldier on leave struck him. The fight broke out just as the tram was turning from George Square down South Frederick Street by the post office, and the riot started.

The police charged, but the crowd stood; when that happens the police are lost. One policeman dropped his helmet and got it thrown back in his face, someone else hit the chief constable, and the Riot Act was torn out of the sherriff's hands. Gallacher and Kirkwood came out to control the riot, and the police batoned them down and arrested them with some rank-and-file demonstrators. Then it spread up all the side streets and even to Glasgow Green.

I was among a crowd who went up North Hanover Street with the police charging after us. The street is very steep, and there was a pub; some of the crowd went and fetched beer bottles and threw them at the police lower down - they fell like rain. The police tried to get behind us by going up North Frederick Street which was parallel with ours. We retreated, and a pitched battle took place in Cathedral Street. First the workers rushed and the police retreated, then the police rushed and the workers retreated. This happened two or three times, until the police didn't know what to do. Then one old policeman rushed forward with his baton drawn to lead the others - but they didn't follow, and he landed in the strikers. Finally the police ran for it, and we ran after them. They rushed up the Cathedral Street closes and tried to go over the back walls, but the strikers got them by the legs and pulled them back; some of them got a terrible hiding. I'm sure that the best fight of the riot took place in Cathedral Street.

Kirkwood came out on the balcony of the city chambers and appealed to everyone to stop fighting and go to Glasgow Green. At that time the ex-servicemen had organisations all over the country - the one in Glasgow was headed by J.R.Campbell, who was later the editor of the Communist Party's *Weekly Worker*, and a man called Shane. It was well-disciplined and active, with several hundred members. The aim was to organise the men who had come back from the front and were prepared to fight for better treatment now the war was over. They always supported the industrial workers' movements, and it was they who led all of us from George Square down to Glasgow Green.

When we got there we found the police lined up ready to attack us. But the ex-servicemen pulled up the park railings, spikes and all, and the police ran for their lives. All over Glasgow, strikers went about cutting the trolley ropes and hundreds of immobilised trams blocked every route. Two policemen tried to intervene at the Saltmarket; the strikers stripped them and they had to run off naked. Demonstrators went back to their own areas, cutting the trolley ropes on the way. In some places jewellers' shops were looted - Govan got a particularly bad name for looting that night.

I didn't go home. I had heard that troops were being brought in, and I decided to wait in order to talk to them and explain what the strike was for. I went to Buchanan Street Station, which was the one for traffic from the north of Scotland; when I got there I found about a dozen other people with the same idea. The whole socialist movement had been affected by Tom Mann's 'Don't Shoot' campaign before the war, and we had all come to talk to the soldiers.

I remember those young soldiers very well. They were recruits with no experience, and they were very aggressive; they had no knowledge of the labour movement or anything else and were quite prepared to use their weapons - one of them pointed to his rifle and said 'This is better than bottles'. The others and I tried to talk to them on the road down to George Square, and the officers kept trying to get between us. But there was no need: those young ones would have shot us down.

There was still a large crowd at George Square, and when the troops marched in they ran away. But gradually they came back and there was no running away after that. We learned to live with the troops, but it was a strange experience to see a big howitzer in the city chambers, tanks in Glasgow, machine-guns on top of the post office and the hotels, and soldiers who were not from the front but walking the streets to hold us in check. I don't think these young soldiers had been in battle, but they were very proud of being soldiers and felt very heroic. I heard later that men from Maryhill Barracks hadn't been used because they were old soldiers who had been at the front and couldn't be relied upon to act against us.

The strike lasted only another week. After the George Square arrests others were also picked up including George Ebury, the organiser of the BSP, Harry Hopkins of the ASE, and Shinwell. We continued meeting in our local halls, but there were no more meetngs in George Square. In that second week Kirkwood came to our meeting in the Gordon Halls and made a speech about how he was a revolutionary socialist but this wasn't a revolution and we should all be sensible and concentrate on the fight for a shorter working week. He was a very frightened man. Gallacher told me later that when they were all in the dock together Kirkwood kept bursting out: 'Listen to the lies the police are telling.' Gallacher was different, he could take any kind of punishment and used to tell jokes about his times in prison. The 40-hour strike was the last agitation Kirkwood and Shinwell were involved in; if it had been a revolution Kirkwood would have run a mile.

During the week some places began to drift back to work. The strike had centred on the engineers, and the other trades weren't so involved although a number of miners had also stopped work. The biggest support outside of Scotland had been in Newcastle and Belfast, with some in London;but there had been no response from the other centres of the wartime shop-stewards' movement. The strike had hung on loyalty to the CWC, the ASE, the trades council and the Scottish TUC, but after a fortnight with no money at all - there was no strike pay - the men were in great difficulties. The joint committee called the strike off and we went back on Monday 10 February.

But we went in at 8 a.m., not 6. While we were on strike the employers had settled a national agreement for a 47-hour week at the same wages. It made a tremendous difference to our lives. We didn't have to get up at five and have a breakfast break at work any more, we could eat our breakfast at home. The 8 o'clock start was something gained from the struggle and it was worth gaining. I remember one old boy at A & W Smith's saying that it wouldn't be good for us - it wasn't healthy - to start work at such a late hour; I was scared that we would go back to the old hours, but we never did. We didn't get the 40-hour week until after the second world war, when the Saturday shift was abolished entirely; but right up to that time no one was paid until noon on Saturday.

There was no ill feeling about the strike or what had happened. It was a completely harmonious movement by the engineers, and we didn't think we had been defeated. I am sure that if there had been another movement, a strike of the Triple Alliance for the miners or some other national strike, we would have come out again. We were disappointed that we didn't get the response outside of Glasgow that we had expected, but we didn't realise that the whole shop-stewards' movement was on its last legs.

We regarded the 40-hour strike not as a revolution but as a beginning. Other things would follow: it was the first rank-and-file agitation to be led by socialists after the war. The working-class movement was bigger at the end of the war than before, and the socialists themselves had hardened. There was no return to the big meetings in the Pavilion and Metropole theatres; the pre-war mood and the artistic side of the movement, the William Morris-Edward Carpenter element, had gone.

For the first time in the British socialist movement serious theoretical discussion was widespread. Previously only the SLP had specialised in this kind of debate, mostly about syndicalist tactics versus political ones. Now it was about power - parliament versus soviets - and the role which a Communist party would play in bringing about a revolution. From the end of the war we were all hoping for the formation of a revolutionary Leninist party. In January 1919 the German Spartacist revolt led by Karl Liebknecht and Rosa Luxemburg had taken place. When it was suppressed the German Social-Democrats, once their comrades, hunted and murdered them. But the movement in Germany wasn't crushed, and all over Europe revolt was spreading. We thought it was only a matter of time before the whole world followed Russia, and that we would be leading a revolution in Britain.

We were specially pleased with the development of the unofficial Miners' Reform Movement, particularly in Lanarkshire and South Wales. The miners' movement was built round political demands for nationalisation beside industrial demands on wages and conditions. Though the Clyde Workers' Committee was on its last legs, its paper the *Worker* became a paper for all revolutionary workers in industry. A lot of our hopes shifted from the shop-stewards' struggle to the campaigns within the unions for amalgamation; socialists had always sought industry-wide unions. All these movements, and the reappearance in February 1919 of the Triple Alliance of miners, transport workers and railwaymen, convinced us that a new phase in the industrial force of the working class was about to begin.

But although the revolutionary elements were strengthened by the war, the reformists also were much better organised than ever before. The ILP had grown in the last two years of the war through its fight on conscription; and the new members weren't like the old ones. The Labour Party itself acquired a new constitution in 1918 which stated for the first time that it stood for the common ownership of the means of production, the famous Clause 4. But in the 1918 constitution the Labour Party also became a party of individual membership, not just trade union and socialist affilia-tions. This was the beginning of the ILP's decline, despite its post-war strength. Up and down the country local Labour Parties were formed without any socialists in them. Prior to 1918 the ILP was the Labour Party in Scotland; the Labour Party had a Scottish organiser, Ben Shaw, but he worked with the ILP.

In the past nearly all Labour parliamentary candidates had been in the ILP and had some kind of socialist faith, but with the new local organisations it was possible for Irish catholics and all kinds of other elements who were not socialists to join. The change also affected the more unscrupulous and ambitious ILP members. Previously they had been under pressure to adhere to ILP policy, but now they did anything they liked. This was the case with Pat Dollan, who became the leader of the Labour group in Glasgow after the election of the other ILP members to Parliament.

The system of individual membership affected the Labour group on the town council almost immediately. Catholics were elected who never pretended to be socialists, like old John Storie. He was an utterly honest man but tied up with the Catholic Church. Every morning on his way to the corporation he stopped at the building site of the new Lourdes chapel and school to check that the men were doing the work properly. As fewer ILPers and more men like this were elected, it became possible for Pat Dollan and others to do as they liked.

A lot of the Labour men on the town council became insurance agents working for the Co-op. The manager of the Co-operative

Insurance was a member of the NCLC (the National Council of Labour Colleges). He wasn't a very good manager, but he did give jobs to Labour and socialist men who were out of work - he even offered to employ me - and a number of them escaped from unemployment into this and various other niches.

The Labour group concentrated on one issue, housing. Before the war Wheatley had come out with his £8 cottage scheme, which had a great impact because of the terrible conditions of the Glasgow slums. After the war the issue became even more important: house-building had stopped and there was a shortage even of slums. The 1919 Housing and Town Planning Act, known as the Lloyd George Act, was designed to give local corporations the authority to build houses - 'homes fit for heroes'. The Labour group in Glasgow used this act to demand action from the town council and gained support on that; but when they themselves got power in November 1933 they didn't carry out their promises.

With the growth of the reformist bodies and the influence of the Russian Revolution, the parliamentarians in the BSP drifted away and other elements began to join. The Irish situation was exploding again in the struggle for a united free Ireland, and some Irishmen joined. One of them joined the South-Side branch of the BSP, of which I was still secretary. He collected arms and ammunition for the struggle in Ireland, and we took him to people we knew who had revolvers and hand-grenades and he passed them on. A surprising number of men had brought weapons back from the war; some used to carry them on the unemployed demonstrations in the early twenties.

Though there was a crisis situation in Britain and Ireland in 1919 and 1920, no unified revolutionary organisation existed. Many of us were awaiting the formation of the British Communist Party, but it was held up by long negotiations between the different organisations. The SLP, the BSP, and Sylvia Pankhurst's group, the Workers' Socialist Federation, were all involved but nothing seemed to happen. While waiting on the negotiations the BSP began to take over some of the future functions of the Communist Party without any discussion with the membership. The leadership were obviously in touch with Moscow, particularly through Theodore Rothstein. Although our branch had supported Rothstein in his fight with Hyndman before the war, a lot of resentment built up.

Most of it centred on the attitude of the BSP leadership. The

BSP became more and more inefficient, with no clear policy, but the people at the top were bureaucratic and authoritarian. They appointed an organiser, Ernie Cant, who came to Scotland for a while. He looked at our bookshop, took notes of this and that, but it was obvious he had no politics at all. Although we were one of the most active branches in Scotland, with forty members, we finally broke with the BSP in January 1920. Looking back, we may have been wrong, but we were tired of all the indecision. We carried on our meetings and selling literature at the bookshop in 19 Morrison Street. We also invited other branches of the BSP, the SLP and other socialists to meet and discuss with us. We had some good theoretical discussions, but that wasn't what we wanted. Though we had left the BSP because it didn't know where it was politically or industrially, we weren't able to develop any alternative in Glasgow.

We did not know at the time that John Maclean had also split with the BSP. They had offered to pay him a salary to concentrate entirely on the 'hands off Russia' campaign. They were asking him to drop all the educational and agitational work that he had done for years. John refused to do that; he and the executive of the BSP fell out, and finally he left. Like us he objected to their lack of an industrial and political perspective for Britain: 'hands off Russia' was the only policy they had.

It did become a very well-developed campaign. Winston Churchill, Earl Curzon and F.E.Smith were preaching a virulent hatred of the Bolsheviks and trying to deny that the British army was intervening on the side of the White armies - fascists - against the red army. In fact Britain was one of a dozen or so countries fighting on Russian soil to try to destroy the Revolution. The 'hands off Russia' campaign was able to build up a mass feeling against this, and eventually British troops were stopped. Every working-class organisation threatened to participate in a general strike; leaders like Ernie Bevin and Herbert Morrison were prominent in the fight.

In Russia itself the Bolsheviks brought out a pamphlet called *Russia's Appeal to the British Soldiers*, citing John Maclean as an example to them and calling on them not to fight. The pamphlet could have been written by three or four people who were in Russia at the time; I always thought it was the work of Phillips Price.

It was our revolutionary duty to carry the campaign in defence of the Russian Revolution as far as we could carry anything at that time, and it was successful. But, important as it was, it wasn't enough. The Irish struggle was raging, there were revolts in India, and we needed an industrial policy. The fact that opportunists like Bevin and Morrison could be active in the campaign in Russia showed that we needed something else.

I discovered that John Maclean had left the BSP on May Day, 1920. There was the usual demonstration on Glasgow Green (on a Sunday, unlike 1918 when it was a work day) and all the organisations had their platforms. I saw John Maclean there, selling a new copy of the *Vanguard*. It had been suppressed during the war, but John had just revived it and I went across and helped him to sell it all over the Green. He told me he was going to do a meeting that night at the old spot at Bath Street, and asked me to take the chair for him. I went that night and the subsequent Sundays; the third time, my foreman was in the audience and I got the sack from A & W Smith's. I was ready to go after another job, but John asked me to take part in a campaign with him and said the campaign would pay our wages. I agreed.

One of the reasons why John Maclean refused to give up other work in favour of 'hands off Russia' was his strong attachment to the Scottish Labour College. There was a Labour College in England, and John and Bob Smillie worked together to establish one in Scotland after John was sacked by the Govan School Board. The miners were always willing to support his activities, and he had taught in all the mining centres as well as in Glasgow. In 1916 the Conference to establish a Scottish Labour College was held. John couldn't be there because he was in prison, but when he came out he took a class for the college and worked full-time for it.

The idea of the National Council of Labour Colleges and its paper *Plebs*, and the Scottish Labour College, was to be Labour's rivals to the bourgeois educational institutions. They were workers' universities teaching marxist economics, marxist history and the class struggle. I have a photograph of one of John's full-time classes; I think every one of the nine men there was a miner. Among his students were Willie Allan, who became the first secretary of the United Mineworkers of Scotland, Johnny Bird of Fife, of whom John was very fond, and Jock MacArthur.

I don't know how the Scottish Labour College finished up, because I left Glasgow in 1923. The NCLC was later taken over by the TUC Educational Service, who didn't believe in marxist economics or the class struggle, and it died. But all his life John

Maclean believed in and carried on workers' education in Glasgow, Fife and Lanarkshire. He had particular faith in the miners of those districts, and he got tremendous support from them.

10. The Tramp Trust Unlimited

When I joined John Maclean in May 1920 the old South-Side branch of the BSP was beginning to break up, and John and I used the premises at Morrison Street. They became the headquarters of the 'Tramp Trust Unlimited' - an organisation of five propagandists who toured the whole of Scotland. At the beginning there were only John and myself, with Jimmy MacDougall helping occasionally.

The campaign began with a leaflet which explained our programme of industrial demands: a minimum wage of £1 a day, a six-hour day, rationing of work, payment of full wages to the unemployed, and a reduction in prices. Some of the demands were similar to what Tom Mann was advocating at that time. We took it round the Glasgow shipyards and to Scott's at Greenock, then we travelled round Dundee and the rest of Scotland.

Every day we held a factory gate meeting at lunch time, handed out the leaflet, and announced an evening meeting. After lunch we chalked all the pavements for our meeting at night, which we held at the most prominent street-corner in the area. In Greenock, for example, we went to Scott's shipyard for the factory-gate meeting, then held the evening meeting at the boundary between Port Glasgow and Greenock because that was the well-known spot. The meetings were a roaring success; we got big collections and sold a lot of literature. The collections paid our expenses and wages. As an engineer I had been earning £4.8s., and at the beginning of our campaign I was paid £4 a week and John was paid as well. We ate in restaurants and money was no problem, though it became one later.

In Dundee a local man called Sandy Ross spoke at the meeting. He was an ex-policeman from Glasgow and had been in Wakefield Prison as a conscientious objector during the war. He had been a member of the ILP, and was a humorous speaker, with one or two stock jokes that made the crowd laugh. John was carried away with this, because he was never humorous; he invited Sandy Ross to move to Glasgow and join us. A friend of Sandy's, Peter Marshall, also joined the campaign. He had also been in Wakefield as a conscientious objector, and had lost his job as a post office worker. He wasn't a man who could think a problem through, but he could learn anything very quickly because he had an almost photographic memory; he picked up marxist economics immediately, and began to teach it at the Scottish Labour College.

Besides the four of us there was also Jimmy MacDougall from time to time. I think that he was the best orator in Scotland. He was flamboyant, but he was the best informed man I ever met - he had actually read a lot of marxist classics in German. As a speaker he had a wonderful delivery and could speak for two-and-a-half hours at a time and no one tired of listening to him. He had the trick of exaggerating in his oratory: when he said something it was 110 per cent correct. Unfortunately his nervous breakdown still affected him and he was erratic. Often we didn't see him for a couple of months; he would sit and read his books, and then come in and make his contribution. I once told John how much I admired Jimmy as a speaker. He said: 'Yes, if you had been stewing up for two months you could speak for two-and-a-half hours, too.'

It was John who called us 'the Tramp Trust Unlimited'. Besides selling a lot of literature, we brought out a lot of our own. We produced pamphlets which were twopence each, and we never printed less than 20,000 of any of them. The first one we had was *The Irish Tragedy: Scotland's Disgrace* - we sold that all round Scotland. It was followed by others on the Scottish Labour College and education and *The Coming War with America*.

Alongside our industrial campaign, we gave more importance to the Irish struggle than any other group in Scotland. Our pamphlet attacked the use of Scottish troops in the Black and Tans in Ireland. In 1918 nearly all the Irish MPs elected to the House of Commons were Sinn Fein, and all pledged not to take their seats. They formed their own parliament, the Dail, and declared for a free Ireland. In return, the British Government began to terrorise the catholic population. They recruited ex-soldiers as 'policemen' in the Royal Irish Constabulary, and from Easter 1920 the Black and Tans were on one side and the IRA on the other. The Black and Tans had all the powers of legal murder behind them, but the IRA had the people. In order to frighten the people the Black and Tans did terrible things: they fired into a peaceful football crowd, attacked women and children, smashed up towns and farms.

We held great open-air meetings on Ireland. In June 1920 we held one in Motherwell, which was always an Orange centre; the Orangemen smashed the platform, but some of the Irish came and fought them off and we were able to maintain a meeting. Port Glasgow was another area where Orangemen were strong, and when we went there to speak a great many turned out in a very stormy mood. We were holding the meeting next to the docks when they came for us. John stopped them by threatening to have them thrown in the docks if they didn't behave - it was much more likely that he and I would have been thrown in! In 1921 we were attacked again in Partick, but this time we were speaking from a lorry and it was able to get clear. Sandy Ross was in jail at the time, and as we left the crowd John thought that they were shouting 'good old Sandy Ross' and must have had a change of heart; I had to tell him it was 'good old Sandy Row' they were shouting.

Though it was a major struggle to deal with the Irish question in Glasgow the Scottish Workers' Committee, which was the remnants of the old CWC, did nothing about it. Neither did anybody else, except the 'Tramp Trust Unlimited'. We had a lively time of it at our meetings, but in the main we got a lot of support. Often a big Irish catholic element turned up, and some people who weren't Irish supported us. On the biggest issue of all, the death of the lord mayor of Cork, we produced 150,000 leaflets.

Many of the Sinn Fein MPs were in jail when they were elected. There was a tradition of hunger strikes. One of the hunger-strikers was Terence MacSwiney, the lord mayor of Cork, and it became obvious that the British authorities - contrary to their treatment of the suffragettes - were going to let him die. On Friday that week John Maclean drafted our leaflet and set it up at the printer's with the heading 'The murder of the lord mayor of Cork'. The news of his death came on Sunday; we got the printer from his bed to get the leaflet out. We had an enormous meeting that afternoon at Nelson's Monument. We collected £43 to pay the cost of the leaflet, and with that money we were able to distribute it all round Scotland.

The Irish struggle had always inspired John. He had supported Connolly in 1916, when others would not, and in 1918 he had been prepared like the Irish MPs not to take his seat in parliament if elected. In 1920 he decided, following the aim of the Irish movement, that Scotland should be a republic. Without consulting the rest of us he brought out a leaflet entitled *All hail the Scottish*

Communist Republic: John believed that the Scottish workers were more advanced than the English and that the revolution could be won quicker in Scotland, so he decided to make that his policy.

We didn't quarrel with the leaflet, and we distributed it at a labour demonstration on housing organised by Andrew McBride. This was a remarkable occasion because Captain White, the organiser of the Irish Citizen Army, also turned up with a regiment of men. He lined them up and drilled them on Glasgow Green. That created one sensation, and John's leaflet was another. Later, at my suggestion, the slogan was changed to 'the Scottish Workers' Republic' because that had been James Connolly's call in Ireland.

The war in Ireland in 1920 had crystallised John Maclean's 'Scottishism'. I first got a hint of it during a big band contest at a miners' gala in Alloa when, to my surprise, I saw John on his toes in time to the music. He believed that the type of fight that ultimately established the Irish Republic could be waged in Scotland.

John thought it was possible to build a separate Communist Party, affiliated to the Communist International, in Scotland. He based his opinion on the wartime militancy in Glasgow and on the number of workers who had been to marxist education classes or had got some theoretical training from the SLP. He also published articles in the *Vanguard* written by Erskine of Mar, who was descended from one of the old Scottish noble families but was an old-fashioned radical. The articles were on primitive communism in Scotland, and John used this idea in his phrase 'back to communism, forward to communism'. He was very proud that his forebears had been crofters.

Because he wanted a separate Scottish party, he was opposed to joining the Communist Party of Great Britain when it was formed in London in August 1920. Sylvia Pankhurst's group hadn't joined, and very few Scots had attended the London Unity Conference. The remnants of the Socialist Labour Party still existed with their own premises and their own printing press. There were also the remnants of the CWC in the Scottish Workers' Committee; it didn't represent the Glasgow workers any more, but the *Worker* was still in existence and around it were John S. Clarke, J.R.Campbell and Willie Gallacher. In September 1920 all these groups met together to discuss the formation in Glasgow of a Scottish Communist Party.

The first meeting was quite amicable. John met the people from the *Worker* and the SLP, and another meeting was set up to discuss the question further. Jimmy MacDougall and I attended this on behalf of the 'Tramp Trust', and it was a very surprising meeting. Willie Gallacher and John S. Clarke had only just returned from Russia, where they met Lenin. We hadn't seen much of them since they got back - and we didn't know that Lenin had persuaded Gallacher to change his views completely!

Gallacher had always been a syndicalist, since before the first world war. One of the arguments about the formation of a Communist Party in Britain was whether it should put up parliamentary candidates or not and whether it should affiliate to the Labour Party. Lenin was anxious that syndicalists and the 'ultra-left' should not gain control, because he wanted the new party to understand the importance of building a revolutionary organisation and not just working through industrial action. Therefore the Communist International was demanding that the Communist Party of Great Britain be prepared to field parliamentary candidates as a revolutionary tactic, and should also work within the Labour Party.

When Gallacher and Clarke came to the meeting in City Hall a number of anti-parliamentarians were present. An anarchist, Jack Leckie, reported that he was already drilling men in Fife. Some were representatives of Sylvia Pankhurst's group, which was always anti-parliamentarian. Gallacher jumped up at the meeting and pointed out all the anti-parliamentarians, and said that none of them was eligible to join the Communist Party! It was a great shock to all of us. We all knew Gallacher's reputation as a syndicalist, and none of us had imagined that no anti-parliamentarian could be a member of the CPGB.

We had decided to call our group the Communist Labour Party, and at the meeting we elected an executive; I nominated Jimmy MacDougall but he didn't get on. But the organisation petered out. The 'Tramp Trust' wasn't represented on the executive, and neither the SLP nor the *Worker* seemed to be working coherently now that Gallacher was back. We began to work more closely with the SLP, and John continued to discuss the problem with them.

John accepted the conditions of membership of the Communist International, and was not opposed to the CPGB on the grounds that Sylvia Pankhurst and others were. He believed in affiliation to the Labour Party, and had always argued for it in the SDF and then the BSP; and he had stood as a parliamentary candidate himself. His disagreement was over a separate Communist Party for Scotland. However, he also objected to the way the new party was being built.

Lenin and the other Russian leaders wanted to ensure that the new International would stick to its principles: the Third International was to be completely different from the Second - that is why there were twenty-one conditions of membership. But, in their anxiety, they were fostering some developments in different countries that perhaps shouldn't have been encouraged. I think that Lenin's *Left Wing Communism: An Infantile Disorder* showed an over-anxiety to support the BSP against people like Sylvia Pankhurst. Many of the members of the BSP weren't very good. John had known a number of them during the war and he wasn't impressed by them or the way they worked.

A lot of money came into the BSP and then the CPGB, and many people got full-time jobs in the movement for the first time in their lives. It is right to have some full-timers; but nearly everybody of standing became a professional. Gallacher left the workshop to become Britain's Lenin - but Gallacher, although a marvellous industrial leader, was no theoretician. Albert Inkpin, the BSP secretary, became the first secretary of the CPGB. Harry Pollitt and Tom Bell both got full-time jobs. They weren't paid much money, but it was as much as they ever got in the factory and they were being released from the factory: which was something in those days!

John was worried about the money aspect, and the ease with which their politics had changed. He had been in favour of the BSP working inside the Labour Party, and many of them opposed him; when Lenin said they should be inside the Labour Party they all agreed. But they went about it in the most stupid way possible - they even quoted Lenin that they would support the Labour Party 'as the rope supports the hanged man'! However, they never did get affiliation.

After the failure of the talks about the Communist Labour Party we couldn't give much time to the problem of building a new party. Our agitation was still developing. Just as the 'Tramp Trust' were the only ones in Scotland who conducted propaganda on the Irish struggle, so we were the first to raise the question of unemployment. This was work that John and I did together, and in November 1920 we had our first big demonstration.

The 40-hour strike had been in order to prevent unemployment, and there was a lot of talk about it, but no action had been taken among the unemployed. By the end of 1920 unemployment was conspicuous. Jobs were becoming scarcer, particularly for the unskilled men and the women workers. Weir's, Mirrlees Watson's and other shops still had peace-time work for skilled men, but the munitions work was slowing down. John Maclean had predicted this in his economics lectures. He pointed out that the policy of 'making Germany pay for the war' would simply mean fewer jobs in Britain as German goods came in; and he was right.

In November 1920 we called a meeting of the unemployed on Glasgow Green. John and I marched the men up to George Square to the city chambers, where we sent a deputation to the town council and made our demands. We got some concessions on relief work and such, and we also got the use of the City Halls free for meetings of the unemployed; and we got free baths as well. We were also able to take special cases of hardship direct to the distress committee that had been set up.

As the law then stood, no able-bodied man could get outdoor relief for his wife and children without himself going into the workhouse. There was such anger about this that we were able to get tremendous demonstrations and fight individual cases at the parish councils. We were particularly concerned with two parish councils, Glasgow in the north of the city and Govan in the south. Both were made up mainly of shopkeepers, with one or two trade unionists, but the worst councillor in each was a catholic priest. Both of them did everything possible to prevent anybody getting anything. The Scottish parish councils were much more parsimonious than the boards of guardians in England; but over the next two years the outdoor-relief rule had to be abolished because of the anger it created.

Besides going to the parish councils we organised demonstrations round the hotels at night. The men shouted 'We want grub' - they shouted it very, very well - and we carried a banner that read: '1914 fighting - 1920 starving'. We kept demonstrations going throughout the winter of 1920-21 and had packed meetings in the City Halls. At these meetings John spoke not only on unemployment but on Ireland, India, and all the important political issues.

Also at the meetings a young boy named Matthew Bird came and recited his poetry. He was still in short trousers, but he would step right forward to the front of the platform with his latest poem - it would be about the struggle in Ireland against the Black and Tans, or something similar. It took a trick with the audiences.

I remember Captain White coming to one of our City Hall meetings. In Glasgow he was known as Jack White the Irishman, who wanted to be in on any possibility of a fight. John had been explaining marxist economics; the roof of the hall was broken up into segments, and he had the whole audience looking up at the roof and using it to sort out marxist categories. White stood up and said: 'Every time I come to Glasgow I feel like a child alongside the Clyde workers. The Clyde workers know all about economics. I know nothing about economics. In my opinion there's too damn much education and too little action.'

When John sprang to his feet to condemn the idea of separating education from action the audience split in two! There was always a lot of Irish support for John, and the City Hall meetings had a large Irish catholic section. Some supported White and some supported Maclean; it was a really heated meeting. John advertised his next Sunday meeting in St. Mungo's Halls with the title 'Let Captain White start the revolution in Belfast', and he criticised White's attitude to education again. However, by the next Thursday in the city halls it had all blown over.

We had two or three big clashes with the *Worker* people as well. They were all in the Communist Party now, including J.R.Campbell who had built the ex-servicemen's organisation in Glasgow. Willie Gallacher looked upon Campbell as his protege; both came from Paisley, and Campbell as a boy had spoken with Gallacher at open-air meetings at Paisley Cross. Campbell had gone into the army, got a distinguished conduct medal, and had been discharged with a frozen foot. After he organised the ex-servicemen Gallacher got him on to the *Weekly Worker*, and he was arrested in 1924 in the notorious 'Campbell case'.

Although he was a good propagandist I never thought much of Johnny Campbell. He had no qualities of leadership and though he could write well he shifted his position, writing one thing today and another tomorrow. In London he relied on Pollitt to tell him what to think, just as he had relied on Gallacher in Glasgow. In the City Hall meetings he and the other *Worker* people were actually intervening to try to take over what we had built up. They argued that the unemployed movement should be developed by linking it with employed workers; yet workshop organisation had largely disappeared and the employed were frightened that they might be made unemployed. The Glasgow Communist Party had done no real work with the unemployed. They were just putting forward propositions to try to get popularity, and we were able to hold them off. On one occasion Campbell tried to take over the platform, but the crowd were so hostile that we had more or less to save him.

The reason why the *Worker* people were so hostile was that we were working with the SLP. We had found it impossible to keep both our agitation and a newspaper going, and the December issue of the *Vanguard* was the last one; from then on, we wrote more and more for the *Socialist*. John had always admired the educational work of the SLP and its commitment to marxist theory. It was the only organisation with any marxist analysis of the state before the war; Willie Paul's book was the best the British revolutionary movement produced. They could also claim that they were the only people in Britain who had any idea of the future role of workshop organisation, and that the Soviets were in line with their own ideas about working-class power.

The Irish question was always much more important to us than it was to Campbell, Gallacher and the others, and the SLP were using their press to print an illegal Irish paper called *Dark Rosaleen*. The editor of it came across from Ireland for every issue; we spoke to him, and kept contact with Ireland through him. The Scottish Workers' Committee had done nothing on the Irish question.

At the end of 1920 John and the SLP called a meeting to form a new Communist Party for Scotland, and it was then that the final break with the others occurred. John trusted the SLP more than he trusted Gallacher and his associates. Not only had Campbell interfered with our work with the unemployed, but Willie Gallacher wrote to the SLP warning them that John was mentally unbalanced and that they shouldn't encourage him in his ideas. It was a stupid thing for Gallacher to do, and the SLP did a really dirty thing: they showed the letter to John. He exploded!

The meeting was held at the SLP rooms in Renfrew Street, and consisted of members of the 'Tramp Trust', the SLP and others. But Gallacher and John S. Clarke also turned up. John denounced Gallacher as having always been anti-parliamentarian; Gallacher

E

responded by attacking Sandy Ross who, he said, knew nothing of the movement and cowered behind John Maclean. They marched up opposite sides of the hall and stood and denounced each other in the centre of the aisle. I never saw John involved in anything else like that - Gallacher's letter had done it. During the meeting Jimmy MacDougall got up and accused Gallacher of destroying education classes in Lanarkshire and deriding the theoretical work of other revolutionaries. Aitken Ferguson, the very well-read secretary of the SLP, was in the chair and he seemed to be very embarrassed at the turn the meeting was taking.

After the meeting was broken up there were no more efforts to form an independent Scottish Communist Party. We worked more and more closely with the SLP and wrote a good deal for the *Socialist* in order to keep an independent socialist press alive. It was possible for us to do this without joining because they were no longer the strict membership organisation they had once been. We hoped that the SLP would accept the articles of membership of the Communist International and that it would be possible to do something with them. James Clunie of the SLP went to Russia for one of the congresses of the Third International, and John gave him a letter of introduction to Peter Petroff who got him into the congress. Nan Milton, John's daughter, in her book *John Maclean* claims that John joined the SLP but he never did. None of us did, and the 'Tramp Trust' kept on going.

The SLP welcomed us writing for their paper because they were losing so many members. Their outstanding members like Arthur MacManus and Tom Bell had joined the Communist Party. The leading figures were Tom Mitchell and James Clunie, who later became a tame Labour MP. I thought the best of those who were left was Dr Esterman, and most of my stuff for the *Socialist* was written because he asked me. He got into trouble in Glasgow over an abortion and had to go and live in London. I liked him; but none of them had the stature of the men who had left, and that was why they needed to work with us.

I only ever spoke at one meeting for the SLP. That was at Motherwell; Ephraim O'Connor, the leading Orangeman in Motherwell was there and we had a real battle with him. Later on he tried to become a spy inside the Communist Party; he said he was a railway worker named Robertson, and joined the railwaymen's fraction of the party. I wasn't in Glasgow at the time or I would have spotted him, but Willie Joss saw him and recognised him. They called in Pat Devine. Pat knew him straight away; somebody grabbed him from behind, and they found a revolver in his pocket. They beat him up and took him and his revolver to Central Police Station, but of course nothing was done about it.

John didn't need to join the SLP because it was us, not them, who were developing the unemployed agitation. In January 1921 Dr MacNamara, the Chancellor of the Exchequer, came to Glasgow. We chased him all over the town demanding a million pounds for Glasgow's unemployed. In the evening we held a meeting - I was in the chair - and it was, I think, on that occasion that Jimmy MacDougall made a wonderful speech. He kept repeating 'A million pounds or bloody revolution' and it captivated the audience.

The following month we had a stormy meeting with the Labour group on the town council. John and I had been organising big demonstrations, and we had criticised the Labour group for not making a fight over unemployment; they weren't in power, but there were a lot of them after the war and they were on the unemployment committee of the town council. To answer our criticisms they called a meeting with Wheatley in the chair and all the Labour councillors on the platform. They wanted to tell the unemployed all the things they were doing for them.

First they put up Davie Kirkwood to speak; although you could see his mouth opening and shutting you couldn't hear a word he said. The other speakers were the same. The audience demanded that I and Jimmy Cox of Anderston, who were in the gallery, be allowed to speak. We didn't make the demand, the crowd made it, and the platform had to give way. We both went down to speak.

Jimmy Cox was not a good speaker, but he said there was one man on the platform he would take his coat off to any day - Tom Collins. Collins was incensed, and said that if Jimmy said it again *he* would take his jacket off. I was speaking to try to pacify them when Shinwell, who was behind me, made a sign that the crowd thought was a threat to me and they rushed the platform. Shinwell said afterwards that he was only signalling to be the next speaker, but the crowd didn't understand it like that. The meeting broke up, and I got the blame: I began to be attacked in *Forward* as John Maclean's 'lieutenant'.

As the unemployed work developed I increasingly took the responsibility for it and began leading demonstrations on my own. This was partly because of the amount of work John did for the Scottish Labour College; the fact that he ran this organisation was another reason why he did not worry about building a party. The Labour College was very important to him - he saw it as a way of educating the workers to revolution. Certainly in the districts where he held his classes the miners seemed to develop much more awareness about their struggles and about the whole capitalist system. It was John's involvement with the miners that led to his fourth arrest for a speech he made during the Miners' Lockout in April 1921.

Because of the depression of 1920-21 the government abandoned all its commitments, including any idea of taking the mines into national control. The mines reverted to the private owners, who immediately cut wages and went back to the district rates of pay. When the miners resisted they were locked out. John went all round Lanarkshire to the towns and villages rallying support. He had saved five pounds to buy himself a new suit that he badly wanted, but when the miners' struggle began John sent the money to their fund.

We hoped for great things because in Feburary 1919 the Triple Alliance of miners, railwaymen and transport workers had been reborn. The whole movement was expecting these other unions to come out in support of the miners. The night the railwaymen were supposed to come out, John and I went up to Polmadie Station to join the picket at midnight. But the strike had been called off! J.H.Thomas, the railwaymen's leader, called it off because he was prepared to accept a compromise which the miners' leaders rejected. The day was called 'Black Friday': instead of an all-out union war the miners were left to fight alone.

They made a terrific fight of it. I travelled all round the mining districts with John and took the chair at his meetings. I was in the chair when he and Sandy Ross spoke at Airdrie. Opposite the meeting was a big cafe, and policemen were hidden upstairs taking notes of everything that was said in the street below. They were both arrested later. In May John was sentenced to three months' imprisonment, and Sandy Ross to three months and a fine of £20 or another three months.

The Miners' Lockout raised again the question of the nationalisation of the mines, although they were ultimately defeated. The lockout made money very scarce; Jimmy MacDougall stood in for John at the Scottish Labour College, but the miners just weren't able to pay. We went on working while John and Sandy were imprisoned, but it became more and more difficult and I began to concentrate on working with the unemployed.

11. Working with the Unemployed

In the winter of 1920-21 it had become obvious that the official trade-union movement was going to do nothing about unemployment. In January 1921 when there was talk of a general strike the British TUC called a conference on unemployment. It was adjourned for a month, and at the next meeting Ramsay MacDonald appeared. He was fighting a by-election at Woolwich, and when he appeared at the conference the whole campaign switched from a general strike on unemployment to parliamentary agitation and his victory in Woolwich. It was a trick that had been pulled time and time before; but the idea of a general strike was dropped.

We had hoped that the TUC would lead the struggle against unemployment, but we saw now that the unemployed had to fight for themselves. From 1921 I concentrated on this. It was my chief work as a revolutionary in the early twenties and in the thirties.

I led my first demonstration in March 1921. The Prince of Wales, later Edward VIII, came to Glasgow and we decided to make our protest at the big reception in St. Andrew's Halls. We called a meeting of the unemployed at nine in the morning; a couple of thousand turned up and they were really wild, angry men. Some of them were carrying hand-grenades they had brought back with them from the front - I also knew that some even carried guns on demonstrations. They were a very militant threatening crowd.

To my amazement John Maclean didn't turn up. The crowd started to be restless. I knew the Prince of Wales's time-table, and I decided I would have to lead the demonstration off by myself. McClure, the police superintendent, tried to insist on us leaving Glasgow Green by the side-roads and avoiding all the main roads; but this was before the regulations empowered the police to direct you along certain routes, and I insisted on going along Renfield Street and up Sauchiehall Street.

All along the route the superintendent kept trying to push us up other streets. Every time, I said 'No' - and I told him he had better keep in mind the type of worker at my back and not do anything to test them. He was in a tearing rage, but I kept relying on the men behind me and he had to let us go through.

When we got to Charing Cross, at the end of Sauchiehall Street, the Prince of Wales's bodyguard had just left him at St. Andrew's Halls. They were all soldiers with rifles at the slope and bayonets, but some of the unemployed behind me surged forward wanting to attack them. The police were alarmed; they got between the two groups and helped push the crowd along to the halls. All the dignitaries and the Prince of Wales were inside the halls. Our crowd was too big to fit into North Street, behind the halls, and McClure suggested splitting them into two with half on each side. That was just what I wanted. I surrounded the halls with singing, chanting and sloganising men: the Internationale and The Red Flag could certainly be heard inside.

The Prince of Wales was taken out the back way and up a side road to Sauchiehall Street. He had heard us, and said he wanted to meet a deputation of four of the unemployed. I was determined that he wasn't meeting me, or any of us, and I took the demonstration back to Glasgow Green and dismissed it.

As well as holding weekly mass meetings of the unemployed in the city halls, we had elected a committee to run the business. It had a meeting that afternoon in the Partick ILP rooms. John Maclean was there, and I put the Prince of Wales's unpublicised invitation at the bottom of the agenda. One of the members of the committee was a communist called 'Sticky' Smith. He was a young man, but he had every disease under the sun; he walked with a stick, and he had to carry a cup to spit into. He was dying, but he was a devoted socialist and went out night after night doing propaganda for the Communist Party - he had a marvellous voice and was a very good speaker. At this committee meeting, right away he raised the matter of four of the unemployed meeting the Prince of Wales. I was chairman, and said we would discuss it in its proper place on the agenda; but he interrupted all the way through, saying it would be too late to send the deputation.

Abour four o'clock we finally got to it. Smith moved that we send four people to meet the Prince of Wales, and a Bridgeton CPer named Adams supported him. John Maclean almost exploded, and the committee of sixteen turned it down by a good majority. John didn't forget it. When he was attacking the CP at meetings he would add: 'And the Communist Party wanted to meet the Prince of Wales!' To want to meet royalty was a terrible thing in Scotland.

During the committee meeting the question arose of why John had not been at the demonstration. He said he wanted to prove that it wasn't necessary for him to be there every time. I doubted if that was the reason, and suspected that he had been ill in the morning. His wife had left him and he wasn't really capable of looking after himself; he ate pease brose in the mornings, and it often made him sick.

John's wife was a good woman, but the years of jail and poverty had taken their toll. He had no job, and she had taken their two daughters to live with a relative in Hawick. John's house was fully mortgaged by this time, and with the decline in what he got from the Scottish Labour College and the 'Tramp Trust' collections he had money difficulties. While she was away he never let another woman into the house, and it was in a bit of a mess.

It was partly because of his personal problems that I continued to take a lot of the responsibility for organising the unemployed. But also, John was not very interested in organisation. He preferred his agitational and educational work, and often didn't have time; often when we were in the middle of some arrangements he would have to go off to his class at the Labour College. He didn't want to link up with the National Unemployed Workers' Committee Movement that was being developed in London and elsewhere by Communist Party members like Wal Hannington.

We went on demonstrating at the hotels, and on Sundays we started taking our protest to the churches. One Sunday morning we marched along Great Western Road to the Church of England cathedral, St. Mary's; I led them up to the doors, and to our surprise the doors were thrown open. We were asked if we were coming in to pray, and I said: 'No - we are drawing attention to the plight of the unemployed.' They shut the doors, and I felt very relieved.

It was easy to call demonstrations on unemployment anywhere. Even in a strange town, all we had to do was chalk the streets. The police had no power to interfere as long as you didn't obstruct anybody while you were chalking; I was arrested once on that point, and got off. Walls were a different matter, of course.

We were also fighting individual cases at the parish councils and the labour exchanges. The unemployed were paid benefit at the labour exchange but when it ran out they had to go to the parish council for money. It was always a battle because they were offered so little - seven shillings a week in some cases, which was very near the pre-war level. Although we often got individual concessions, it was difficult to get them to raise the scales. However, we kept demanding higher scales of relief and bit by bit got the basic raised to 13s. - nearly up to the level of labour exchange benefit.

Some Labour men, like Bill Sharp and John Storie, had been elected to the parish council and they were sympathetic. Bill Sharp had ratted on the movement during the war - he was a boilermakers' official and had taken a job with the employers - but I could get anything out of him at the parish council. There were some sympathetic Tories too, like Wallace the hatter and some other small business men.

It was through the unemployed movement that the socialist movement came closest to the women in the twenties and thirties. A lot of women hadn't been in work and found themselves unable to get relief. We dealt with a lot of cases of widows and single girls. The parish councils treated the single girls particularly badly and wouldn't have given them anything if we hadn't fought it.

Sometimes we had to resort to manoeuvres. There was one woman with four kids whom the parish council wouldn't give anything to: they told me in confidence that she had been living with four different men. I told her this - she asked me what it had to do with them; of course it had nothing to do with them, but we had to get the money. Eventually we proposed a deal with the parish council, that if they paid her three weeks' money she would use it to get herself and her children to her sister's in Grimsby. They agreed to that.

The unemployed movement was closer to the women because it was closer to the streets. We fought evictions, and that always involved women. Our fight made women willing to join the unemployed demonstrations, and some of them were very active in the movement. One woman was always on the demonstrations and always going for policemen. She asked a policeman a question one day, and when he said he didn't know she replied: 'You remind me of the girl in *The Blue Lagoon* who had a baby and didn't know how she got it!'

When we couldn't deal with individual cases through negotiations, we often backed them up with a demonstration. We had regular demonstrations anyway so we simply used the ones we had. Occasionally they were almost accidental. One day when Glasgow Parish Council were delaying payment the men saw me walking along George Square and came and asked me to do something. The parish council was opposite the city chambers; I took the men to the side door of the city chambers, in North Frederick Street, and marched them in and up the stairs. The Tory lord provost looked very serious and promised to do something about it immediately. He took about thirty men into his room and got in touch with the parish council, and they paid the money straight away.

Twice I took men into the city chambers on other issues and the authorities never found out how I did it. On one of these occasions there was a police cordon round the city chambers keeping me and the demonstration outside, but I got in and was arrested inside. It was quite simple. I used to go into the health department and across the corridor over the street, which linked that building with the city chambers.

We were the most important organisation fighting unemployment in Glasgow at this time. The ex-servicemen's organisations which had been active in 1919 had faded away. I was pleased about that; I was never happy with the idea of ex-servicemen being separate. We were developing machinery to fight for all the unemployed at the labour exchange, the courts of referees and the parish councils. Unemployed committees were formed all over Glasgow and they appointed people to go and fight cases. Many of the committees had their own premises, and we were always able to get the use of halls - we even got the picture halls free of charge.

In September 1921 the Scottish Board of Health published a proposed scale which was much higher than many parish councils were paying. In particular, it suggested 3s.6d for each child. We got the increase in Glasgow, and we spread the campaign round the West of Scotland. First I went to Irvine, where the children's increase had been turned down by one vote on the parish council (that vote belonged to a working man).

In Irvine I met Eddie Carr, from Springburn, and he and I chalked the streets for a meeting. Nobody turned out, and we went to the outskirts of the town and found all the men sitting in the park playing cards. They weren't in the least interested, so we went back and held our meetings in the streets; then we spoke to the wives about the increase, and the wives went to see the men. At first the men were hesitant, but we got a piper and a handful of men to walk behind him. Gradually more of them joined in, and by the time we got to the parish council there were four hundred behind us.

We held our meeting at the parish council's door. Arthur Brady of the Irvine Labour Party gave us a hand with the meeting; we explained the need for the higher scale and increased children's allowance. When the parish councillors started coming out I left the platform and went with some of the women to block the door. The parish council hadn't made a decision in favour of the increases. One woman picked up a brick and said: 'Are you going back?' The councillors went back inside, and the increase was won.

The next day I went to Alloa, where the situation was similar. A fellow called Clarke helped me chalk the street and we got a meeting outside the parish council. It was on the main road; no one in Alloa had ever heard of such a thing, and the police tried to tell me I was causing an obstruction. I said they might be right - but we held our meeting, we held up all the traffic, and the increase was paid that night. From there I went on to Alva, but the parish council met in the afternoon instead of the evening and paid the increase. As a result of the Irvine and Alloa demonstrations we got the increase in a number of other places without any fuss.

The area where we were best known was Govan. We had won a lot of concessions from the Govan Parish Council, which covered the whole of the South Side, and most of our premises were in that area. It was decided that John Maclean and I should stand as Glasgow unemployed committee candidates for Kinning Park and Kingston in the municipal elections in November 1921. It was an extension of our agitational struggle.

John had been released from prison in August after serving the three-months sentence for his speech in the Miners' Lockout. He threw himself into the Govan campaign, and the two of us fought on the same election address. It wasn't a very good election address, because it was more of a revolutionary statement than a policy on unemployment, but we waged a great campaign.

In the middle of it, John was arrested for the fifth time at Dunmure Street in the Gorbals. In his speech he had said that if the unemployed were hungry they shouldn't starve: there was plenty of food about and they should take it. He was charged with sedition and given twelve months. The night he was arrested, a tremendous crowd of two thousand came to a protest meeting at Govan Cross. We were using the pillar-box as a platform. Jimmy MacDougall stepped up to speak, and I warned him to be careful because I didn't want him to go to jail again. But he talked to the crowd about the demonstration we were going to have, and said there were a lot of windows along the route and nobody could stop you just tapping the glass. The demonstration led to a huge battle, the police were pushed all over the place, and Jimmy was jailed.

I was left to fight the two seats by myself, and carry on organising the unemployed. There was also the need to raise money for John and his defence. I visited him in prison every week and discussed our campaign with him. Our agent was Montgomery of the SLP. At one stage he got out an election poster which said we were SLP candidates. He and I had a row about it; the next Thursday when I went to see John I told him, and he agreed that the posters should be pulled down. We worked with the SLP but we weren't members and it wasn't their election campaign. Our team were not SLPers; some were ex-BSP members, others were just sympathisers.

We all worked until five o'clock every morning. We covered the area with posters on all the big hoardings. In those days we stuck up proper sized bills, large ones in separate pieces like cinema posters; to do it you needed a team with a ladder, and the bills, and paste. Once one of our fellows was caught by a rather new policeman. He grabbed the man and set off with him carrying his equipment. As they walked along they were joined by the rest of the team, four alongside and two or three at the back. Gradually the bills were passed back, then the pail and brush and finally the ladder. When I joined them, the policeman said: 'I suppose, McShane, you didn't know that this was illegal.' I said: 'What's illegal?' He said: 'bill-posting.' I said: 'What bill-posting?' He turned round and all the evidence was gone - no bills, no pail, no ladder. He still insisted that we all went to the police station, and he lined us all up outside. Through the window we saw all the other police laughing like anything, and he had to tell us to go home.

There were other incidents like that during the campaign, and everybody enjoyed it. John finally got over 2,000 votes and I got a good vote, and we beat the official Labour candidates into third place. Because it was so successful, we stood again for the education authority elections in March 1922. The old school board had been abolished, and there were elections every three years for the new body. We put up John Maclean and Tommy Egan in Kinning Park, and Frank Duffy and myself in Gorbals.

Like all socialists, as well as campaigning for free boots and free meals for the schoolchildren we were in favour of secular education: the catholics and the rest were for religious schools. This led to some stormy meetings. One catholic woman teacher never missed one of our meetings; it was Frank Duffy she went for, and at every meeting she made him say he was in favour of secular education.

The election for the education authority was organised on a system of preferential voting which meant that if your first choice was down the poll you could recommend that your vote go to someone else; there were thirteen preferences and you put down 1, 2, etc. It meant that our chances got less as the poll went on, although John was only just beaten into fourth place. Under that system the Labour Party only got one or two seats; the middle-class elements, the catholics and the others, won the rest.

Besides all this I was organising food and clothing for John while he was in prison. By hunger-striking he had gained the status of a political prisoner, an unheard-of thing in Scotland, and had the right to have his food brought in from outside and wear his own clothes. I arranged changes of underclothing for him and the cooking of his food. We got a different woman to prepare his meal every week; we paid them for it, although they would have been proud to do it for nothing.

Wheatley was a prison visitor, and John wanted him to come and see him. I went and asked Wheatley, and we had a fierce argument in the corridor of the city chambers. Wheatley promised he would go to see John, but he never did.

Throughout Glasgow unemployment continued to spread. The contracts which had been put off until after the war were now finishing, and a lot of engineers were unemployed. In this situation the union, now the Amalgamated Engineering Union (AEU), was trying to control overtime working and manning levels. The Engineers' Employers' Federation decided to break the power of the union, and locked out all AEU members in March 1922.

I spoke at some of the meetings of the locked-out engineers. It was important for the dispute that the unemployed movement should stop unemployed workers taking the engineers' jobs. Despite that, the engineers were defeated; the lock-out lasted 13 weeks for AEU members, and they returned to much worse working conditions. The union's defeat meant a reduction in wages, not only for them but ultimately for all trades and the labourers as well. After the war I got £4.8s. a week as an engineer, but after the lock-out engineers' wages went down to £2.13s. By 1924, when I was working in England, the labourers were being paid 24s. or 25s. a week, only a little more than before the war - but all the prices had risen since then.

The AUEW only took in semi-skilled men in 1920. There are now six grades of membership, and that opens the door for some catholics to become union officials from the labourers and with the labourers' support. But catholic full-time officials are still rare in Scotland. One of the earliest I remember was John Storie who came in with the Hammermen in 1922. He was a semi-skilled man, and he also got to be on the parish council and the town council. But the protestant tradition in the engineers has continued. John Boyd is a right-wing member of the AUEW executive; he is in the Salvation Army and has been on television in his uniform. In the past nearly all the officials of the union have been protestants because nearly all time-served men are protestants.

John was in jail for a full year from October 1921, and while he was there the 'Tramp Trust' collapsed. Sandy Ross had gone back to Dundee, and later went to India. Jimmy MacDougall was completely unreliable after he came out. He only did one or two meetings, and at one of them he argued that there was no chance of a revolution in the next ten years and all we could do was return a Labour government to power. Of course there hadn't yet been a Labour government at this time, and there were a lot of illusions about what it would do, but it was still an astonishing speech for Jimmy to make. He said it with nearly two thousand people present.

Peter Marshall was teaching a Scottish Labour College class at Falkirk. I kept sending telegrams to him, but he never replied and never came to any of the big propaganda meetings we were holding in Glasgow. Later, when John formed the Scottish Workers' Republican Party, Peter joined that.

Finally, I was arrested myself in May 1922 on two charges, fighting an eviction order and sedition. Evictions for not paying rent had become more numerous. This case was an old man, his wife and their grandchild being evicted from their house in South York Street (now Moffat Street). Three of us went up to the house and put the furniture back in. During the day we held meetings in the street, and a very large one in the evening. It was at the evening meeting that policemen took the notes which were later used to charge me with sedition.

Some of us decided to stay in the house all night. After we had a meal at home, we entered the house and barricaded the door. When the police came at midnight we told them we were in the middle of a draughts tournament and refused to let them in. We knocked up the next-door neighbour and persuaded him to go and get hold of a magistrate, Baillie Buchan. He came and got the police to hold off until after he had seen the house-factor at nine the next morning.

The next morning Baillie Buchan came back with the news that the house-factor would not yield. He pleaded with us to give in. But by this time we were being supplied from the street with food by means of a rope and pulley; when the police tried to stop it there had been a huge protest from the crowd. We pulled up some of the floor-cloth and used it to advertise a meeting that evening.

The meeting was so big that it extended into several streets. The local MP, George Buchanan, spoke at one end, the Communist Party spoke at the other, and we held our meeting from the window. But when all the people went home for their tea, a whole army of police arrived in a van. They smashed down the door and took all of us. We were all charged with taking possession of the house without the permission of the rightful owner, and in addition I was charged with making two seditious speeches.

I had said that if the unemployed had to choose between paying rent to a house-factor and feeding a wife and family, they should let the factor go to hell. I also said that it now seemed a crime to fight an eviction or to fight hardship, but only a short time before the Government had given men rifles and bayonets to go and fight the German 'enemy'. In court they tried to distort this into 'What we want is rifles and bayonets', which would have been a very stupid thing for me to say.

All of us were refused bail and a big agitation, largely led by the Communist Party, developed about the case. After three weeks, everyone but me was released on bail. I lay in jail seven weeks until the day of the trial. I wanted to defend myself, but the Communist

Party had arranged a lawyer for all the defendants; they pointed out that I was on a charge with others, and if I defended myself I might jeopardise their case.

The night before the trial the lawyer came to see me and said they were going to attempt a technical argument in court. The tenant of the house was Mary Shaw; but the eviction order had been issued against James Shaw, her husband. The next day both the house-factor and the sheriff-officer had to admit that they had evicted the wrong person. The result was that the dock was cleared of all the other prisoners, and I was left to face the sedition charge.

The only witnesses for the prosecution were the three detectives who had taken notes at the meeting. They tried to introduce scenes from the eviction as evidence - the red flag flying from the window, the food being pulled up by rope; but because the previous case had been dismissed, all that was barred as irrelevant. Eventually all they had left was their own story. They said they had come to the meeting in disguise and mingled with the crowd; and that each of them had taken notes on a notebook in his trousers pocket, using a short pencil! All three, in separate parts of the crowd, had taken exactly the same extracts from my speech, and one of the notebooks actually had a bit rubbed out and rewritten - our lawyer wanted to know how the policeman had managed that in his trousers pocket. It was farcical.

But the three of them went on and on in the witness box, and one of them kept saying: 'McShane insulted one of our best officers, sir.' Which was true. Their 'disguise' at the meeting had been that they were wearing caps instead of hats. I had recognised them, pointed them out to the crowd and even mentioned their names - Davenny, Bowie and Douglas. In my speech I attacked their chief detective, Lackie MacDonald, and accused him of sending spies into working-class meetings.

MacDonald had a great reputation as a successful detective, and the police were incensed because I had attacked him. The night I was arrested I was taken before him and he said: 'We can take you for something else' - meaning my army desertion. But he thought that the sedition charge was enough to send me down for two years (so did I), and he didn't really want to use the desertion because it would make the police look stupid for not charging me before then. It was MacDonald who more or less hunted John Maclean everywhere; we often had to escape him by jumping on a passing tram or something like that. The police thought he was great, and kept trying to work my attack on him into their evidence.

Finally, the lawyer said 'Well, I don't suppose he was very complimentary to your best officer, but that is not the charge', and they had to give up. The police really made a mess of the whole case, and I got a majority verdict of 'not proven'. I discovered afterwards from one of the jurors that all six women on the jury thought I was guilty. However, this juror had pressed them to re-examine the evidence and got enough of them to agree that it was insufficient.

There was a marked contrast in the behaviour of different sheriffs when cases came before them. One of the best was Sheriff Lee. It was he who dealt with John Maclean on a sedition charge in 1915 and gave him a fine of £5 or five days in prison. Sheriff Lee was in charge of the eviction case during the rent strike and agreed to hear a deputation of shop-stewards - which was unprecedented - and then went and phoned Whitehall. It was also he who presided over the court when I appeared in July 1922 and stopped the prosecution witnesses from referring to the scenes at the actual eviction. Because the eviction charge was dropped, he was not prepared to allow them to use it to colour the evidence against me on sedition.

Sheriff Lee was a remarkable man, and his decisions stood out sharply against those of other sheriffs. When Peter Petroff came before the court in 1915 for simply not notifying the authorities of his change of address from London to Glasgow, Sheriff Thompson sent him to prison for two months.

With my seven weeks in jail, and expecting a prison sentence of one to two years, I had arranged for someone else to see to John Maclean's food. John didn't want the person I had asked, and got Jimmy Maxton to do it. But Jimmy was a hopeless organiser; after six weeks John had to go back on prison food.

In some ways it had been a bit of a relief to be arrested. I was overwhelmed with the jobs I was doing - carrying all the propaganda of the 'Tramp Trust', the unemployed agitation, and looking after John. It was a terrific weight, and I had other problems. I was only getting 15s. a week for my wife and myself. It was very difficult to live on that, and personal troubles between us had already begun.

While I was waiting to be tried I had some trouble with the prison authorities. One of the warders wanted me to scrub something off my cell wall; I hadn't written it, and I refused. They left a lunch, a bucket of water and a scrubbing brush outside the cell door, and I took in the lunch and nothing else. They put me on bread and water for three days and took away my mattress. I wanted to write to the Secretary of State for Scotland and was given permission; then I decided to raise it at the trial instead, along with the question of the prison visitor who came to hear my complaint and said 'I suppose your own actions brought you here' before I was tried.

Over the seven weeks the Labour Party became active on my behalf for the first time. They campaigned against my imprisonment and demanded that I be allowed out on bail. The Communist Party held meetings, raised all the money for the defence, and really organised the unemployed for the first time.

While I was in prison I had time to think about my position. In reality the 'Tramp Trust' had dissolved. For two years we had done hundreds of factory-gate meetings and other meetings, and organised countless demonstrations. But although we had conducted the best propaganda and agitation in the West of Scotland, we had left no organisation behind us. When I was arrested there was no one else to carry on the work except the Communist Party or the Labour Party. Realising this, I thought I must make a choice about what I was going to do. I decided to join the Communist Party.

I came to the decision with difficulty. It was I who had held the communists at bay on the Glasgow Unemployed Committee. When we met on that committee, I had often exploded at them. I felt a great deal of loyalty to John Maclean and I resented their attitude to him. But, conscious that I was isolated, I knew I had to join an organisation. The Communist Party's work in the unemployed committee after my arrest convinced me that their aspirations for the movement were the same as mine, and that they were serious. When I was released from jail Aitken Ferguson came to see me to persuade me to join. I was still hesitant about some things and was determined to have nothing to do with the intriguing, but my mind was otherwise made up. I joined the Communist Party in July 1922, and did not regret my decision.

Of the 12 arrested at the Shaws' eviction fight only Tommy Linden, who got six months was a Communist Party member. One of the others was an ex-member, but none of the rest were in it: they were part of the team that had been built up round the South-Side election campaigns. All of them, including two women, joined the party after I did. That kept the Glasgow unemployed movement together.

My decision to join the Communist Party meant a complete break with John Maclean, and I never saw him again until my own eviction fight in May 1923.

12. The Glasgow Communist Party

I joined the Communist Party in a period of intense activity. The Irish war was turning more and more of the Glasgow Irish to socialism; in the winter of 1922 the unemployed agitation was growing; and in November 1922 ten Glasgow ILP members were sent to parliament as Labour MPs.

Several Glasgow branches of the Communist Party were very active. A lot of the prominent Glasgow members had gone to London to do full-time jobs in the party, and the outstanding man in Glasgow was Bob Stewart. He had a long record in the socialist movement. He had spoken at the Glasgow unemployed demonstrations in 1908, at which time he and a man named Scrymageour ran the Prohibition Socialist Party in Dundee - ultimately Scrymageour went to parliament as a prohibitionist, but Bob went into the Communist Party. He was a nice fellow, very honest and reliable, but I never knew how he came to be the local full-timer.

There were a lot of good communists in Glasgow. Aitken Ferguson had been the Glasgow secretary of the SLP, and he was probably the best-read man in the Communist Party in Scotland. There was Allan Campbell of the Vale of Leven, and Eddie Carr of Springburn, both of whom I worked with in the South-West District Committee of the Unemployed. There were a host of others including Johnny Milligan, 'Sticky' Smith, and McHendrick. All of them were active, and it was a good organisation to work in.

The party was particularly active in the railways. Jimmy Figgins, of the National Union of Railwaymen, had attended John Maclean's economics classes and had defended John inside the Communist Party; he later became the general secretary of the NUR after the second world war. The railwaymen, particularly the clerks, seemed to pay more attention to education than most workers, and with the engineers and the miners they were the backbone of the National Council of Labour Colleges.

It was the railwaymen who became the strongest part of the National Minority Movement later on. In 1922 the organisation of workers into a broad national movement was only just beginning; the first conference of the NMM wasn't held until August 1924. But communist workers in the railways, the shipyards and engineering shops were doing fearless work despite the possibility of victimisation. We were still expecting a revolutionary situation to develop - there had been upheavals all over Europe, and as late as 1923 there was the Hamburg rising in Germany.

Each Minority Movement was meant to bring together all the rank-and-file trade unionists in that industry. It went across unions, and all the Minority Movements such as transport workers, engineers, miners joined up in the National Minority Movement. But among the transport workers no one was so well organised as the railwaymen. In Glasgow the tramwaymen were organised in the Municipal Employees' Association, and it was difficult to involve them. Unemployment was rising for a lot of workers, but it didn't on the railways. A railwayman had a job for life, and that made a big difference: the railwaymen practically were the Transport Minority Movement.

I didn't see much of the engineers, joiners and railwaymen because they operated in the workshops while I was organising the unemployed, but I remember one prominent railwayman, Joe MacMillan, very well. He was an excellent speaker and was one of the communists who carried the street-corner meetings at Bridgeton Cross. Those meetings were made difficult by the extreme protestant gangs, the Billy Boys. On some occasions they broke up the meetings by physical force, but at other times we were able to carry on. One young communist, the poet Matthew Bird, spoke from a table-top because he was so small. He was a very humorous speaker and quoted poetry a lot; the Billy Boys never harmed him, but often they lifted him and the table and put them both on the tram lines.

The Bridgeton Cross meetings were usually concerned with general communist propaganda. The party didn't deal with the Irish issue as much as John Maclean did. But in those days it did show great guts and determination. The members believed that they were on the winning side and that the revolution wasn't far away.

The Irish question was very important in Glasgow. The execution of James Connolly by the British after the Easter Rising of 1916 had disgusted the Irish. So had the attitude of the English to Home Rule, and the giving of six counties to the Northern Irish state of Ulster. The atrocities of the Black and Tans in the war against this settlement became notorious. In that situation the Glasgow Irish wouldn't vote Liberal, and all over Glasgow and the West of Scotland Labour MPs were returned to parliament in November 1922. The Irish vote counted for something in those days. Nearly all the Labour candidates were ILP members, so Glasgow sent a good left-wing contingent to parliament; the whole Labour movement was greatly encouraged.

The Clydeside MPs helped elect Ramsay MacDonald to the leadership of the Labour Party, and this puzzled me very much. From about 1910 the marxist movement had no illusions about MacDonald. In *Justice* Harry Quelch had denounced him for having his eye on the treasury box; all of us knew he was a careerist and opportunist. His weekly column in *Forward* was nothing but clever opportunism, but it helped make him popular, and he used the ILPers to maintain a 'left' face in the Labour Party. Of course, after they had got him elected to the Labour leadership he abandoned the ILP.

That winter I was the organiser for the South-West District Committee of the Unemployed. It covered Glasgow and the surrounding area right through Lanarkshire and Ayrshire to the Vale of Leven. Delegates from all the local unemployed committees met once a month; when a decision had been taken to press for something or to hold a series of demonstrations, you could rely on the work being done straight away. All the towns of the South-West of Scotland would have their pavements chalked, meetings would be held, everything would be done. It was the best body for agitational work that I ever knew.

We fought the parish councils. The queues for relief were getting longer and longer - skilled men were out of work now as well as the unskilled. The defeat of the engineers in June 1922 had led to many victimisations. There was no such thing as a standard payment, and every case had to be fought individually. On each local unemployed committee we had members who specialised in this work.

We organised demonstrations against the parish councils through-out South-West Scotland. In Lanarkshire there were Hamilton, Motherwell (with a very strong unemployed committee), Blantyre and any number of other places. There were big battles in the Vale of Leven as well. What we were doing in the South-West was also being done in the rest of Scotland; Mary Wickspeke was very active organising the women of Dundee.

In September 1922 a number of arrests were made in Port Glasgow. The local committee didn't have the experience to handle it, and Johnny Milligan and I went down there. When a riot broke out a man named Lang and some others had been arrested and a complete ban on all meetings was proclaimed. Lang had been active on the Irish question and on unemployment. The police weren't allowing his wife or anybody else to contact him. However, we went to the police station, arranged for his wife to see him, and then arranged bail.

We couldn't hold a meeting in Port Glasgow; all over the town were notices banning meetings and demonstrations, and we would have been arrested immediately. We went to Greenock, where there was a very good team of workers. They included Alec Geddes, who nearly became the first man to win a parliamentary seat as a communist when he came close to winning the Greenock election, and Mrs Harley who organised the women in Greenock. Between us we did meetings at all the street-corner pitches and the labour exchange, and we held a final one at the big meeting-place, the boundary of Greenock and Port Glasgow.

I arrived there after the meeting had started and I didn't know that all the other speakers had been officially warned not to refer to the Port Glasgow riot. My very first sentence was about the riot. I laid into Lithgow, one of the owners of Scott-Lithgow's shipyard, who was the provost of Port Glasgow. I got a great feeling stirred up and we had a very lively, enthusiastic meeting. At the end Milligan and I had to catch the train back to Glasgow; the whole crowd marched us from the boundary, through Port Glasgow, to the station. We broke the ban on demonstrations, but we couldn't be arrested because of the crowd.

Johnny Milligan and I worked together on the unemployed agitation and built up the Glasgow branches. Johnny was one of the founder members of the Communist Party and remained in it until he died. He came from Dundee, but his chest was bad and he had been unfit for work for a long time. He had all kinds of trouble and illness, but like two or three others he was spending his remaining time doing good political work. He got very fond of the beer, which wasn't surprising, and he finally died in 1939. He was a very good proletarian.

One night I was booked to speak for the Anderston Unemployed Committee. When I got there I discovered that it wasn't an ordinary meeting but a boycott of a local picture-house; the manager had refused to let the committee have it free of charge for meetings. We held our meeting nearby in Hydepark Street, and from there I led the crowd up Argyle Street and round the back of the picture-house. There was a cordon of police round it, but I turned round and went backwards through it; the crowd followed and we smashed the police cordon (the people waiting to get in to the picture-house ran for it). Then we marched round the building and back to Hydepark Street to finish our meeting.

Everything was quite orderly, and Mrs Cameron got up to speak, when the police charged the meeting with drawn batons. We heard them shouting: 'Get Milligan and McShane!' I pulled Johnny against a wall, the police and the crowd ran right past us, and we went round the corner into a little pub and had a couple of half-pints.

The Gorbals crowd arrived after it was all over - I had sent for Allan Campbell, who was speaking at a Gorbals unemployed meeting. They had come ready for a battle and didn't want to go home. Finally we got them back to the south of the river. Afterwards, Johnny collapsed; we carried him to the local ILP rooms and from there he went to the infirmary. At three o'clock in the morning we went to see him and found him demanding to be let out. He had picked up one of the old blue chemist flasks and was threatening them with it; I managed to get it off him when we were finally outside.

I was arrested the following day. They tried to keep me in prison without bail, but *Forward* took up the case and I was released on bail after eight days. The trial wasn't held until February 1923. The charge against another man and me was mobbing and rioting. In court a policeman, Sergeant Chisholm, claimed he was stabbed in the 'riot': as proof he produced a pair of trousers and a tunic and showed holes in them. But he hadn't been to a doctor, he hadn't been to hospital, and there wasn't a scratch on his body! He just couldn't explain how there was this big hole in his uniform but he hadn't felt anything until he saw it.

There was no proof at all of mobbing and rioting. In our evidence we pointed out that Mrs Cameron had been speaking on the platform at the time of the police charge, and obviously a peaceful meeting was in progress. Finally the sheriff asked to see Mrs Cameron; she came in - a big stout woman - and gave her evidence very clearly. The verdict was 'not proven' again, and I thought I had been fortunate.

The case prevented me from going on the 1922 Hunger March in London. At the end of 1922 I pressed for the affiliation of the South-West District Committee to the national body, the National Unemployed Workers' Committee Movement. The NUWCM had been organised in England and Wales for over a year. Once we had affiliated, we issued national cards and collected a penny a week off all the members. At the same time we began to prepare for the first-ever Hunger March, a propaganda demonstration to draw attention to unemployment.

I couldn't take part because I didn't know when my trial was, but I helped to organise the march in Glasgow. As well as recruiting men from the local unemployed committees, I went to the Govan Parish Council and demanded boots and shoes for the marchers. They agreed, and when the local press found out there was a storm. The Scottish Board of Health stepped in and threatened to surcharge the Govan Parish Councillors for the amount of the goods they had given us. That stopped it; but 29 men had already got boots and clothes, so we had scored a victory.

When the hunger-marchers got to London the Prime Minister, Bonar Law, refused to see their deputation. The NUWCM tried everything to force him to meet them: he wouldn't. But Bonar Law was also the MP for Glasgow Central. I wrote asking him to meet the Glasgow unemployed, and to my surprise he agreed. We then faced the problem of whether only NUWCM members should go or whether we should invite the Glasgow Trades Council as well; our movement worked for the unity of employed and unemployed workers. I went to see Willie Shaw, the secretary of the trades council, and finally we agreed to have a joint deputation.

Ten went on the deputation - five from the trades council and five from the Glasgow district of the NUWCM. The speakers were to be Willie Shaw, Herbert Highton, Johnny Milligan and myself. In order to get a common front with the trades council we had dropped the specific demands of the NUWCM and agreed a general policy with them. When we got in front of Bonar Law, to our annoyance the trades council handed out long duplicated sheets of their own proposals to provide work for the unemployed - building a road here, a bridge there, etc. They read the statements out word for word. I dropped a note to Johnny: 'Get back on *our* original demands.'

Johnny got up and said: 'I am here speaking for Britain's premier fighting organisation. Premier in a double sense - it is the most outstanding fighting organisation in the country, and it has chased the premier from London and caught him in Glasgow.' He went on to expound one of our central demands, that hours of labour should be reduced in order to distribute work among more men. Then I raised the question of the interest being paid on the war loan, which at that time was £400 million a year, and argued that half of this interest should be used to give decent benefits to the unemployed. In fact the scale of benefits we were advocating was higher than the average wage, because wage rates had collapsed after the engineers were defeated.

Bonar Law made a long reply expressing his appreciation of the trades council statement and promising that he and his officials would go home and study it. He outlined all the things the government were doing - building a road here, a bridge some other place. Then he turned to us whom he described as 'the gentlemen of the extreme left'. He said that my proposal to cut the interest rate in two would undermine credit and trade and would 'quite frankly, undermine the system that I stand for'. He also said that it was quite unfair to those who had lent money to the government during the war and were now expecting their interest on it. Allan Campbell was not down to speak, but he burst in: 'Well, we've had your reply, but this thing won't finish in parliament, it will be finished in the streets!' Allan was a great lad and he was quite right to come in; unfortunately, what he spoke about didn't happen.

The meeting ran on for two-and-a-half hours. There were pages of reports in the *Birmingham Post* and the *Glasgow Herald*, the only two papers that Bonar Law allowed in. It was the nearest we got to the trades council over unemployment. It wasn't left-wing as it had once been; though the ILP were still fairly strong they were on the way out and the Labour Party members were taking over. Men like Willie Shaw were in the Labour Party. They were really like the old Liberals and didn't want to emphasise socialism too much; and, of course, they were very pleased to be invited to meet the Prime Minister even though he was an old reactionary.

During the winter of 1922-23 our agitation for increased benefits from the parish councils took me all over the West of Scotland. For the first time, people actually took an interest in the elections for parish councillors. Before the war hardly anyone knew who the councillors were, because only the sick and elderly went for help. After the war, with the development of struggles over unemployed relief, we were able to run fantastic campaigns against some of the worst councillors. We even ran our own candidates in some places.

Voting for the parish council took place every three years, and in November 1922 we put up an unemployed candidate at Govan. His name was Barclay; he and I were both members of the Gorbals branch of the Communist Party. He was the best-dressed man in the branch, and seemed intelligent, and that was why he was chosen. The local unemployed committee was very active in the South-Side, and Barclay was actually elected. As a communist he was expected to see the unemployed and fight their cases from within the council - but he didn't: he went to America while he was still on the council, leaving others and me wondering where he got the money. He was our first communist to be elected to office, and he was a rat.

Because of our fight at the parish councils the Labour Party began running candidates. They started getting elected, and a big number of Labour parish councillors were elected to the town council in 1922 and before - John Storie, Bill Sharpe, John Wilson and others. Naturally they promised all kinds of benefits to get themselves elected; but the only parish council which was prepared to challenge the rates of benefit was at Bonhill parish council in the Vale of Leven (where five communists had been elected).

The conduct of the parish councils was directed by the Scottish Board of Health at St. Andrew's House. It was they who prevented the Govan Parish Council from giving boots and clothes to the hunger marchers. When Bonhill Parish Council decided not to take into account the ten shillings armed-forces pension and to pay full relief to ex-servicemen, the board of health stepped in again. Just as in Clay Cross recently, they decided to surcharge the councillors the extra amount of relief involved. This is a government trick which has always been used to prevent elected representatives doing what they were elected for. In response, the councillors got the local co-op to give out food vouchers that would be charged to the parish council later. The mass movement in support of them was so strong that the surcharge was dropped; but the board of health won over the rates of benefit.

In April 1923 I attended the third national conference of the NUWCM in Coventry. At that conference a man named Soderburg, who was leading a fraction within the NUWCM, attempted to run me for national organiser against Wal Hannington. I wouldn't allow it. I was very friendly with Wal and I thought he was a marvellous organiser - he had built up the organisation of the London unemployed from the very beginning. When he himself was first unemployed he had to go and collect foodstuffs, potatoes and so on, from the Board of Guardians: the movement he helped to build changed all that. Wal was re-elected national organiser. But Soderburg was later seen in the company of a CID officer at a Lyons' Corner House. Obviously he was working to split the movement.

I was elected assistant organiser of the NUWCM, but I didn't function because I had to leave Glasgow. In May 1923 my wife and I were evicted. We had been living on 15s. a week from the labour exchange, and our rent in Thistle Street, Gorbals, was 6s. All we had to live on was 9s. a week. It was a very cautious time for us, a very tough time. We lived on toast; my wife said her stomach was all scratched from toast with nothing on it. There were many others in just the same situation. I had always said the unemployed should feed their families and not pay the rent, and that is what I finally did.

The day we were evicted, I was at the bottom of Thistle Street speaking at another eviction. There was a tremendous audience. Someone announced that John Maclean had been holding a meeting at Dunmore Street and had raised the matter of my eviction and was marching his crowd to my house. I asked my crowd whether we should do the same, and we did. John and I had two big meetings outside my house on two different platforms. We looked at each other, saw each other, and I never saw him again. I left Glasgow in August and he died in November that year.

In the two months after I left there was some trouble between John and the NUWCM. Wal Hannington came up to speak in Glasgow; John organised an opposition to him at the meetings, and there was a lot of bad feeling. John had formed the Scottish Workers' Republican Party. It had some queer people that I didn't like - they had never

been to John's economics classes, they knew nothing about socialism or revolutionary work. Even if I had not joined the Communist
Party I could never have joined with that crowd.

John died of pneumonia. He was exhausted. The authorities hated
him more than any other man. He was jailed five times; the first time
was in 1915, and he spent four of his remaining eight years in prison.
When he was out of jail he was followed everywhere by plain-clothes
policemen. They were more frightened of his revolutionary stand
than of the shop-stewards.

Willie Gallacher in his book *Revolt on the Clyde* asserted that
John was made mentally unstable by his years in prison, and blamed
Peter Petroff's influence on John. I never accepted that - it was a
scurrilous accusation. John was weak, living on one or two pounds a
week without enough food or warm clothing; he was desperately
anxious for the mass movement of workers to break out; but he
didn't have delusions. His wife left him not because of differences
with him but because the years of poverty had been too much for her
- in fact she returned shortly before he died.

The accusation was typical of the worst side of Willie Gallacher.
He could lead men anywhere, but despite his popularity in the CP
and his loyalty to what he believed in, he had to twist what you said
and give it a wrong interpretation in order to win the argument.
Unfortunately, because he had met Lenin he thought he had all the
answers, but that didn't make him a match for John Maclean. Willie
really believed that the reason John would not join the Communist
Party was that he was unbalanced; he couldn't understand John's
suspicions of those who were forming the new party.

John had good personal reasons to be hostile. A man in Bridgeton
branch called J. Maclean, an ex-SLP member, rose to prominence in
the party. John felt, and so did I, that the party were trying to make it
appear that John had joined them; the name would look like his to
people in the rest of Britain and in Russia. As well as Gallacher's
slanders on him, he objected to J.R.Campbell describing his
campaign for a Scottish Workers' Republic as 'tartan socialism' and
'socialism in kilts'.

By the time Gallacher wrote his book he had reasons for wanting
to discredit Peter Petroff. (Petroff did alarm John about poison and
drugs in prison food, but those things existed where he came from.)
By the 1930s Petroff had broken with the Communist International
and joined up with the Independent Socialists in Berlin. He had been

sent as a special envoy to Germany; he saw how Stalin's tactics there had led to Hitler's victory instead of a revolution, and wrote a book called *The Secret of Hitler's Victory* which Trotsky referred to.

Afterwards Petroff came back to England and got a job as a writer at the TUC - he, his wife and two daughters walked miles to the French border to escape when Hitler took power. He was extremely critical of the role of the Communist International in Germany. Gallacher wrote *Revolt on the Clyde* when the revolution in Russia was ruined and Trotsky was in exile; I don't believe he really knew Petroff. After I joined the Communist Party I discussed John with him many times, and we never agreed.

John Maclean never worked as a schoolteacher again after 1915, and when he died his house was mortgaged and he was heavily in debt. The Glasgow Trades Council raised a fund to pay off his debts and the mortgage for his wife and two daughters. Money came in from everywhere - all over England, Australia, as well as Scotland - and the fund came to over £2,000. The whole movement knew what he had been and what he had done for them.

13. Travelling

After the eviction my wife and I went to live with her folks. It was only a two-roomed house in a tenement in Weir Street, and we slept in one bed and they in the other. It was intolerable to all of us, and my wife and I were unhappy because we had known better conditions. I was spending most of my time working with the unemployed and only coming back at night for a meal and some sleep. I was determined to get a job, and I travelled to England.

At Sutton-in-Ashfield I saw a big navvy job, and I walked on and asked the foreman if he wanted any men. He looked at the stiff white collar I wore and said: 'You're not a navvy.' I told him I was an engineer needing a job, and he gave me a start. For the first week or two it nearly killed me - it was all heavy pick-and-shovel work and I had never done that before. But the foreman shifted me on to grading, laying out and easier work; he wanted to keep me on because a lot of big machinery was arriving - pumps, locomotives, concrete mixers - and he needed an engineer to sort it out. I worked on the concrete mixer first, then the other machines as they came. My job on the site became that of repairman, and my wages went up.

I was still anxious to get a proper engineering job, and I took a day off to go to a firm at Nuneaton. I got the job there, but my foreman told me I would be daft to go; engineers' wages had sunk so much since the lockout that I was getting much more working with him. So I stayed where I was. It was a very big job extending the sewage works, fitting new pipes and beds, and I had a lot of work to do on the valves, pipes and sprinklers.

I was there eighteen months. I found lodgings two miles from the job in Mansfield, and my wife came to join me. I joined the local communist branch, and while I was there I spoke every Sunday morning and evening at the local market-place. The manager and the foreman of my job knew this and mentioned it to me, but I just carried on. In fact everybody knew I spoke there because of the vicar of Mansfield. He wrote an article in the local church magazine complaining of the Sunday political meetings and saying we were not doing anything worthwhile. I went after him and we had a long controversy in the *Mansfield Advertiser*, which had reprinted his article, about the merit of our work compared with his. It helped us considerably in getting the meetings going.

I became secretary of the Mansfield branch and I was there when they contested the local elections for the first time. I think Rose Smith, a school-teacher who had just joined the Party, was our candidate. The branch was mostly miners, about thirty of them, and I got them all out chalking the streets - it had never been done before in Mansfield, and it had a tremendous effect: everywhere you turned there was Rose's name and the times of our meetings. Rose was very good. Later she worked on the *Daily Worker*; the last I heard, she was pro-Chinese Communist and in Peking.

There was a Liberal MP in Mansfield and the Liberal Party was still strong. One of them always came to our Sunday meetings and twitted me about being a Scot who had come down from Scotland to tell them what should and shouldn't happen. In December 1923 the general election took place and I fell on my feet. I told him that the Liberal Party was doomed and Asquith, the old Liberal leader, was going to lose his seat at Paisley. It happened just that way, and the following Sunday I made most of it with this old boy. Then I took another chance. He had been sneering at the left-wing Clydeside MPs. I announced that at least two of them would be in the Labour cabinet, and they were - Wheatley and Shinwell. It made my reputation in Mansfield, but I didn't try my luck any more.

Unemployment wasn't a problem among the miners and we were able to do a lot of work round A.J.Cook's campaign to be secretary of the Miners' Union. Mansfield was very important to the campaign. It was always possible for a left-wing candidate to get support from miners in Scotland, Wales and the north of England, but Nottinghamshire was a difficult area to win - it is even today.

Cook's chief rival, Frank Varley, had just become the Labour MP for Mansfield. Three members of the Communist Party, including myself as secretary, had a secret meeting with Cook at one o'clock in the morning to discuss the campaign. Although Cook joined the National Minority Movement he never entered the Communist Party, but the way he spoke at that meeting you would have thought he was one of us. We decided to hold two enormous meetings with Tom Mann speaking at one and Cook himself at the other. The Communist Party had a room in the Labour Club in those days, and Tom Mann came there the night before his meeting. There must have been two hundred in the club that night, and Tom decided to entertain them. He sang a Chinese song, a French drinking song, and he kissed all the women, and everyone was delighted with him. His meeting was in the Grand Theatre, where no communist meeting had ever been held before. He packed it; he was an old man, but he could still go to town.

He gave the old type of syndicalist speech I had always heard him make in Glasgow. Although he was the great figurehead of the National Minority Movement and other activities led by the Communist Party, he was still a syndicalist at heart. He had always fought for the amalgamation of unions, and while he was general secretary of the ASE it became the AEU through the amalgamation of a great number of small engineering unions with it. In his speech at Mansfield that night he attacked the lack of co-ordination in the trade-union movement and argued for amalgamation. Then he turned and made great swipes at those trade-union leaders who put faith in parliament instead of fighting the struggle themselves: he pretended to be one of them, tottering along the platform and going down on his knees to pray to parliament for help. It was a great meeting.

A.J.Cook also spoke at the Grand Theatre. He wasn't a patch on Tom Mann as a speaker, but he filled the hall. The meeting was nearly all miners; he spoke on the problems facing the coal industry and put himself forward for the secretaryship. The votes were never counted separately, but I'm sure the meeting swung a lot of the Nottinghamshire miners to Cook. I think we did beat Frank Varley.

As well as working for the miners, the local Communist Party tried also to help the Transport Workers' Minority Movement. The movement was nearly all railwaymen, and we held a public meeting in Mansfield in the hope of getting members of the three railway unions to come and discuss amalgamation. The unions were ASLEF with John Bromley in charge, NUR whose secretary was J.H. Thomas, and the Railway Clerks; the whole communist movement was working for them to fuse as the engineering unions had done in 1920. They have not done so to this day.

The December 1923 election returned a minority Labour Government to power, and Ramsay MacDonald and the others used the

F

situation as an excuse to behave even worse than we had expected. Liberals were given the most important posts in the Labour Cabinet, strikers were threatened by the use of the Emergency Powers Act, and the British Empire was defended by bombing civilian populations. Only John Wheatley, at the Ministry of Housing, produced any real reforms for the working class.

Finally, after only nine months, the Labour Government was brought down by an alliance of Liberals and Tories over an article that appeared in the Communist Party's official paper, the *Workers' Weekly*. The article was a 'don't shoot' appeal to soldiers in the emergency powers period. J.R.Campbell was arrested as the editor of the paper. There was an enormous outcry against the case from all sections of the labour movement, and the government prosecution was withdrawn. A technical mistake - that Campbell was the acting editor and not the editor - was used as the reason for dropping the case.

The Tories went mad over Campbell's release. They argued that the Labour Party was protecting communists, and they and the Liberals pushed the issue to produce a 'red scare' election and oust the government. In the middle of the election the 'Zinoviev letter' was published, purporting to show a Russian plot to use the Labour Party to weaken the army and navy. Of course the original letter was never produced, only copies of what was clearly a forgery; but it carried the election for the Tories. We used the attack to publicise the communist case, and Johnny Campbell came and spoke for us in Mansfield.

I enjoyed my eighteen months in Mansfield. Although it was a comparatively small town it was a centre of activity. I went out speaking at week-ends and travelled to Sheffield, Leicester, Leeds, Denbigh and other towns, and got to know many other communist party branches. One of the best was in Sheffield. Some of the members there had long traditions in the labour movement; one of them, Fletcher, was a master baker, and both he and his son were very active.

Finally, however, I shifted to Kent. The foreman on the Mansfield job had gone to work down there for the same company, and he wrote asking me to go. At first I didn't reply, but then they offered me £6 a week and I decided to go. £6 was big money then; my wife had returned to Glasgow, and the wage would enable me to support myself and send money home more easily.

The job in Kent was building a road and a bridge. There was a tremendous amount of machinery - steam-driven and petrol-driven locomotives, big shovels - to keep me occupied. The job was in a very isolated place; the nearest centre was Dartford, which was also the Communist Party headquarters for Kent. I went and spoke at the branch at Dartford, but it was a long way for me to travel. In addition I didn't much care for the Kent organiser, Harry Homer, whom I had met in connection with the London unemployed - he later became a real right-wing opportunist. There wasn't much I could do in Kent and I felt restless.

While I was in Kent a number of unemployed men were given jobs there. They were London men sent up on relief work. One day I came across a meeting of angry workers and stopped to listen. Suddenly attention was drawn to the 'spy' listening to the meeting - and it dawned on me that I was the 'spy'! Unfortunately the men returned to London every night by train and I never got an opportunity to talk to them.

While I was doing this work on maintenance in England I had a labourer working alongside me all the time. This hadn't been the case in Glasgow. In Glasgow there were labourers in the workshop and you simply called one over when you needed anything to be shifted - there were cranes ready for use. I had only one labourer that I really liked, but even he and I fell out. One night I gave him the tools to hide for the following morning, and when I went back the next day there was no labourer and no tools - he had been picking primroses to sell in London. Primroses!

The foreman who had asked me to come down shifted to another job in Leicester. I stayed where I was until I lost my temper one day and packed my bags. After a fortnight out of work I went back to the same company, Vickers Armstrong, and went to a job in Hounslow. This was a contract with the Metropolitan Water Board; there wasn't much engineering work as there was only one locomotive, and most of the work I did was testing the equipment. But there was a lot of navvying work, and tramp navvies had come from all over the country.

The tramp navvies were a de-classed bunch, and among the most dangerous kinds of lumpen proletarians you could run across. Many of them had done long-term imprisonment; one man at Hounslow had been done for manslaughter. They slept under the hedges and moved from job to job with no ties; they said they just packed up a job whenever they felt like it. They were very proud of that, and thought they were the elite because they were free. A lot of nonsense has been written by sections of the socialist movement about this: to romanticise that way of life is daft. When human beings don't care about their own health or personal cleanliness and think of nothing but drink, they are no good to the movement or to anybody else.

At Hounslow they were earning £3 a week, but they lived in filthy conditions. Great big forty-eight-inch pipes were used on the job; the navvies covered up one end of a pipe, got a bag of straw, and slept there when they came back drunk. In the morning thirty of them filled a big skip with water from a hosepipe and they all washed in the same skip. The pipeline itself ran through an orchard, and they stewed the apples with streaky bacon for their lunch. You couldn't go into their cookhouse at all because it was verminous. I thought they were a stupid bunch.

The foreman who brought me to the firm had been a tramp navvy, but he was a very decent type, and by this time he had settled down in a little village outside Leicester. I went and joined him on the job there. I still got £6 a week and was able to send three or four pounds a week to my wife. I preferred this job. There were a number of local people working there as well as tramp navvies, and I joined the Leicester Communist Party. When I got to know the members and had met some of the men in the General Workers' Union I tried to interest them in getting the navvies organised, but they never did. I could do nothing on my own because I was still a member of the AEU.

I wasn't happy with the Leicester Communist Party. Several of them were more often in the pub than on the platform, including the chief propagandist: he had gained a lot of prominence in the branch, but his speeches were purely entertaining with no content. The branch was very slow, there were few advertised meetings and nobody seemed to do much at all. It was partly because of the town itself; in Mansfield the miners had their own kind of life and we were able to work around that, but the hosiery workers of Leicester were a very different bunch.

The Labour Party were very prominent in Leicester and it was a solid Labour town. The ILP actually held a conference while I was staying there, and Pat Dollan and a number of other Glasgow ILPers came. Knowing that I was fed up with the Leicester Communist Party they tried to persuade me to join the ILP, but I wouldn't do that. Instead, all I could do was go to the local library and read.

Leicester was a very strange town; there was a mixture of class-consciousness, high-level philosophy, and working-class 'intellectualism'. The Roman Catholic priest there was Vincent McNab, who was chairman of the Philosophical Society - he had defended socialism and the Labour Party on the grounds that it stood for common ownership of the means of production but not distribution! He had been well-known since before the war. There was an ethical society and a very respectable fabian group. E.D.Morel had come from Leicester and Ramsay MacDonald had represented it. The 'intellectual' element seemed to affect the workers, and it had a deadening effect on the Communist Party.

In Leicester I was persuaded to go to the only spiritualist meeting I ever went to in my life. Spiritualism had a tremendous revival in Britain after the first world war, as it had after the second. The medium, a man, pointed at me and said there was someone called Mary standing with her hand on my shoulder telling me to have an open mind. The friends who had taken me asked if I had discovered who 'Mary' was: I told them I had examined all the Marys from Mary Magdalen downwards, but it wasn't any of them! They were quite annoyed with me. Spiritualism seemed to have an effect on ILP members that it never had on the CP or the old BSP and SLP.

The General Strike took place while I was in Leicester, but very little happened as far as the Communist Party was concerned. Everything was very peaceful. The Labour Mayor stopped the trams and the Labour Council ran the town, and there were no disturbances. Herbert Morrison was sent to Leicester by the Labour Party and was looked upon as the leader of the strike while he was there; when he spoke at one big rally the whole council attended. Everything just stopped mechanically, and when the strike was over everything just started again. During the General Strike the TUC called men out section by section instead of bringing us all out at once, and the engineers were only called out the day before the strike ended. However, most of the engineers didn't wait to be called out - the fact that there were no trams made that easier - and the return to work was as if they had all been on holiday.

One of the men on the job left to work in the Yukon in Canada, and when he returned he described it all to me. He had been scared while he was out there, of the animals, the winter, the trees, everything. I wanted to go there; I liked the idea of travelling - I had read Jack London's stories - and I knew the wages would be good. At the beginning of 1928 I applied for a job in the Yukon.

The job was to build and repair two big American-made shovels. I had done repairs on four of them in Kent. When I went for my interview at the Yukon Consolidated Gold Co., Corbet the secretary of the company was there and so was the boss, a millionaire called A.N.C.Treadgold. Corbet told me it had been difficult to get my passport. Apparently there was a man born at the same time as me with the same name in Glasgow, and he was a trouble-maker. He said. 'I assured them it couldn't be the same man, but I don't think I would have got it if I hadn't known the passport officer.' I just nodded 'Oh, aye', and went and got the boat.

When I got off the boat in Canada the immigration officer looked at my passport and said 'Glasgow, Moscow, same thing', but I passed through and went on to Vancouver. I missed the boat in Vancouver, so I was able to stay there ten days and visit the Communist Party. I was shocked by what I saw. The members were so down-and-out that they were sleeping in the party premises. There was no work in Vancouver and hardly any relief. I wired the company and asked for £20 because I had missed my boat. To my surprise they sent it, and I was able to buy meals and such for some of them.

The Vancouver communists asked me to speak on the situation in Britain. I agreed, but I asked them not to publicise the meeting because I had lied about my passport, and I still had a good bit of my journey to do including catching a boat into Alaska. They said they wouldn't - but right across Vancouver every telegraph pole had a leaflet stuck on it bearing my name. I spoke on a Sunday night to a couple of hundred people at the Royal Picture House. Vancouver had a lot of Scots, some of whom were in the Communist Party, and a good many of them were there that night.

The members in Vancouver were pretty well-informed, but very different from the communists in Britain. They were already hero-worshippers of Stalin. It was the first time I had run across this. I didn't know much about Stalin, I had just heard his name, but they had Stalin on the brain. I couldn't understand it because I was still living in the communist tradition which saw Lenin as the leader but didn't have heroes in that way.

My boat took me up the inner Pacific to Stagway, Alaska. From Stagway the journey was by single-track railway. The train ran twice a week and went over Dead Man's Gulch, which was very frightening - it was as if the train was rearing over the gulch. It stopped at White Horse, and then we travelled to Dawson City on a horse-pulled sleigh. It was over four hundred miles. Every morning the horses had icicles from their noses to the ground, formed by breathing; we pulled the icicles off the horses and did the same of ourselves.

The route was just one narrow passage cut through the trees, tremendous trees. One old fellow with me was very superstitious; he kept looking back over the path and thought he could see the trees coming closer and forming as women and their babies and visions like that. Every 40 miles there was a roadhouse with one person manning it. We slept in these places at night and ate salmon and bear steaks. I never ate food like it in my life, it was marvellous.

When I got there, the two big shovels I was to build were to dig a ditch 400 miles long to the silver mines at Kino. Treadgold, the owner, had already bought all the land for a hundred miles all round, had got control of the water rights and driven the old miners out. He was mining for quartz gold by using big dredgers on the Yukon and Klondike Rivers, going up one side of the river one season and coming back another. He sluiced the rock with big hoses and got quartz gold out that way.

Now he wanted to use the same method in the silver mines farther down, with the massive ditch replacing the river. It was hoped that the ditch would also supplement the water supply to the power-house which was run by water-driven turbines; in winter the ice was four feet six inches thick, and the water beneath it got less and less. At the beginning of the winter men broke the ice, but then it became impossible and they had to stop the dredgers and just use the power for lighting.

The great ditch would not only allow the dredgers to work all the time, but it would enable Treadgold to control the water to the silver mines and buy them out as he had the gold mines. But it just happened that those shovels, big as they were, simply couldn't dig that ground. They were the most powerful shovels I ever saw, but the ice just pushed them back. A foot below the surface was solid ice. They dug about four hundred yards, one shovel coming back and the other going down; but the summer was nearly over. I told Treadgold that the shovels were going, and that I should go back to Bear Creek as I was no use where I was. He replied: 'The doctor isn't always attending to disease, he often waits for disease to occur', and he toddled off to inspect the shovels. He dawdled around in and out and under the buckets until I thought he was going to get killed. After an hour he told me he was satisfied that I was telling the truth, and sent me back to Bear Creek.

I was pleased to go back there. Our camp had been right up in the wilds, and in summer the twenty of us had slept in tents. After two months the summer was over, and we built some huts very quickly. Bears were roaming everywhere and we were all a bit worried. The silver-grey bear was the most dangerous; the brown bears usually ran away except when they had young. If young ones were with them it was you who ran away. They would leave the young to chase you, and a bear can catch any man.

One night a bear came to the camp while I was doing my washing. We used four-gallon tins to which we fixed a handle and put across the fire. While the washing boiled you sat with your front and back alternately to the fire, because half of you roasted and the other half froze. The fire was near the cookhouse, and for a number of nights a bear had been coming and stealing bacon from the boxes outside the door. This night, I had left the fire to get fresh water; as I returned, the cookhouse door opened, out came the cook with an axe, and a big black thing rushed past me. It was the fright of my life. I put my overalls in the water but I didn't do any washing for another week and had to thaw the overalls out. Two men waited on the cookhouse roof one night and shot the bear, but though they followed the blood trail for two miles they never found the animal; bears have tremendous vitality.

Things were much better than that in the camp at Bear Breen. There were about twenty people living in cabins, including two families: a man and wife, both French, and a half-Indian half-white Canadian with his family. There were two dredge-masters, myself, and two others. I had a cabin to myself, a man to look after the fire, and all my food supplied. I could have spent the rest of my life there.

I worked hard mending the dredgers that worked the Yukon. This is one of the fastest-flowing rivers in the world. When the ice breaks up it is very picturesque, with the lumps of ice moving swiftly on the current; but we had to cross the river in a small boat, trying to avoid being hit by the ice. I worked on both rivers - one dredger on the Yukon hadn't been repaired since the first world war.

I was earning £10 a week. I sent £5 home to my wife and had £4 put by for when I got back to Britain. I didn't have to spend anything because food, clothes, everything was found for me by the company. When any of us wanted anything we just put a note in for it - they even sent the beer up from North Forks - and they paid all travelling expenses. At the end of 1929 I had a paid holiday due, and I decided to go back to Glasgow for a short break.

Coming out of Bear Creek was different from going in. Some of the roadhouses had closed down and they were now 80 miles apart instead of 40. If we missed our train we would have to wait three or four days for the next and I would miss my boat, so we didn't stop for sleep but only for food, until we got to White Horse.

In Vancouver I found the Communist Party rooms open and nobody there, but on the blackboard there was a big notice of a demonstration. When I found the demonstration there was a man from Clydebank, Jimmy Litterick, who later became an MP. He grabbed me and asked if I knew Allan Campbell: of course I knew him very well from the Clydeside unemployed movement. Jimmy explained that Allan was in prison, and the demonstration was a protest to try to get him out. Apparently he had been arrested on board ship for mutiny, under the name McEwen. When he told the prison authorities his real name was Campbell they hadn't believed him, and no one was being allowed to see him. I said I would try to see him, and then return to the party rooms and report.

In the prison I told one of the officers I had heard some people say that an Allan Campbell from Scotland was there, and that I should like to write a note to him to see if it was the Allan Campbell I knew. I wrote in very guarded terms, and the prison officer looked at me and said: 'Well, he seems to come of respectable people.' I explained that I knew Allan from the Vale of Leven not far from Loch Lomond, and he said: 'He has got among the riff-raff of this town; he has got among the communists.'

Then he pulled out a statement about Allan Cambell that read: 'Born in the Vale of Leven, brought up in the Church of Scotland, now an atheist.' I pretended to look shocked and he talked to me for a long time about Allan, for whom he seemed to have some respect, and finally took my note to him. When he came back, he let me in to see him. Allan was in a bit of a state. The first words I got out of him were 'Have you any money?' and I gave him what little I had.

I went back to the Communist Party headquarters in Vancouver to tell them I had seen Allan, but they were in a terrible mess. There had been a police baton-charge, and all their heads were bandaged. I had to leave them to catch the train for Montreal. I arrived back in Glasgow at the beginning of 1930.

14. Back Among the Citizens of Glasgow

I arrived on 5 January and was due to return to the Yukon at the end of March. I discovered that my marriage was over, and I had a number of personal matters to attend to. Despite this, I got in touch with the Glasgow Communist Party and did one or two meetings for them in the Gorbals.

The party had changed a great deal in the time I had been away. It had begun the emphasis on 'Comrade Stalin' that I had found in Vancouver. It had also completely changed its attitude to the rest of the Labour movement. The Communist Party was now attacking all the Labour MPs and town councillors as agents of capitalism, almost as agents of fascism, and denouncing the Labour Party as the third capitalist party.

The attack seemed to be fiercer against the Labour left than against the right; the ILP MPs, specially Maxton, got a more thorough battering than anyone else. At the beginning of 1930 George Middleton was fined for interrupting a Maxton meeting the previous year, and one of the first things I saw when I got back was a leaflet on the 'sham left' by George Middleton. In the twenties our campaign had been against MacDonald, Thomas and Henderson, the right-wing leaders of the Labour Party; but this leaflet was entirely aimed at the left-wing MPs.

Years later I realised that this 'social fascist' policy was actually related to Stalin's position inside Russia. In order to support his regime he had to attack his opponents as being all in some way or other connected with fascism. From the time Trotsky was exiled he was described as an agent of fascism, and all those who were later executed were said at their trials to be working for fascism.

Stalin was also asserting that the way was open for a revolutionary seizure of power by the Communist Parties and the working class. In these circumstances, the social-democratic parties were the main obstacle in the way! In Britain this policy was introduced at the 1929

Party Congress, when Harry Pollitt replaced Albert Inkpin as general secretary of the party. Many leading communists, including Gallacher and Campbell, were against the policy but they all had to accept it. The new line was embodied in a pamphlet called *Class Against Class*, which was really arguing for the revolutionary dictatorship of the British Communist Party.

I found it difficult to understand the new policy: ultimately it was directed not only at the leaders but also at the members of the Labour Party and the ILP. Naturally Labour Party people were upset by these attacks upon them, and the entire working-class movement became separated on the basis of which party they supported. People in the labour movement began to hate the communists.

The personnel of the party in Glasgow had changed while I was away. When I went to the Glasgow bookshop there was only one man I knew, Willie Joss who had done a great deal of educational work in the early twenties. The Scottish organiser was a man I didn't know, Davie Campbell. He worried me. He had been to Germany and other places on behalf of the Communist Party, but he had no politics at all and had read almost nothing. Once when I was in the bookshop someone wanted to buy *The Communist Manifesto* for threepence. Davie Campbell said this was only the abridged edition, and pointed to Ryazanoff's commentary on the *Manifesto* instead! Fortunately the man had the sense to take the 'abridged' edition.

George Middleton was the organising secretary for Glasgow, though he and Adam Haimes both worked from the Carlton Hall in Maryhill and it was sometimes difficult to tell which of them was the secretary. George was one of the most competent of the party men. Like Aitken Ferguson, he was exceptionally well-read and not just in party literature; he read a lot about history, particularly the French Revolution. He was an unskilled man who had been in the army during the war, joined the CP after the war, and had suffered almost continuous unemployment. He wasn't a paid full-timer, but his wife worked in the advertising department of the *Evening News*. She was a very fine type of woman and he was one of the ugliest men in Scotland!

Middleton's slum background made him a very blunt, tough sort of fellow. In 1930 he was one of the chief organisers of the campaign against the left MPs, and he got a bit of a reputation for threatening to assault people. He was a rascal, but I liked him because he had qualities the others didn't have. He always had a shadow, someone hanging round to assist him, and when he was Glasgow organiser the shadow was Adam Haimes.

The problems of organising the Glasgow branch were greater now that the Communist Party had its own daily paper. The *Daily Worker* first appeared in January 1930, although in membership the party was weaker than it had been since it started. The wholesalers in the newspaper trade wouldn't touch the paper, and the party had to organise its distribution. Every morning a fleet of about thirty members on bicycles met at the railway station and took bundles of papers out to the different localities where others were waiting to distribute them to the newsagents. Paper shops were open from six in the morning, and we asked them all to take it. This method of overstepping the wholesalers was organised by Jack Morrison (who later joined the Labour Party). Jack set an example to all party members.

When I returned from Canada it was obvious that there was practically no unemployed movement left in Glasgow. It existed in name only, and its reputation had been badly tarnished when two members had gone on a deputation to the Scottish TUC at Hawick and allowed a collection to be taken for the delegates. We *never* allowed this kind of thing. It was made worse by a story that the delegation had been seen in a pub afterwards - the Scottish TUC made the most of that!

Although there weren't any unemployed meetings being held, there was an instruction from the party for the Glasgow CP to become involved in a demonstration called by the Communist International for 6 March 1930. It was to be International Unemployment Day, and there were to be demonstrations in America, Germany and Britain. I spoke at a couple of meetings in the Gorbals and drew attention to it. But none of the new party members seemed to have any experience of demonstrations, and I got involved in a controversy in the party as to how it should be conducted.

I had organised unemployed demonstrations before, and I had a knack for organising them that was largely my political life. I always held that to demonstrate without some definite objective was entirely wrong. But they had no objective, and when I suggested that the demonstration should be used to back up a deputation to the corporation on unemployment, they went mad. I was immediately told that my suggestion was ILPism, and a big argument started.

In the midst of this argument Wal Hannington came up from London. He was staying at George Middleton's council house - he and Middleton were friendly, though Middleton was not greatly interested in work with the unemployed. Wal and I had always been friendly in the twenties and we never had a wrong word; all through the unemployed movement of the twenties and thirties we helped each other, worked with each other closely and were in trouble together many, many times. I liked the man, and he had a big influence in my decision to again take up serious work with the unemployed. We discussed the poor state of the Glasgow movement, and it was agreed between us that while I was in Glasgow I would do what I could. It was the kind of work that I could do; even the Communist Party always recognised that.

But it wasn't easy. Even when Hannington was there, we had a row with the secretariat - they were annoyed that he walked through their meeting in the back of the bookshop to get a shave because he and I were going out! They were a very rigid lot. A Communist International representative was in Glasgow at the time. Every day he went to lunch with Davie Campbell almost standing on guard over him. Then one lunch-time the representative announced that he was going out with me. He asked about my ideas for the demonstration. I explained that we should make it a day of defiance, that we should take charge of George Square against the ban imposed in 1908, and also have a deputation to the corporation. He said: 'That is exactly what they are going to do.' His decision must have carried weight, because they all agreed.

On the day of the demonstration I held a meeting in Gorbals and marched a contingent from there to George Square. We had chalked all the streets in Gorbals with notices of the demonstration. There were only a couple of hundred of us, but we were the only group that marched to the square although a lot of other demonstrators just arrived. When I got there I asked several of the agreed deputation when they were going into the city chambers. They were all members of the Communist Party, but when I tried to get them together they wouldn't come.

Finally I was so exasperated that I suggested to some others that we make a real demonstration. I proposed that one of us get up and speak; if he was pulled down another would get up, and so on - we would really let them know that we were there. Straight away Jimmy Beecroft from Blantyre jumped on to a seat. The police pulled him down immediately, so he lay on the seat and talked. I got up on the other side of the square and started speaking, and I was pulled down. The police made a ring round me and as I tried to speak through them I heard Rosie Kerrigan calling to me to carry on. Then Willie Allan, the secretary of the Scottish Miners, started to speak, and we were both arrested. Willie and I were fined £3 each for a breach of the peace. That finished my chance of going back to the Yukon - I would never get another passport.

From then on I put all my political energy into organising the Glasgow unemployed. At the end of 1929 it had been decided to have a hunger march in April to arrive in London in May 1930. I didn't go on this march because I had no part in organising it, and George Middleton was the leader of the Scottish contingent in Glasgow. Of course, from 1929 a Labour government had been in power; the march was directed against them, and the Labour Party was against it. A Labour Party organiser, Mary MacArthur, was sent down ahead of the march to tell all the Labour supporters not to help the marchers. It was a very hard march, and on it they sang a song with a line, 'We met with Labour sabotage in village and in town.'

The NUWM had to battle against the Labour Government. Margaret Bondfield was in the cabinet and was responsible for introducing all kinds of economies; she became a main enemy. J.H.Thomas, the railwaymen's leader, was the Minister for Unemployment and introduced 'rationalisation' schemes for industry which added to the number of unemployed. The unemployed had a very strong case against the Labour Government.

In May 1930 John Wheatley died, leaving the parliamentary seat at Shettleston vacant. The Communist Party decided to stand Saklatvala for the constituency, with George Middleton as the election agent. Saklatvala had previously been an MP for Battersea, an English constituency; he was an Indian and a very able propagandist. The Labour Party candidate was John McGovern, and the communists conducted a 'social fascist' campaign aimed at the ILP and McGovern himself.

Many Labour men had been interested in Wheatley's seat, and it came as a surprise to some that McGovern was selected. He got in on the ILP and trade-union vote in the area because he was chairman of the local ILP and appeared to be on the left. One of the troubles with the ILP was that they were a bunch of hero-worshippers who couldn't distinguish the real lefts from the fakes. Those who knew McGovern didn't trust him. He had been a pacifist during the war, then an ILPer, then an anarchist in Guy Aldred's Anti-Parliamentary Communist Federation; he was Aldred's election agent in the campaign against Wheatley in 1922. McGovern then went to Australia for a short time, and when he returned he re-joined the ILP.

During the election campaign relationships between McGovern and the Communist Party became very bitter. We were, of course, attacking him as one of the 'so-called lefts' of the ILP. But McGovern responded by taking a racialist attitude to Saklatvala and simply slandering everybody else. Of me, he said that I was living with another man's wife and had claimed from the parish council for myself, my 'wife' and her four children! It was an utterly fantastic story: I had never lived with any wife except my own - and she was gone. I never had any children. I had never been to the parish council in my life except to lead deputations; I had no stamps when I came back, but Rosie Kerrigan had a shop and I got four stamps from her and that put me on the labour exchange. McGovern and I nearly came to blows over this statement, and finally he sent me an apology via Guy Aldred.

He also brought in a fellow called MacLean from Govan who had been on the first Hunger March in 1922, to discredit the march and us. When I heard this I immediately wrote to Wal Hannington; he replied that this was one of the men who had caused trouble on the march by getting drunk and by mishandling money. At the next meeting when McGovern produced MacLean to speak, I got up on the platform and read out Wal Hannington's letter. He completely crumpled up - I've never seen anything like it in my life.

The whole Communist Party waged a most active campaign against McGovern and for Saklatvala. Sometimes it went too far. The Young Communist League went and wrote 'Arise ye starvelings from your slumbers' on the cemetery walls. It caused an awful row, and the party instructed them to go and wash it off. I was quite closely involved with the campaign because I was the prospective municipal candidate for Parkhead Ward in the Shettleston constituency.

One of our favourite terms for John McGovern was 'Judas'. Years before, when he had been an anarchist, McGovern had written a leaflet referring to Labour MPs as Judases who sold themselves for a salary of £400 a year. We used this and the *Daily Record* also referred to it. On the morning of the vote Reg Bishop, a London communist, shouted 'Judas' as McGovern went into the polling booth. McGovern said 'Do you know that you are insulting me?' and Bishop replied: 'I didn't know that it was possible to insult a bastard like you'. Such was the bitterness engendered at that time.

Although I stood as a candidate in the municipal elections of October 1930, my real work during that year was with the unemployed. In May 1930 the Local Government Act of 1929 came into force, and dissolved the parish councils and put relief into the hands of the public assistance committees of the local authorities. Our fight on unemployment had to be directed against the Glasgow Corporation and its Public Assistance Committee. The corporation set the rates of relief for Glasgow, and our demonstrations and deputations demanded more benefit for the children and wives and, sometimes, more for the men. The committee had administrative offices in the various districts, and we also held demonstrations at those.

As the crisis deepened throughout 1930 more and more of the unemployed rallied to our appeals for the rebuilding of the NUWM. In places like the Gorbals and Govan the possibility of getting jobs again was very remote for many of the unemployed. I can remember saying that there were large numbers who would never find work again. That was true right up to the second world war.

We were able to build up a dues-paying membership for the NUWM (the National Unemployed Workers' Movement). Everybody with a card paid a penny a week, and a proportion of that went to the National Administrative Council of the NUWM. We were very careful that only those with membership cards actually voted at our meetings, but our activities were never confined to our membership. We constantly organised mass activity in which most of the people demonstrating were not actual paying members.

I was a member of the Gorbals Unemployed Committee, and we held street meetings in Cleland Street. Every Wednesday we held a meeting at the labour exchange that dealt with the plight of the unemployed, the cause of the crisis, and the rates of benefit. At those meetings we also laid out our plans for future demonstrations. The committee itself met nearly every morning to deal with the next stage in the campaign and consider complaints from people who were not getting their benefits. We were at it morning, noon and night; we fought cases at the labour exchange for insured workers and at the public assistance committee for the others, as well as organising demonstrations and all our agitational work. In Glasgow the committee appointed people specially to concentrate on fighting cases while the rest of us concentrated on agitation.

The National Administrative Council of the NUWM decided national policy. People from various districts went to it as delegates: Len Yule was on it from Sheffield, I was on it from Scotland, etc. The national organiser was Wal Hannington, Sid Elias was the chairman, Emrys Llewellyn was national secretary and Maud Brown was women's organiser. Of course most of the NAC were members of the Communist Party, but also the party used certain people to report back to it. Sid Elias used to watch and report back every little thing we did, and later Pat Devine was put on the NAC by the party as well. Neither of them carried any weight on the committee, but they used to insist on following the party line.

In 1931 the party wanted us all to form 'charter committees'. The idea was of a workers' charter with a number of demands not only for the unemployed but also for the employed. There was a song 'Fight for the workers' charter' which went: '£3 a week and the seven-hour day'. Elias saw himself as the leader of the charter committees and used to sing this song and hope that the audience would join in - he was a badly disappointed man.

The party's intention was to use the unemployed as a spearhead into the trade unions. But, of course, in 1931 there was no response from the trade-union movement and the committees couldn't possibly take root. There was also a lot of resistance from the NUWM. Margaret McCarthy, who later became Mrs McKay MP, was sent over to the Gorbals Unemployed Committee to convince us that we were on the wrong track and should be building a charter committee in Gorbals. We were against it. We were against liquidating the NUWM into any sort of committee, and we were justified.

The 'social fascism' policy led to other activities for which we had no mass support. In 1931 we tried to resurrect the idea of the first of May being a workers' day of protest. Gallacher and I led a demonstration of several hundreds; but I doubt if there was an employed person among them, and we never did it again. Gallacher refers to this demonstration in his book *Revolt on the Clyde* and says it was in 1924; but I wasn't in Scotland in 1924, and it was 1931 that he and I took the demonstration to Glasgow Green.

In those years the attitude of the Communist Party was that they were the only revolutionaries and all others were bourgeois: which made it very difficult to participate in some campaigns. When the free speech fight started in Glasgow in June 1931, I had to drag them into it - but I was the only one who got involved and got arrested. It should have been an important fight for us, because with the build-up of agitation from 1931 the authorities began to impose restrictions on where we could speak. In order to hold meetings at Glasgow Green, Cathedral Square, Nelson's Monument and other places it was now necessary to obtain a permit from the police. The most important ban was on Nelson's Monument: that was where all the strike meetings, all the anti-war meetings, had been held before and during the war. The corporation were using the fact that a lot of quack doctors had sold patent medicines at Glasgow Green to ban *all* meetings there, and planned to open the old bandstand instead.

At the beginning it was Guy Aldred, the anarchist, and the Tramp Preachers who took up the fight on free speech. Aldred thought of himself as a modern Richard Carlile - he dressed like Carlile and had written a pamphlet on him. The Tramp Preachers were a group of Christian socialist ministers who lived together in a house in Greendyke Street. They were all English and were led by Tom Pickering, who had been involved in the unemployed struggle in Liverpool in the twenties. He carried a crucifix entwined with red ribbons and saw himself as a Christian revolutionary.

It was the Tramp Preachers who were first arrested for speaking on the Green in defiance of the ban in June 1931. I met them one day in George Square and they asked me why the Communist Party wasn't involved in the free speech fight. I promised them that I would speak on their platform and that I would get the CP involved, and I went straight to the party offices. I had a real row that day. Aitken Ferguson was there with a bunch of others; I told them we should get involved with the demonstrations. They weren't really listening, and finally I told them that I was going to take part and that they were a crowd of bloody office clerks! After that, they called a meeting and expressed strong disapproval of my attitude; and I expressed strong disapproval of their indifference. Finally they agreed to support the demonstrations, but only Aitken Ferguson ever spoke at a meeting besides me, so it was I who really got involved. I was the CP representative on the Free Speech Committee, and John McGovern and John Heenan were there from the ILP.

We kept breaking the ban on holding meetings and were repeatedly fined £3. All of us were pledged not to pay the fines but to go to prison; but Aldred persuaded the Free Speech Committee to take an appeal against the fines to the high court. I was against this because I was afraid that if the appeal was lost that would be the end of the fight for Aldred, and I was right. The fines were reduced from £3, the usual penalty for breaking a by-law, to ten shillings, and our fight was finished there and then.

One morning I went to court and received the reduced fine of ten shillings. As I left, I was grabbed by the police because of another ten-shilling fine that I hadn't paid. Down in the cells there were also three Tramp Preachers. I had seventeen shillings on me, and despite my protests the police took that and deducted the fine and kept me in overnight. Next day they told me they had the magistrates' permission for what they had done, and threw me out. McGovern raised the matter in the House of Commons, and for the night I spent in jail I received one shilling and fourpence from the police, in postage stamps! Finally it got to the stage where only McGovern's and my fines were outstanding, and somebody paid them. However, we did accomplish something by the fight; the corporation eventually agreed that a large area next to Nelson's Monument should be available for open-air meetings without a permit.

In 1931 the Labour Government finally split. Snowden, Ramsay MacDonald and J.H. Thomas were pressing for enormous cuts of 10 per cent in unemployment benefit, but the rest of the Labour Party and the trade unions wouldn't accept this solution to the crisis (although some of them were suggesting a five per cent cut!). It was then that MacDonald went over from the Labour Party and formed a coalition government, called a 'National Government', with the Tories and Liberals. Immediately everyone knew that teachers', police and civil servants' wages were to be cut along with unemployment benefit. The formation of the National Government led to intensified activity all over the country.

We held all-Glasgow demonstrations every second Thursday, when we marched to the city chambers in George Square and put our demand that a deputation of unemployed be heard by the councillors. On the other weeks we held local demonstrations. But one week, in September 1931, Baillie Fletcher said that our deputation should not be received because we were not 'citizens they could be proud of'. That statement caused a storm. It was printed in all the papers; we replied by calling a massive demonstration for the following Wednesday.

I expected the demonstration to be big, and it was decided to take the crowd from Glasgow Green through the town to the west end of the city - I found a suitable site in Anderston where a number of houses had been demolished. But because of Fletcher's statement, 20,000 turned up. Peter Kerrigan and I realised that we would never fit them in to the Anderston site. We kept to our route, but at Anderston we turned back and marched through the town again to St. Enoch Square, carrying an effigy of Baillie Fletcher at the front.

The St. Enoch subway for the Glasgow Underground stands in the middle of the square, and to get all the thousands of demonstrators in we wound the demonstration round and round the Underground building. The police were caught up among the demonstrators and couldn't move, and some of the demonstrators started nudging the police. Kerrigan and I walked up the wall overlooking the square and hung the effigy of Baillie Fletcher over the wall and burnt it. We spoke to the crowd and called a meeting for the next Thursday at George Square, from which we would send another deputation to the corporation.

On the Thursday, 1 October, our deputation was met by the corporation and we had also received an apology from Baillie Fletcher for his remarks. As well as having demonstrations during the day we also had evening ones, and we called one for that night. Bob McLellan and I were organising it, but when we got to Glasgow Green it was already pitch-dark and we couldn't see a thing. We found the police, though - hundreds of them, massing at Jail Square facing the high court. Bob and I went down the ranks warning the marchers not to break their fours and not to run; it is always embarrassing for the police to attack a regular well-organised demonstration.

That night we never even got marching. We hadn't got out of the

Green when the police attacked. While Bob and I were going down the ranks John McGovern came from nowhere and put himself at the head of the demonstration, and that decided the police to act. They arrested McGovern and waded into the crowd with batons. The whole crowd retreated and broke up, and when we got to the first passage away from the Square the police made a rush.

I stepped into the passage; Bob and the crowd and the police all went straight past me. That meant I was behind the police, but as I walked up I met a cordon of them coming back down the passage. I braced myself and went right through - they didn't recognise me. At the top of the passage I met another crowd who had come down the main road, and they wanted to go back and have a go at the police. I had to stop them - we would have been slaughtered. I got them back to the green, over the suspension bridge, and back into the Gorbals.

The police had attacked a crowd of nearly forty thousand. That Thursday, Friday and Saturday there were riots every night. Shops were looted and over fifty people were arrested. On the Thursday night I had an appointment with yet another Communist International Representative in Glasgow, in Springburn. When I got there, a phone call came with instructions that I was to go out and get arrested because John McGovern had been arrested! I was putting my shoes on again when the CI Representative stopped me: he had heard reports that two policemen had been thrown over the bridge into the Clyde and killed. I had also heard them, and we decided that it would be better to get me to Moscow! However, when the papers came out and there was no mention of this story I walked home to Gorbals.

Monday was the first day without looting and street clashes. Crowds had gathered at Glasgow Green during those few days, and on Sunday Guy Aldred and three ILP MPs called a meeting there to denounce us for organising the demonstration and to deplore the riots that followed. It was a dirty trick. They tried to keep me off the platform, but the crowd insisted that I be allowed up. I said: 'We have had the demonstration. A number of people have been arrested, a number of people are in hospital; the casualties are all on our side. We have got to organise for the next time and make sure that the casualties are on *their* side.' If ever I carried a crowd in my life, I carried it that day.

Then I called for the demonstration of the unemployed the following Thursday. The entire meeting supported the demonstration and the MPs were finished as far as they were concerned. That evening I spoke at Exchange Square, and a police van rushed the crowd. The next morning at three o'clock I was arrested.

We were allowed the evening papers in prison. That evening I read that the Communist Party, not the NUWM had been to the magistrates to ask permission for the demonstration on Thursday. That I would never do - and the free speech fight against the permit system was still going on despite the corporation's concession. The party had not only asked for permission, but they promised that the marchers wouldn't carry their walking-sticks! I couldn't do a thing about it.

On Wednesday, against all the usual police procedure, we were all taken to the sheriff court and bailed out. Apparently Gallacher had been in Fife, and he had come over to see the procurator fiscal and tell him that if I wasn't let out of jail to lead the demonstration there would be another riot. We all got out on bail. The police kept well clear of the demonstration, and although it was over fifty thousand it was a most orderly procession.

The charge against me and others was mobbing and rioting. It was a scandalous charge - any rioting came from the police. I think they had become desperate with the repeated demonstrations we had held, and also that they had been badly frightened by being trapped in St. Enoch Square. Sweeney, the superintendent in charge on 1 October, resigned not long afterwards. In truth, our demonstrators would have liked to get their revenge on the following Thursday, and I was very relieved when I got them to their destination!

I was acquitted of the charges against me because they couldn't prove that I had started to even provoke a riot. The same was true of McGovern, who was arrested before the baton-charge started. We both defended ourselves, and I think that helped our case. Others who were arrested on the same charge went to jail, as did the looters. Years later, in his book *Neither Fear Nor Favour*, John McGovern claimed that the Communist Party had set up the riot and then hadn't turned up; he said that George Middleton, Peter Kerrigan and I were not at the demonstration. That was a ridiculous accusation. Middleton and Kerrigan were not supposed to be there - but I was in the dock with McGovern!

The riots and the subsequent demonstration had a funny sequel. The national executive of the Communist Party wrote to the Scottish committee and told them they had made a mistake in ordering the marchers not to carry sticks. I was in the clear because I had been in prison when it happened; but because the Scottish committee persisted in opposing the national executive, Peter Kerrigan and the Communist International representative had to go to Moscow to have the mistake explained to them. Eventually it turned up in *Communist International*, a journal for analysis of the world situation, as the error made by the Communist Party in Scotland in disarming the workers!

That Communist International rep was the last I ever met in Glasgow, although I met others in London. One of the earliest that I met in Glasgow was George Borodin, who assisted the Chinese Communists in the 1920s. In Glasgow he was actually arrested and served six months' imprisonment under the name of Brown, and no one knew who he was! Eventually the *Morning Post* (the present-day *Daily Telegraph*) made the discovery that a Russian called Borodin was in Glasgow, but by that time he was on his way back to Russia. The only other two in Glasgow were the one in 1930 and the one who was recalled to Moscow (I hope he was all right).

Although I was in favour of the unemployed marching with walking-sticks, I was against some of the other romantic notions that were about. At one stage Charlie McDermott decided to organise a workers' defence corps and had teams of men drilling with hammers and sticks that had been sharpened to a point at the end. Willie Gallacher and I had to step in and stop it - it was just inviting the police to break up demonstrations. Communist Party members supported such activities because during the period of the 'social fascist' policy the party used evidence of warlike conduct and the riots to show Russia that they were leading the workers' struggles in Britain. Charlie McDermott had originally been a member of the Catholic Church, and after a period in the Communist Party he rejoined them.

At the end of 1931 there was a general election, called by the National Government which had taken over in August. Tories, Liberals and the Labour members all stood on the same platform of 'national unity'. The Labour Party and some Liberals opposed them, and the Communist Party also fielded candidates. I stood in the Gorbals against George Buchanan the ILP MP.

In the Gorbals campaign I was the only communist speaker. Willie Gallacher was standing in East Fife. The Communist Party had a lot of support there because CP members ran the United Mineworkers of Scotland, and Abe Moffat and the other miners' leaders did all they could to help Gallacher win the seat. But in 1931 the 'national unity' appeal was too strong, although Gallacher won in East Fife in 1935.

During the 1931 wave of nationalism associated with electing a National Government, Lord Beaverbrook of the *Daily Express* launched his own campaign and his own party for imperial free trade. When he came to speak in Glasgow the audience broke up the meeting, and the following morning it was said that this had happened 'by order of Mr McShane'. As it happened, I knew nothing about the incident, and I went to the *Daily Express* to protest. All the reporters rushed at me saying 'You broke up *our* meeting' - they always were a bunch of yes-men at the *Daily Express* office; and the next day John McGovern came out with a statement in favour of free speech!

Some time later I was asked to go to a house for a meeting. When I got there I found a secretary representing Beaverbrook, an engineering manager, a brewery owner and some others! They wanted me to give them an assurance that if Beaverbrook came to Glasgow again he would get a hearing!

The general election resulted in an overwhelming victory for the National Government. The Labour Party was reduced to only 52 MPs, and among them the ILP members were reduced to three - Maxton, Wallhead and McGovern. The government's enormous majority meant that 1932 was a year of the most massive attacks on public servants and on the unemployed. In that year we built the NUWM in every part of the country. But before that, I went to Russia.

15. Marching Against the Means Test

At the NUWM Conference of 1931 elections were held for a delegate to be sent to Russia. Sid Elias, the chairman, topped the poll and I came second. However, Elias went to Russia as a 'referent' from the British Communist Party (I still don't know what it means, but that is what he was sent as). I didn't actually want to leave Glasgow at that time, but the party called me down to London and more or less put me on the boat. In 1932 we sailed for Russia from Hays Wharf.

I was in charge of a British delegation of eight, but there were many others on the boat. There were two Irishwomen who said that they were special guests of the Russian trade unions, and they wouldn't have anything to do with me. One was Rosemary Jacobs, the daughter of the owner of Jacobs' biscuit factory in Dublin, and the other was a Mrs Connery. They took particular exception to the fact that I had described De Valera and the other Irish leaders as bourgeois.

The crew of the ship came to see me as leader of the delegation. They explained that the Baltic Sea was frozen and the boat would have to go to Riga; but if I went to see the captain he could arrange for the famous ice-breaker *Krassin* to clear our way to Leningrad. I put this proposal to our delegation, then saw the captain, and it worked. One old Russian refugee who had lived nearly all his life in London was furious. He ranted that I had altered the plans of the Soviet Union, and demanded a mass meeting of the passengers: we had the meeting, and all 40 passengers agreed with me! I felt very powerful, altering the Soviet Union's plans.

Two interpreters met us in Leningrad. I knew one of them; he was Joe Fineberg, who had been on the executive of the BSP. The other was Boris Reinstein, an American who had been a follower of Daniel De Leon. I had read an article of his describing a discussion with Lenin, in which Lenin said that De Leon must have been a genius. We were very fortunate in having Reinstein as our interpreter in

Moscow. He could take us round all the famous places of the Revolution and describe the scenes that took place.

Reinstein took us to the Smolny Institute and described the meetings that lasted all night during the Revolution, with comrades falling off their chairs to the floor - asleep. At one meeting, he told us, someone came in and told them of the fight at Peter and Paul Fortress; he had said that the Mensheviks (the social-democrats) were dying for their principles, and someone replied: 'By God, we'll need to go and see that.' He showed us the room that Lenin slept in during those days. We were also taken to the Winter Palace, and he described the dissolution of the Constituent Assembly at the point when the Soviets took full power in Russia.

Apart from the Nevsky Prospect and the bridge over the Neva I found Leningrad a very drab city. The Nevsky Prospect appealed to me with its attractive, heavy-looking buildings. I wandered round the side-streets by myself, and in one place I came across a driver beating his old horse very severely. The horse was pulling a concrete-mixer on metal wheels, and one of the wheels was flat and wouldn't turn. The people in the street went over and made very strong complaints to the driver; I liked that. In the same street was a long row of barrels going right down to the docks, and I wanted to find out what they were for. But when I asked one old woman all she would say was 'soldat, soldat' (gold, gold), pointing to the gold chain on my chest. I couldn't get anything else out of her at all.

Outside the hotel where we were staying the pavement was often crowded with Russians who came to speak to us. Among them were some young students who spoke English; they did the interpreting for the old-timers who had seen the Revolution, and we had some tremendous discussions. Some of them thought things weren't as good as they should be, others said that it had been better after the Revolution. There were complaints, there was support, there were arguments about Lenin and all kinds of things.

I was worried by some of what I saw in Leningrad. We went to St. Isaac's, a church which had been turned into an atheist museum. It was a very poor effort, so crude and stupid it wouldn't convince anybody; there were no arguments - it just sneered. There was an atheist class while we were there, with nine people attending. We also went to a factory in Leningrad where they introduced us to a man who had been compulsorily retired at 50. They said proudly that this man still wanted to work: I thought that he probably needed the money.

After several days in Leningrad we went to Moscow. There I met Albert Inkpin, previously the secretary of the BSP and then the Communist Party in Britain, who was now in charge of the 'Friends of the Soviet Union'. He wanted to know why we had left the two Irishwomen in Leningrad, and I had to explain that it was they who had parted from us. Apparently they had a terrible time and even had to pay their own hotel bill. They rejoined our delegation, and there was no peace after that - they found fault with everything.

In Moscow we were taken to a banquet at which Kalinin, the President of the Republic, spoke. In his speech he said that there were no labour camps in Russia: it was against the principles on which the Soviet Union had been built. Delegates from all over the world were present, and we were all delighted with this assurance. I replied as the leader of the British, Irish and American delegations and said how pleased we were to have this statement that labour camps didn't exist. I couldn't imagine that the man could be such a blatant liar as to give such an emphatic assurance to all of us if it wasn't true.

At the banquet I met Isabel Brown, a British Communist Party member who was a student in Moscow. She was acquainted with the old lady acting as caretaker of the Kremlin, who had previously been a Russian refugee in Newcastle. Although the old lady was now lame she insisted on showing us all over the Kremlin, through all the private rooms and the Tsarina's private chapel.

From Moscow we took a tour down to Kasherstroy. I had become the leader of the 'American delegation' because one young American journalist had joined us. He and I got on very well. He had lived in Russia for two years and was a very decent fellow, but he was very disillusioned. He confided things to me that I never told anybody. He told me that people kept disappearing - that one night he would go to a party, and the next night some of the people he had seen had disappeared. What was worse, nobody ever asked any questions about them. I had so much faith in the Soviet Union I was prepared to overlook a great deal, but the American started me wondering.

Once, when the train to Kasherstroy was held up, the American and I went off together to see a local church whose bells we had heard. The door had the biggest padlocks I have ever seen. An old, dishevelled priest finally showed us round. The walls were covered with pictures overlapping other pictures; they had been taken from a much bigger church which had been turned into a club, and the

Bolsheviks had built the smaller church in its place.

That was near Kasherstroy, and we went from there right down to the Crimea. Here I smelt discontent. The people lived in caravans in abject poverty. They used to beg cigarettes from us, saying *'They'* - the authorities - 'won't let us have any.' There seemed to be a shortage of food. An old lady with a basket walked into our hotel and wandered up and down complaining. The American interpreted what she was saying: 'The boat that was to bring us food was promised yesterday, was promised the day before, it is always tomorrow.' In Leningrad and Moscow we had seen no shortages, and at the banquet there was masses to eat and drink.

Conditions in the Crimea were bad even for us as guests. The Irishwomen complained endlessly; we went to get a cup of tea at one place and they found fault with everything. Then some of us went to the toilet. I have never seen anything like it - it was terrible, terrible: we just ran away. When I saw the two Irishwomen going there I knew that we were in for it. They came back, and Mrs Connery looked straight at me and said: 'That is where culture starts.'

On our trip we were not invited into people's homes. Only once did we go inside an ordinary home; it was tiny and very poor, with one bare light bulb. That was the house of the local pit manager, and he was very proud of it; obviously conditions for the ordinary workers were extremely bad. When we went down the pit I was shocked. It was in South Russia, by the Don-bas, and it was terrible. We had to jump out of the way of the coal waggons or we would have been killed. It resembled the nineteenth-century British pits; they even had women turning the waggons.

On the other hand, we went to a factory in Kiev and met some Jewish workers who showed us a paper in their own language. There were Jews in nearly all the weaving factories, and they seemed to be delighted with their paper. I brought some copies back for my Gorbals comrades; there was a traditional Jewish community in the Gorbals, and they tore the papers out of my hands.

At the end of our tour we went back to Moscow for the May Day celebrations. We watched the procession in front of the Kremlin wall where the ashes of the pioneers are kept, including those of Arthur MacManus of Britain. Lenin's Mausoleum is nearby, but we didn't see that until a day or two later. In front of us was a parade of thousands of young men and women - with rifles over their shoulders - and thousands of workers, all coming into Red Square cheering. I had never liked rifles, but I felt really marvellous looking at all these young people. I looked upon Russia as our country, the workers' country, and I was pleased to think that the Revolution had arms.

When our delegation was taken off for lunch we were taken past Lenin's Mausoleum and saw Molotov, Kalinin and Stalin saluting the procession. The young fellows in our party were all excited about seeing Stalin. I wasn't, and I was displeased at seeing Stalin's picture given equal prominence with Lenin's on the May Day parade. I had never seen that happen before.

Despite these worries, I was pleased with my trip to Russia. I had seen the Revolution. One of the beliefs that carried us through the thirties was the existence of the Revolution in Russia and our role in defending it. We were still thinking in terms of a world-wide revolution led by Russia, and we welcomed the Five Year Plans and any development that strengthened Russia.

I returned to Glasgow via Hull, and after my five weeks' absence plunged into unemployed activity. The National Government, as soon as it was elected, had brought in the household Means Test in order to cut the amount of benefit to the unemployed; and the Anomalies Act, which cut married women and part-time workers out of benefit altogether. Those and the 10 per cent cut in unemployment pay meant that the unemployed bore the brunt of the 1931 crisis.

The Means Test was specially feared and hated by every unemployed worker. The regulations insisted that *any* member of a household who was working was responsible for the household income - that is, he or she had to support the rest of the family. If any one in a house was working - including uncles, aunts, cousins and even lodgers sometimes - then unemployment benefit wasn't paid to the other people in that house.

It broke up families. Sons and daughters went to live away from home; fathers in work became bitter towards their children. Cases were reported in the newspapers where worry over the Means Test had actually led to suicide. It produced despair - and also the most massive demonstrations by the unemployed all over the country. These demonstrations brought attacks on the NUWM by the authorities: in 1932 four hundred of its members were imprisoned.

In Glasgow our activity intensified. More and more people came into the struggle through our street meetings and demonstrations, and we established premises in all parts of the city. Anderston, Govan, Partick, Maryhill, Bridgeton, Springburn, Gorbals, all had their own branches of the NUWM. Each branch had two hundred members or more. They built their own flute bands - we had eight of them in Glasgow. There was one Glasgow man, John Scott, who spent all his time teaching people to play the flute.

Every branch had its own committee to distribute duties among its members. People were appointed to specific tasks, including fighting cases at the labour exchange and the public assistance committee. Some NUWM members became very well acquainted with the unemployment insurance regulations and the public assistance rules. They collected all the literature on the regulations, and every case they fought provided more experience. Other districts organised themselves differently. In Edinburgh, for example, the whole committee did casework; when I went to see them I would find the entire committee working all night on the cases they were to fight the following day!

The main work of the branches in Glasgow was agitation. In those days people signed on at the labour exchange five days a week, and we held meetings in the forenoon or afternoon. Tremendous crowds would gather as we spoke about government policy, the new regulations being imposed, rents, and recent evictions.

We developed teams of new speakers at the labour exchange meetings. New members would begin by taking the chair at a meeting, then gradually make speeches themselves. Some speakers were able to explain the causes of the crisis and unemployment in simple theoretical terms. Many became very well-informed about politics, and many joined the Communist Party. We were the chief source of recruitment, in fact: in the early thirties the unemployed movement rebuilt the Communist Party.

Each branch of the NUWM in Glasgow also elected members to a small district committee, which organised all the Central Glasgow activity and led the branches. As well as demonstrations at the local labour exchanges and public assistance committees we organised all-Glasgow demonstrations. I was the Glasgow organiser for the NUWM, and therefore largely responsible for organising these large demonstrations. There was also a Scottish district committee which I was on; it staged all-Scotland demonstrations which went to Edinburgh, where deputations presented our demands to the Scottish government offices.

The introduction of the Means Test in 1932 caused our influence among the unemployed to soar, and this led the TUC to attempt its own unemployed organisation in competition with us. But it was to be based on local committees run by the trades councils and not by the unemployed themselves; and it could obviously do very little because of the restrictions placed upon it by the TUC.

In May 1932 The National Administrative Council of the NUWM decided to organise a nation-wide protest against the cuts and the Means Test: a national Hunger March to London, backed up by a petition.

I had missed the 1922 and 1930 marches to London from Glasgow, but by 1932 I had organised marches to Edinburgh, and I was in charge of the Scottish contingent on the way to London. The organisation of the Scottish marchers was always most important for the success of the whole march. We moved off first, and once we were on the road it was the signal for every other district to organise its contingent. The size of our contingent and our send-off from Glasgow encouraged all the rest: they knew that the march had really begun.

We recruited men from May 1932, when the decision was taken, right up to the start of the march in September. At all our meetings at labour exchanges and street corners we explained the aims of the Hunger March. From all the recruits, we had to select the marchers and get them properly kitted-out. Every man who came on the march had a kitbag with his own plate, cup, knife and fork, and proper boots and a cape.

We raised the money for kit from collections at labour exchange and street meetings, from indoor meetings, and from people who weren't in the NUWM but were sympathetic to our aims. We raised enough to get us on the road, including money for our food, and we collected money all the way on the march: in every town we went through we held at least one meeting and took a collection. For accommodation we relied on the local authorities and we always insisted that they provide a certain amount of food in the workhouse - usually the breakfast before we set out.

We departed on 26 September from George Square, Glasgow, and thousands turned out to see us off. Many of them marched with us to the city outskirts along the Kilmarnock Road. Our first step out of

Glasgow was Kilmarnock, where we slept in the town hall, but after that our route lay among small towns and villages until we got to Carlisle. George Middleton was in charge of arranging accommodation, and he went ahead of the march to find places that could take all three hundred of us.

At Auchinlech, the stop after Kilmarnock, the authorities refused the town hall or any other accommodation. When we approached the town, a number of women came out to warn us not to enter because police had been drafted in from other areas and were lined up along the main street. Despite their fears for us we marched straight into the town and along the main street, and turned round and came back again! That was our practice - if we were banned from marching along a street we always went up and down it twice.

The police were angry, but there were more of us than of them and they could see we were determined; they left us alone. In the street we held a meeting to which everybody came, and we explained the situation. We told them that we needed a place to sleep the night, that the local committee were refusing us the town hall, that there wouldn't be any trouble in the village, and that we were fighting for all the Scottish unemployed. When we had finished, a deputation of the local women went and pulled that committee apart: we got the town hall.

The episode at Auchinlech set the tone for the whole march. We had called a meeting of the marchers, told them what was in front of us, and got their understanding and agreement that we would carry on no matter what the cost. Many times on the march we expected to be batoned or arrested, but everyone was prepared. This was one of the great feelings of the march that I still recall - you knew that you were one of them, and that they were going to go with you through everything.

Our hardest times were in Scotland itself. Conditions became much easier once we had crossed the border and the boards of guardians began to provide the things we demanded. It was important for us to establish a routine for the men and keep to it. Every day we tried to get on the road half-past nine, which meant that we rose at half-past eight. When - as in Scotland - we didn't get breakfast from the workhouse, our cooks had to rise before that and prepare the food. For breakfast we dished out porridge followed by bacon, egg or fish, and then the cooks' lorry would go ahead to the next stop. They were responsible for getting the food ready for the rest of the day.

G

We stopped every hour for a ten-minute rest, and eight miles out the cooks would hand out tea. Then they went ahead again to the next stop and dished out a good big lunch, usually a stew. The hot food kept out the rain and the cold - often the marchers were better fed by us than they would be at home. Our only vehicle on the march was the cooks' lorry, although we did have an ambulance man for first aid and a boot repairer.

The average day's march was twenty-two miles, and each day had to be planned in advance. I doubt if we covered more than three miles an hour, and the stopping places for meals all had to be worked out. The planning was done by a march council which included myself and Bob McLellan as organiser and assistant organiser of the Scottish contingent, and the leaders of the local contingents. On the march each area had its own leader: the twenty men from Fife were a contingent in their own right alongside Dundee, Aberdeen and so on. The leaders were chosen in each locality before the start of the march. They were often the local NUWM officials. Many, but not all, were Communist Party members.

The march council slept together, separate from the marchers. We had to meet at night-times to count the money and take the decisions for the following day. Sometimes we had to have a man up before us for some misdemeanour; but only eight men were sent home, and there was a meeting of all the marchers to decide. But we had no serious trouble with anyone on the march. The way a body of three hundred men could march nearly five hundred miles under such bad conditions, and remain so cheerful, was amazing.

We had rules - against drunkenness and so on, against any marcher collecting money for himself. No one brought any money with him on the march, but on Fridays each marcher was given half-a-crown and they spent it on cigarettes or in the pub. The drunkenness rule was simply to safeguard against any trouble; we knew that the marchers took a drink and so, secretly, did we. The discipline of the march was self-discipline, imposed by the men themselves in everybody's interests. The results were exceptionally good: all enjoyed themselves when they could but no one was allowed to step out of line. It was the aspect of the march that I liked best.

It was very important that nobody was seen to get better treatment than anybody else. Although the march council slept separately, we slept in no better place than the others. The same applied to eating. The contingent that fed first at one meal fed last at the next, and all the contingents moved up a place each time. The leaders were the last men in their sections to be fed - and the last of all were the organisers of the march. One night, by the time Bob McLellan and I got to the cooks all the food had gone and we had to go and knock up the local fish-and-chip shop.

The Scottish contingent had a flute band. Some of the men could already play and others learnt on the road; some of them became so enthusiastic that they wanted to play their damn flutes in the middle of the night! We had a drum, too - there have always been plenty of drums in Glasgow - and the flutes and drums played all the time. It helped the march a lot. The tunes they played became a part of you. The flute band led the Scottish contingent into Hyde Park, and one London police sergeant told me afterwards that he had heard flutes playing all night through his sleep!

The marchers didn't sing very much, but when we crossed the border from Scotland to England we all sang the Internationale. We were entering another country and declaring our solidarity with the English marchers we knew we were going to meet later on. Crossing the border was also a relief to the Scottish marchers because once we were in England we could get support from the English boards of guardians, and the English workhouses began to supply our demands. At Carlisle the chief constable came out to meet us and tell us about the arrangements at the workhouse, which were very good, and the free baths and other facilities that had been laid on. I was surprised at him doing this; he told me that on the first Hunger March when he was stationed in Dumfries there had been some trouble and he had arrested six marchers, and his mother had given him hell for it!

From Carlisle we marched to Penrith, and then we had the longest day's march in the entire road: over the Shap Fell to Kendal. It was 26½ miles, and it was a hell of a march. The night before we left Penrith, at a meeting of all the marchers, we had a marvellous debate. Charlie McDermott argued against the men having to march over the Shap, and I argued for it. I put the motion and he put the amendment, and I carried it with only 30 votes against. After arranging that everyone should march over, it was agreed that the cooks' lorry would come back from the lunch stop and pick up all the kitbags. Eight men refused to part with their bags and marched with them all the way.

From Kendal we marched to Lancaster, and there we took our

day's rest. Then at Preston Wal Hannington came to join us. Each contingent of the National Hunger March was taking a different route to London so that all the major towns would be covered. Hannington was the national organiser, but he had left London to come and be with us. He and I had great times together. He was a most honest, decent man and a tireless organiser. I shall always remember our meeting at Preston. Tom Pickering the tramp preacher was marching with us, and he said that when he got to heaven he hoped he would find its front benches occupied by members of the Third International!

Wal loved being among the Scottish marchers or the Welsh ones, and to lead a big body of men singing. He used to march at the head of the Scots singing 'McGregor's Gathering' and get them all waving their caps on top of their sticks - with the Welsh it was 'Land of my Fathers'.

Unfortunately he could only stay with us for a short time. Already unemployed men had been dragged out of their beds and beaten up in Birkenhead. The day after he joined us, unemployed demonstrators were shot down in Belfast. Then, a week after we left Preston, we learned that the Lancashire contingent of the Hunger March had been attacked at Stratford-on-Avon by police specially drafted in from Birmingham. The authorities were trying to repress all activity of the unemployed. Wal took some of our contingent to meet the Lancashire marchers, including Bob McLellan who then reported back to us.

Though it was a long, hard march for us, the Scottish contingent had no difficulty after Auchinlech. I shall always remember one time that we stopped for a ten minute rest in a quiet little place. We were by a bridge, and as the water flowed the men stood against a wall under the sun and sang 'The Wells o' Werie' over and over again. It was a tremendous experience to be among a body of men singing with such feeling in such a quiet place.

On the way down to London, at Stoke, I suddenly found a girl in the ranks. One of the marchers had met her and brought her back with him. We all decided that he had to leave the march: he left it and married her! But leaving the march was very rare, and what the marchers did at night was usually their own affair. It wasn't incidents like that which caused trouble; on the contrary, the most difficulty I had was with a Communist Party member, Norman Kennedy. Kennedy was the leader of the Dundee contingent, a regular parade-ground lad. He was a joiner, and later became a right-wing trade union official. I was always suspicious of him. It has since been discovered that there was a government agent in the Scottish contingent. Was it Norman Kennedy? He kept the Dundee contingent separate from the rest of the march, and every morning he got them all together and read the newspaper to them and commented on the political situation. He came to me and said that he wanted the march to get out on the road at *exactly* half-past nine. But the next day, after we had agreed to this, it was the Dundee lads who were still sleeping. Naturally I had some strong words to say. All the way, after that, their leader grumbled about me having a bias against the Dundee marchers; and in Buckingham I managed to upset them all.

In the towns where we stopped there was usually accommodation big enough for all the Scottish marchers, but in Buckingham I had to break them into several smaller groups. Usually the best place to stay was the workhouse, so I sent the Dundee contingent there to prove that I hadn't a down on them. The next morning they turned up late for breakfast and said I had served them another dirty trick: there were lice in the workhouse.

I nearly took a fit. We had to march seventeen miles that day in pouring rain and were all soaked to the skin, but what was on my mind was the fifty lousy marchers at the back of me. If I didn't do something quickly, the lice would spread through the whole Scottish contingent. At the next stop, Aylesbury, I went and saw the workhouse master and asked him for spare clothes. He didn't have any clothes, but he said he had the best fumigating apparatus in the country. I had to go back to the Dundee crowd, who were running about naked on the stone floors, get them to put their clothes on and take them to be fumigated. They came back to the march de-loused and completely dried out. It was the first time I had seen them smile; the rest of us were still soaked.

After several smaller stops, we marched into Hyde Park Corner on Thursday 27 October. We saw the Lancashire marchers for the first time and were shocked by the state they were in; all their hands were bandaged. At Hyde Park they and the Yorkshire contingent had a tremendous battle with the police, along with part of the enormous crowd that had come to meet us. The crowd was anything from a hundred thousand to twice that number. The Scottish contingent had to form a barrier round the NUWM meeting to prevent it being broken up by the police, and when the march left Hyde Park Wal Hannington and I got at the front of it. Police on foot and horseback were all round us, and we saw a bottle come flying through the air and hit one of the mounted police on the back of his head. I said to Hannington: 'Wally, we're for it!' But the police didn't charge, and we managed to get the march out of the park.

I marched nine hundred of them - the Scottish, the Welsh and some others - to Fulham workhouse. In the papers next morning there were attacks on Hannington and me, and demands that we be arrested. We had arranged a huge demonstration on the Sunday in Trafalgar Square, and on Sunday I marched my contingent of nine hundred there from Fulham. At the Square Hannington made a speech in which he referred to the National Government's cuts of 1931; he mentioned the cut in police pay, and called upon the police to support us. He was later arrested for this appeal.

On Monday Wal, Sid Elias and I met John McGovern MP at the Fulham workhouse. McGovern had asked to meet us, and Wal had phoned me there to arrange it. My address in London on a Hunger March was whichever workhouse I was staying in. I always put myself at the far end, so that any communication for me had to go through all the other marchers.

McGovern wanted to see us to discuss the presentation of the NUWM petition against the Means Test and the cuts. By the end of the Hunger March it had over a million signatures. We had used it to organise the march and we collected signatures as we came: it was bigger than the Chartists' petition. McGovern wanted to present it in the House of Commons for us. Hannington and Elias didn't know McGovern but I did, and I didn't trust him. He went away without the petition and very angry. That night he denounced us in the House of Commons, and the next morning Hannington was arrested.

We were to assemble on Tuesday night at Trafalgar Square and march down Whitehall to deliver the petition. Obviously there would be trouble because processions are illegal within a mile of the House of Commons. But unknown to us Emrys Llewellyn, the secretary of the NUWM, had left the petition in the left luggage department at Charing Cross Station. It was in bundles done up in satchels: we had to collect it from the station and then walk to

Trafalgar Square. We got the petition out - but as we were leaving the station the police recognised us and locked the big gates that were there then.

No one could get in, and we couldn't get out; the police stayed inside with us to make sure of that. We could see thousands and thousands of workers going down the Strand to the demonstration. We couldn't contact them, and of course they didn't know where we were. It was chaos, and there was a terrible riot in Trafalgar Square - the third in six days since we arrived. The petition was never presented, and we put it back in the left luggage office.

On Thursday I went to the NUWM office for the first time since my arrival in London. Everyone was expecting me to be arrested next, and someone noticed that the police were surrounding the building. When I went into the back room to finish my business, two plain-clothes men came in; but it was Sid Elias they took. They searched the office and found a letter he had written while he was in Moscow. It was the only piece of incriminating material in the office, because Wal Hannington had ordered everything to be cleared before he left to join us at Preston, but the police knew exactly where to look for it.

Strangely enough, the letter from Moscow had actually never reached anyone except Elias who wrote it! When the National Administrative Council of the NUWM decided on the 1932 march, it hadn't consulted the Communist Party first. Therefore, the Communist Party hadn't consulted Moscow about it; and in turn couldn't report to Moscow that they had instructed the NUWM in its course of action. To make up for this, Elias wrote telling us how to conduct the march, and in the letter he referred to the riots in 1931 and said that spirit should be on the 1932 Hunger March.

He sent the letter via young Oliver Bell, who had been in Moscow; but by the time he got to London Hannington had already left. Bell kept the letter and handed it back to Elias when he arrived from Russia. For that letter, Elias was sent down for two years on a charge of inciting Wal Hannington and Emrys Llewellyn to sedition. Hannington himself was given three months for his speech to the police. Llewellyn, Tom Mann and the other national officials of the NUWM were also arrested but let off.

I wasn't arrested, and I had the problem of getting my nine hundred marchers home. All the Aylesbury lice had come to life again in the Fulham workhouse, and the marchers were lousy.

Everybody was ready to go home. I had a number of the Welshmen come to me and say they had to go because their wives were going to have babies. I pointed out that they must have known this before they came, and I didn't let anybody away before Saturday when everybody left. Llewellyn and I negotiated with the railways to take all the marchers at reduced fares, and we got the Glasgow marchers back at £1 a head instead of the normal fare of four or five pounds.

When the march was all over, we were denounced from another quarter. Willie Gallacher came to a meeting of the NAC of the NUWM and demanded a vote of censure on Hannington, Elias and me for having met John McGovern and shaken hands with him. They were all prepared to let the vote go through - no one wanted to quarrel with Gallacher; but I wouldn't have it. I said it couldn't be Wal's or Elias's fault because they didn't know the man, and that I didn't have anything to do with his proposals and didn't shake hands with him. I had quarrelled with McGovern, and Gallacher knew it. The row went on, and finally Gallacher was defeated: an unheard-of thing.

After the 1932 Hunger March and the riots in London the authorities began to move even more strongly against the NUWM. All over the country, branches were having to fight local police bans on demonstrations. In Glasgow at the end of December the chief constable, Captain Sillitoe, wrote to me saying that demonstrations in George Square were causing great inconvenience to traffic. He informed me that the NUWM demonstration would only be permitted to march through George Square, not round and round it as we had done previously.

I wrote back to him saying that the inconvenience he spoke of was negligible compared to the inconvenience of poverty for thousands of unemployed, and that we should be marching round George Square that Thursday. I handed copies of both letters to the newspapers; all three Glasgow evening papers splashed it on the front page with statements such as 'Unemployed Fight Chief Constable'! That made our demonstration.

On the Thursday Peter Kerrigan and I marched the demonstrators round George Square four times while we waited to hear if the corporation would receive our deputation on increases in winter relief. When we learned that it had been turned down I went to the post office and sent a telegram to Pat Dollan, the leader of the Labour group, asking him to raise the question again. Then Kerrigan took the marchers to Glasgow Green while I went across to the city chambers. Captain Sillitoe came out and said 'It went very well, Mr McShane' - I agreed that *I* thought it had gone very well. He offered to take me through the chambers and went upstairs to find out the result of my telegram. On his return he said he was sorry that our deputation had been turned down; he and I agreed that I would lead the several hundred men who were waiting back to Glasgow Green to join up with Kerrigan and the rest of the demonstration.

When we arrived at the Green we saw men running everywhere. The demonstrators had spotted two plain-clothes men in the crowd and were chasing them right along the Clyde. I kept our ranks together and marched into the Green: the meeting was in a shambles. It was obvious that hundreds of policemen would be arriving in a few minutes and that I had to get all the men together. I lined them all up with Kerrigan and myself at the front, and in front of us I put the flute band. I told the band to keep playing no matter what happened. As the police arrived, they found an orderly procession marching out of Glasgow Green, and they could do nothing.

Fourteen policemen were injured that day, and on the demonstration the following Thursday I said that we had won by fourteen to nothing. But though there were no casualties on our side, five men who ran out of the Green after policemen were arrested and got three months.

Captain Sillitoe was probably the most diplomatic of all the chief constables we had, but he had a rough passage from time to time from the unemployed. In 1933 the authorities started organising clubs and meetings for the unemployed. One of the organisations involved was the Glasgow Council of Social Service. They held talks to the unemployed, and Captain Sillitoe offered to speak.

He had spent some years in Africa, was very proud of his experiences there, and had chosen to speak on 'big game hunting'. The meeting was in Partick Picture-House. We heard about it the day before, and managed to get word to the NUWM members. To Captain Sillitoe's - and the organisers' - surprise, the audience was not receptive. When he held up his rifle to show how he shot a tiger coming from a tree, men got up all over the hall shouting 'bang!' In the middle of the uproar someone shouted 'Tell us the one about the three bears!' and there was pandemonium. Sillitoe demanded that the lights go up and said he would find the men who had caused the interuptions. But the meeting couldn't continue, and finally he promised to come back and speak another day. He never did.

16. The Edinburgh Hunger March

Though my main work for the Communist Party was in the NUWM, I kept up the propaganda meetings in the Gorbals and stood in municipal elections. At the end of 1932 I got a good vote and then had to run again in March 1933. The Gorbals Labour Councillor, James Strain, was caught soliciting a bribe from a woman over a stall in the market-place, and his conviction led to a by-election.

There were an ILP candidate, a socialist (labour) and co-operative candidate, an independent names James McLaughlin, and myself. The catholics were all directed to vote for McLaughlin. Polling day coincided with a holy day of obligation, and they pulled out all the voters; cars were run from the three Gorbals chapels. As there was no Tory candidate, all the Conservatives voted for McLaughlin as well, thinking he must be their man. The result was that he won with three and a half thousand votes. But I came second with two thousand, more than the ILP and Socialist candidates put together, and it was the nearest the Communist Party came to winning a municipal seat in Glasgow. McLaughlin admitted that without the catholic vote he wouldn't have won - I was quite relieved that he had ! - and then gave them all a surprise when he went to the town council by aligning himself with Labour.

The reason why there were two socialist candidates was that in 1932 the ILP and the Labour Party had finally split, after two years of disputes. From 1918, with the introduction of individual membership, the Labour Party had gained ground from the ILP. During the 1929-31 Labour Government major arguments about policy and party discipline had developed between them. The ILP MPs were incensed by the attitude of MacDonald's cabinet in the capitalist crisis and fought for a completely different policy. The split came after the formation of the National Government; and I thought that one of the chief causes was John McGovern's being the ILP MP for Shettleston.

Many right-wing Labour Party members had wanted the

Shettleston seat, and immediately McGovern was elected stories about him were circulated. It was said that he had used trade-union delegates with forged credentials to vote him in at the selection meeting. The Labour Party started an investigation of the entire selection procedure, and repeated other stories that had circulated about McGovern - that he had worked during the General Strike (he was self-employed) and that he had gone back into the Catholic Church at a very convenient time for gathering the catholic vote in Wheatley's constituency.

Finally, despite appeals by Davie Kirkwood and James Maxton, John McGovern was expelled from the Labour Party. Willie Shaw of Glasgow Trades and Labour Council just wouldn't give up on it. From then on, McGovern was instrumental in seeking the disaffiliation of the ILP from the Labour Party. A year after his expulsion it took place.

The ILP was split internally by the disaffiliation. Some, especially the town councillors, wanted to stay with the Labour Party and did. Pat Dollan became the leader of this section; he formed the Scottish Socialist Party and ultimately led the first Labour-controlled town council in 1933. Davie Kirkwood also remained with the Labour Party. McGovern became dominant in the ILP in Glasgow, although James Maxton continued to be the figurehead.

Maxton was an orator and nothing more; it was Wheatley who had actually built the ILP in Glasgow. Maxton modelled himself on Victor Grayson, and his speeches were full of pathos and wee jokes. But, unlike the early Grayson, there was no real political content - nothing he ever said or wrote will live. While Maxton remained the Chairman of the ILP, it was McGovern who started appearing on all our demonstrations as soon as he was elected. McGovern had no conscience - he was utterly unscrupulous.

Kirkwood was elected to parliament in 1922 for Dumbarton Burghs (Dumbarton and Clydebank). When the ILP split from the Labour Party he remained with Labour, even though he had defended John McGovern of the ILP who had caused the split. He never really did anything as an MP. His only claim to fame was that as the MP for Clydebank he had got the *Queen Mary* built there; he took all the credit for it, and it was very important for Clydebank where the only two places for jobs were Singer's and John Brown's the shipyard. Men were queuing up at six o'clock in the morning to try and get jobs on the liner. Kirkwood was great friends with the general manager of John Brown's, and they even looked alike - it was very funny to see them together.

In 1951 he was actually made Baron Kirkwood and went to the House of Lords. It was then that the Scottish movement began to get the size of the man: anything like that was taboo in Scotland. We used to say his title stood for 'barren of brains'. He began to talk a lot of cheap moral nonsense, and in one speech actually said that the backbone of the Scottish workers was their love of simple porridge. After that he was known all over as 'porridge Davie'. He would shout about his Scottishism with a broad accent.

The break with the Labour Party had left the ILP in a very difficult position. It had been formed to get Labour represented in parliament and had always worked in the Labour Party: the split took away its foundations. The members were torn in all directions. In Scotland McGovern came on NUWM marches, but in England the ILP couldn't be seen to be identified with the Communist Party. They had to find an existence as a separate party. They even formed their own unemployed organisation, which had a few branches in England but got nowhere in Scotland.

The more right-wing members finished with the ILP, and the rump moved to the left. They made revolutionary statements, and even applied to the Communist International for affiliation. This change led the Communist Party to make approaches to the ILP. However, the CP was largely interested in joint activity against the Labour Party, and our approaches were anything but tactful. I remember, at one joint meeting, Gallacher turning to an ILP woman and saying: 'Lady, it is easy to see that you are not a socialist.'

In April 1933 John McGovern and I were arrested together. The authorities had been interfering with all kinds of demonstrations and meetings; the police had actually stopped George Buchanan, the ILP MP, from speaking at Queen's Park Gates, which was a traditional meeting-place. We arranged to hold a meeting there the following week. I had been on a deputation to the Scottish TUC at Ayr that day, and I arrived a little late to find that John Heenan, the ex-councillor and ILP chairman, had already started. As soon as I appeared the police superintendent asked 'Are you in this?' I nodded, and he turned to his policeman and said: 'Pull that bugger down and let this one up.'

When I got up they arrested me for causing a crowd to assemble and causing obstruction - later I was charged with breach of the peace. McGovern had been speaking at Richmond Park Gate; he came over, bringing his crowd, when he heard of our arrests and he too was arrested. We were all held at Queens Park police station. The police station is part of the building in which the cases are tried before a lay magistrate. The police superintendent acted as the prosecutor and we objected to this because of his influence on the magistrate. We demanded that our case be heard at the Central police court where a layman was prosecutor and the trial was heard by a stipendiary magistrate. This enabled me to bring the superintendent into court as a witness. He stood in the witness-box with all his buttons on, and made a terrible mess of his evidence; he even admitted that the crowd had assembled before I arrived, and the magistrate asked him why he hadn't arrested Heenan, the chairman. Then we brought in Isabel Coleman as a witness. She was a schoolteacher, very respectable-looking in her fur coat. She was asked if she found any obstruction at Queens Park Gate, and she said she could hardly get into the Park for the obstruction caused by the police and this big superintendent! It was a complete farce, and McGovern and I got off.

McGovern was quite deeply involved with the NUWM for a while. With the ILP no longer inside the Labour Party, its MPs and councillors had to work hard to establish themselves as popular figures. Several other members came into our activities, and some later joined the Communist Party. McGovern did no organising for the NUWM - he never entered the NUWM premises the whole time we were associated - and couldn't resist making attacks on the Communist Party. Nevertheless he worked with us. His chief contribution was to make public speeches on unemployment, and he came on the 1933 Scottish NUWM march to Edinburgh.

We held Hunger Marches to Edinburgh quite regularly, to back up our deputations to the Scottish Secretary of State, but this was the most lively one. We left Glasgow on 10 June. On previous marches we had gone through Airdrie and Coatbridge, but this time we took a new route along the Kilsyth Road. Thousands of people turned out to see us. We had a flute band leading the march, and one woman came out of her house with a big drum and started to ban it in time with the band. We spent one night on the road and arrived in Edinburgh on the Saturday.

By the time we arrived the Glasgow contingent had been joined by more marchers from Lanarkshire, Renfrewshire, Dunbartonshire and Fife. There were a thousand in all; when the police tried to stop us marching down Princes Street I pointed out that they would have the thousand men on the pavements instead of in the road - they immediately eased up. We marched up to the Mound in Princes Street and were met by a big gathering of the Edinburgh NUWM. We sent our deputation to meet the officials of the Department of Health, the Ministry of Labour and the Education Committee, all of which had their offices in St. Andrew's House.

The deputation protested chiefly against the Means Test and the Anomalies Act; we demanded public works to create jobs for the unemployed, and at the Education Committee we argued for free boots and books for all children in school. (On this occasion, as on every other Edinburgh march, we were helped by old Mr Marwick, the minister. He always supported our negotiations with the government departments and the town council.) As well as seeing the officials of those three departments, I demanded that the Secretary of State for Scotland, Sir Godfrey Collins, should meet us. I said we would stay in Edinburgh until he agreed to do so, although the police wanted us to return home the following day, Sunday.

Because we had arrived late in Edinburgh, the three of us on the deputation had to rush off and leave the marchers at Waverley Market. I had left Peter Creggan in charge; however, the deputation took longer than I anticipated and when I returned I found Alec Moffat addressing the marchers. He wasn't speaking about the weaknesses of the leaders of the march, asking why we weren't there and where we were. I was furious, and he and I had a terrible row in front of the marchers.

That Saturday evening I received a mysterious instruction from Aitken Ferguson, who was on the march as well as McGovern and Heenan, to go to a house in Leith. When I got there I found three men in their pyjamas eating sandwiches and drinking tea: Gallacher, Kerrigan and Max Goldberg. I had no idea they were in Edinburgh, and to my surprise they told me they were the 'alternative leadership' in case I got arrested. Before I went back to the march they gave me instructions which weren't anything I didn't know already. I thought it was utterly absurd, and doubted very much if the marchers would accept their 'alternative leadership'.

When we arrived in Edinburgh we had been put up in the Waverley

Market. On the Sunday however, the authorities refused us accommodation of any kind and expected us to go home. We refused to go home and repeated our demand to see Sir Godfrey Collins. We took the marchers to Leith and had our tea there. On our return back up Leith Walk instead of marching to the Police Station to protest at their refusal to help get accommodation, I turned along Princes Street.

We marched to the Mound and that section which lies directly underneath the Castle, and there I made all the marchers sit on the edge of the pavement all the way along. The police came up and told me that we couldn't sit there. I told this to the marchers, and said that since *sitting* was forbidden the best thing for us to do was to get out our blankets and *lie* down. That is what we did. Hundreds of policemen arrived, but they just stood all night on one side of the road while we slept on the other. It was a lovely June night.

Late at night a lot of the marchers appeared to be missing; I was worried and got up and went looking for them. I found them at a nearby tea-van. A lot of prostitutes hung round that area, and these women had taken pity on the marchers and were buying them cups of tea! Next morning, in Princes Street, we set up the big boilers that we always carried, and fed the marchers. The police were obviously worried over what we were going to do next.

On Monday morning I met with Gallacher and Kerrigan in Woolworth's cafe at the end of Princes Street. I had refused to go down to Leith again, so they had come up to tell me what I should do next. Their idea was that as we had made our protest against the Secretary of State for Scotland the marchers should now go home, and that we should pay their fares. I refused to arrange this; I proposed to ask the authorities to pay the fares home.

The Rev. Marwick and Captain Jack White both went to the town council to negotiate over the fares. We got nowhere. Then the Public Assistance Committee said that they would pay the fares of the marchers if I agreed that they would never come to Edinburgh again. I refused, and told them that we had only £30 left; that would just feed the marchers for that night, and then the marchers would be the PAC's responsibility. We were offered halls in Edinburgh for the night, and I accepted.

The next day John McGovern and I went to see the town clerk. We were unsuccessful, and we left in a real temper. As we strode off we suddenly heard running footsteps behind us. It was the chief constable. He said: 'For God's sake don't do anything drastic.' He guaranteed the marchers' fares home, without any conditions, and told us to spend our money on food. Actually we already had our food stashed away in shops all over the city, and we fed the marchers before they went home on buses and trains paid for by Edinburgh Corporation. We made £100 surplus on that march.

I arrived back in Glasgow on Wednesday in time to attend a meeting of the working bureau of the Scottish Communist Party. Instead of proposing my expulsion for not bringing the marchers home as instructed, I was congratulated on the victory that we had won in Edinburgh!

As well as being the Glasgow District Secretary of the NUWM I was the Scottish organiser. We had branches all over Scotland, particularly in towns like Aberdeen, Dundee and Edinburgh, and in the strong mining districts of Ayrshire, Fife and Lanarkshire. It was the Scottish conferences, at which they were all represented, that put forward the demands we took to the government departments in Edinburgh.

At the Scottish conferences we also discussed problems the NUWM branches were having. For example, Edinburgh did their casework better than anyone else but it was all they did, and as Scottish organiser it was my job to go through and encourage them to hold meetings and demonstrations. In Dundee, demonstrations were banned and I was sent there with definite instructions to break the ban but not to get arrested! I spent a week in Dundee and spoke at the labour exchanges, outside factories, in Albert Square and in City Square. On the Friday night we organised a meeting which was intended to break the ban. We started it at Hilltown, which is on a slope facing a very narrow street. I told the crowd that if I called a demonstration I should be arrested, therefore I was only telling them that the venue of the meeting was changed to Westport.

To get to Westport the crowd had to go down the small narrow street opposite, and they had to line up in fours as they went. But as they got to wider streets they remained in fours and marched all the way to Westport. I spoke there, and as soon as I stepped off the platform the police came at me from all sides. Someone pulled me out of the crowd backwards while Kelly, the chairman, got in the way of the police and told them I had gone. The following morning when I went to the railway station I saw two plain-clothes policemen there. I stood and watched them. The train arrived at 9. Just as they moved off, thinking I wasn't coming, I ran for the station and jumped on the train as it left.

When I returned to Dundee later on I had forgotten the whole incident. By chance I had to spend the forenoon in Glasgow, so I caught the bus instead of the train to Dundee. I got to the Forresters Hall where I was to speak, and the street was packed with policemen. The reason didn't enter my head, but when I entered the side room of the hall all the Dundee lads were surprised. They had waited for me at the railway station - along with the police - and were sure I wasn't coming.

We decided that I would carry on and speak, but as soon as I had finished all the doors were locked and the lights turned off while the Dundee Workers' Theatre Group performed. Another man was put on the platform in my place; he was about my height and had my case, and the audience were told to follow him when the lights went up and the doors were opened. Of course the police grabbed him, and I got away. The following morning I walked up the Perth Road in the dark and caught the bus to Glasgow.

After the 1932 Hunger March I was also sent to Ireland to try and set up an unemployed organisation over there. A conference of the unemployed was arranged for the Mansion House, Dublin. But it was a poor effort. A deputation of about nine came to see me before the meeting and said they couldn't advertise me as the speaker because the lord mayor had said that they couldn't have the hall if an outside speaker was there. I told them that they shouldn't let a lord mayor decide their meetings for them.

Some Irish MPs were sympathetic to the attempt to set up an unemployed organisation, and one of them spoke. There were some fifty poor fellows there - absolutely down and out - from all parts of Ireland. Some of them had cycled miles to attend the conference. In the middle of it the lord mayor came in and said: 'I've got no whisky but I've got the best sherry in Ireland', and sent in trays of the stuff. No one had eaten because they couldn't afford to and, of course, the drink had a very bad effect.

The chairman of the meeting drank too much sherry and obstructed any attempt to set up an organisation. I argued for one to be formed there and then, and for some kind of federation between Dublin and the other towns. A very decent man called Dunne, who later became an Irish MP, supported me and subsequently led a hunger march from Brae to Dublin. But the Chairman got in the way of all suggestions, and I had to report to the NUWM in London that the conference had not been very productive.

I did a lot of work as Scottish organiser, but I really concentrated on the Glasgow District and my job as secretary to it. The Glasgow NUWM fought for the unemployed at all levels. Throughout the thirties we were able to use the Rent Restrictions Act passed in 1915. There was a clause in the Act that the rent could be reduced if repairs weren't done, and sometimes we got the rent reduced to almost nothing. We made as much use as we could of this, and sometimes landlords were actually forced to abandon their property. Many of the houses should have been knocked down, but there was such a shortage of houses after the first world war that they had to stay up. Some of the slums were terrible.

The bad conditions that people suffered in Glasgow didn't automatically lead them to support a socialist revolution - far from it! From 1931 an organisation called the Scottish Protestant League actually began winning seats on the town council. They got three members by 1932, and in 1933 they won another four. The Scottish Protestant League was organised by a man called Ratcliffe. He took over an old building in George Street and pulled all the old Orange elements round him. One of the members was a boilermaker named Charlie Forrester who had joined the Communist Party for a while.

Ratcliffe had a paper called the *Scottish Vanguard* in which he published really vicious anti-catholic stuff and also attacked the Communist Party, including myself. His league's base was in Bridgeton, and their presence meant that we were never able to build an organisation of the unemployed in that area, although the Carlton municipal ward next door had a lot of catholics and we had a branch there.

In Bridgeton in the thirties there was a strong Billy Boy's faction, and Orange protestant gangs grew up of a type that Glasgow hadn't seen before. At the time when the Communist Party was attacking James Maxton as 'sham left' the Young Communist League had a march into Bridgeton where Maxton was speaking. Margaret McCarthy appealed to me to go with them, and we were completely cordoned off by Billy Boys in the cul-de-sac where we held our meeting. We had to hit our way out with our slogan-boards, and then they followed us throwing bottles and stones. After our crowd broke up they came looking for me but fortunately didn't find me. The next day we were due to have a meeting outside Bridgeton Labour Exchange, where the Billy Boys mostly gathered. Gallacher, Frank Docherty and I went down there and held the meeting; they were taken by surprise and we had no trouble from them at all. You had to do something like that, because if you showed the slightest sign of fear you were for it.

They faded away because they had no real policy apart from ranting against popes and nuns. Charlie Forrester went to Belfast and slashed a picture in the art gallery of the Pope blessing King William at the Battle of the Boyne - he was only fined £5! He led a breakaway from Ratcliffe's group, but the whole thing died away with the outbreak of the second world war.

The existence of the Scottish Protestant League brought the Moderates into a lot of disrepute. They were the ruling party of the town council, an alliance of Tories and ex-Liberals and all the reactionary elements. When they put up no candidates against the Scottish Protestant League, even the reactionary catholics began to wonder about voting Moderate. Then they refused to do anything about the inquiry into graft which, following the conviction of Baillie Strain who was Labour candidate for Gorbals, showed that graft was common practice in the town council. Further, the Moderates' proposals, like the government's, were all for greater and greater economy in spending and forced the brunt on the unemployed.

For these reasons, in the municipal elections of 1933 the Labour group got control of the Glasgow Town Council for the first time. They depended on the ILP, which still had nine members on the corporation, for a majority over the Moderates and the protestants. Although the Communist Party were working with the ILP, our policy was still to criticise the Labour Party. Just before the 1933 election I led a deputation to the town hall. (Of course the ILP had rushed out to make it look as if they were leading the unemployed!) We had spoken to the full council, which is not possible now, and from the Labour group we had received a promise that if they were elected everything we demanded for the unemployed would be carried through.

As soon as the Labour-controlled council was elected they stopped some of the Moderates' economies and brought in some of our demands. Immediately, they were told that their actions were illegal and nothing got carried through. I was never very much in favour of the 'social fascist' policy of the CP, but it wasn't difficult to criticise the Labour group over that!

Although the Labour Council had some real opportunists, some belonged to the old school of socialism. George Smith, Jimmy Welsh and Andrew Hood of the ILP were more in the tradition of Wheatley and of William Morris. They were the ones I kept in contact with, and they would argue for the unemployed against the economy measure being brought in by the National Government.

There were some new regulations proposed by the government in 1933. The idea was to create three classes of unemployed workers. Those who were in benefit were to be paid under the insurance scheme; those out of benefit for short periods by the Unemployment Assistance Board; and the third group, the long-term unemployed, to be paid by the Public Assistance Committee. For the first time, compulsory attendance at training centres was to be introduced.

In response to these proposals the NAC of the NUWM called a National Hunger March for the beginning of 1934. Though we faced winter conditions when we set off in January, it was an easier march than 1932 because we got the co-operation of the ILP and even some Labour bodies on the way to London. John McGovern and some other ILPers came, but I am sure that McGovern never expected to have to march farther than Kilmarnock. A ban had been put on all demonstrations there, and there had been arrests and imprisonments. When we actually got past Kilmarnock I noticed that McGovern had to send home for some clothes - he had nothing at all in his kitbag!

The Scottish contingent was led by Peter Kerrigan as well as myself. George Middleton went ahead to arrange the accommodation, and did it very well. The authorities were now used to handling us, and we were more co-operative, so there wasn't any trouble at all. But all through Scotland we had to provide our own food, and by the time we reached Carlisle we were running short of money. The facilities at Carlisle were very good; to arrive there was a relief after our tramp through Scotland; and I left the marchers for their day's rest and went to London by the night train. The next evening I spoke with Harry Pollitt at a big meeting at the Memorial Hall. After my speech we collected £83 for the Scottish contingent. That solved our

roblem, and I caught the night train back to Carlisle in time to take
the marchers out the next morning.

At Preston Wal Hannington joined us. He and I marched
together, and I told him that I had a present for him. He said he had
one for me. After another mile or two he said: 'Come on, what have
you got?' - we both brought out a bottle of whisky! We had to be
careful that no one saw the whisky in our kitbags. Finally, at
Macclesfield, all the marchers got beds and we could get out that
night, and we decided that it would be safe for us to drink it. We went
to one pub, but saw two marchers there with two local women, and
we quickly backed out. We went to another on the outskirts of the
town, ordered two whiskys and kept re-filling them from our own
bottles; but we discovered that the people in the pub knew who we
were and we had to move again.

By the time we went for our bus we were no longer very alert.
Someone said 'It is Mr Hannington and Mr McShane, isn't it?' -
fortunately it was just a local person who helped us get the bus.
When we arrived back we quietly went in the side door and into bed.
Nobody saw us, and we got away with it. The rule against drinking
on the march was never meant to be strictly enforced, but Kerrigan
and McGovern were both teetotallers and they would have been
difficult about it if they had found out.

The next morning, Kerrigan came to see me with the two marchers
I had seen in the pub. He wanted me to put them on the carpet for
being out until eleven with two women. They insisted that they had
been in bed long before that, but Kerrigan brought the two men who
had told him about it. 'Them', they said, 'We stole the two women
off them!' I just said 'Away you go.'

McGovern marched with us all the way, but he kept disappearing
for odd days to go and do meetings. There was a lot of resentment at
his presence on the march, and I had to restrain one communist
councillor from Lanarkshire from hitting him. The Communist
Party was trying to win some of the ILP members over, but I wasn't
keen on having a lot of ILPers on the march. There was a lot of
pacifism among them, which was not the most useful attitude when
the march was in danger of coming into conflict with the authorities.

Because of the assault by the Birmingham police on the Lancashire marchers in 1932, the Scottish contingent asked to be routed
through Birmingham this time. We wanted the Birmingham police
to be facing us, and in 1934 we marched through Wolverhampton

and Birmingham. At Wolverhampton we were warned that the police would not allow us to march through the town's main street.

We held a meeting outside Wolverhampton to tell the marchers the position and make our plans. It was agreed that I would take the first contingent, all the other leaders would take separate contingents all the way down the march, and as we entered Wolverhampton they would come up level with me on my right hand. We would then take the full width of the street and go right through. I felt very confident about our decision; but when we arrived at the main street there was only *one* policeman to divert us. We brushed him aside and walked down the main street, then turned round and marched back.

The following day we reached Birmingham and were told that we couldn't march through Corporation Street. There was a large army of policemen to stop us. I told McGovern to lead the first contingent through Birmingham and follow the police route; I would be half-way down the march. When we reached Corporation Street I took my half of the march straight down *our* route. The police rushed after us, grabbed me and swore that I would be for it. But the whole march just carried on and joined up with the others, and there was nothing they could do. That evening I made a complaint about the attitude of the police in both Wolverhampton and Birmingham. The Wolverhampton police tried to say they had never banned us in the first place, but the Birmingham Trades Council took it up on our behalf. The next day the Birmingham police escorted us as we left the town.

The 1934 Hunger March was an agitation more than anything else. In each town we stayed in we held meetings, and some reporters marched with us the whole of the way. It was very peaceful because of the co-operation we received from the ILP councillors and men like Aneurin Bevan and James Maxton. Our petition was presented in parliament in the normal way by MPs, and we returned to Glasgow.

Kerrigan's presence on an unemployed demonstration was part of the CP policy of 'showing the face of the party'. For the NUWM, that meant bringing well-known Communist Party members into the agitation alongside those of us who always worked there. Kerrigan came to a meeting at the labour exchange and urged the crowd to join 'the party of Lenin and Stalin'. I objected to this. I said it was not a party meeting but an NUWM one, and that we had always recruited to the party through building the NUWM as a united front of all unemployed workers.

Kerrigan then attacked me for attacking the Communist Party. He produced a document I had written for distribution inside the NUWM in which I said that we had to appeal to members of all sections of the labour movement, and I mentioned the Labour Party, the ILP and the Communist Party. Kerrigan said that this amounted to an attack on the Communist Party. I scored out the words 'Communist Party' and told him to get it duplicated like that, but he took the original to the Scottish secretariat.

At the secretariat meeting I demanded to know where the attack on the party was - could they see one? Those bloody fellows said yes they could; I stormed out of the meeting saying that I wasn't a rubber stamp on Peter Kerrigan or anybody else. I didn't go back to the office for over a fortnight, and just continued with my work in the NUWM. Then Gallacher, who was a very fly old fellow, came to see me on one of the demonstrations. 'Harry', he said, 'I'd like to talk to you about one or two wee things. Could we meet in the party office tomorrow morning?' I went back to the office, and things returned to normal.

17. Inside the Party

During the thirties some members of the Communist Party were called upon to make terrible sacrifices. Apart from the enormous number of arrests in the NUWM, members were sent to prison for two to three years on charges of criminal libel. The *Daily Worker* carried many libellous articles against labour leaders in the 'social fascist' period. The articles were true, but the Labour Party and the courts made a real offensive against us. Some people went to prison for articles which they didn't write but had put their names to. Members of the Communist Party showed a lot of courage then.

There were also some arrests on charges of spying for the Soviet Union. It was regarded as a duty by members to help Russia at the expense of the capitalist world. Percy Glading was caught and sentenced to six years in 1938. The chief witness against him was a colonel's daughter named Olga who had worked in the office with Harry Pollitt. The other girls in the office were suspicious of her, which made Pollitt very angry because he thought she was a capture from the ruling class; she was then transferred to the office of 'friends of the Soviet Union', of which Percy Glading was in charge, and that led to his arrest. Later in the forties Dave Springhall, another member of the CP, was sentenced during the war and found that two of the witnesses against him were girls from Piccadilly whom he had associated with.

Spying for the Soviet Union was considered disgraceful by outsiders, but not by us. We believed in the revolution and in the Soviet Union. To us Russia was the heart of the revolution, and it was only a matter of time before she spearheaded a revolution for the whole world. We had no idea in the thirties that Stalin had abandoned the idea of a Western European revolution led by the Communist Parties, and wanted those parties merely to give support to Soviet foreign policy.

In 1931 and 1932 Stalin-worship was only just beginning in the party. It was introduced by Communist Party members who had been to the Lenin School in Moscow. A large number went, and they were utterly impossible when they came back. They would come up to Glasgow and lecture us on every little thing that should be done. One bunch came when I was raising the demand for a reduction in working hours to reduce unemployment: they told me that I shouldn't because it wasn't a demand for the unemployed! They infuriated me, and I was glad to see the back of them. All they knew was the stuff that had been taught to them at the Lenin school - they had never thought anything through for themselves.

I never went there, but Bob McLellan and Peter Kerrigan did. Kerrigan was an engineer who had gone into the CP through the rank-and-file trade-union movement about 1921, and he had been active in the Minority Movement. His wife, Rose Glasgow, was also a member of the party and I thought she was a very fine comrade. Gradually Kerrigan became part of the apparatus of the party and was sent to Moscow for two years. When he came back all he could say was comrade Stalin says this, comrade Stalin says that. Aitken Ferguson said to me: 'Christ, we'll soon be getting Stalinism instead of Leninism' - and he didn't know how true he spoke.

Peter had very little imagination; for him the important thing was to get the party line straight and lay it down to the rest of us. Through him we learned all the changes in position immediately, and we were able to get a lot of information from him when he came back from Russia. He was an intrinsically honest fellow, and would simply repeat the most amazing statements from the leaders in Russia. He told us that they weren't happy about what they had done to Trotsky: they should have executed him instead of sending him into exile! He also said that Krupskaya - Lenin's widow - wasn't following the line and was in danger. Another of his statements was that the early writings of Marx were immature and not to be counted. That was funny coming from Kerrigan, because although he was the Scottish organiser for years before he went to the Industrial Department in London, he was not a theoretician.

A few who came back from the Lenin school were not so happy about what they had been taught. Fred Douglas of Edinburgh told me he couldn't stick it at all; the atmosphere was like a confessional, with all the students sitting around picking holes in one another looking for deviations. Bob McLellan also came back without some of the worst excesses. But generally, it got so that inside the party it was impossible to speak out against decisions. Harry Pollitt would put the line, and if you disagreed he would simply say: 'Comrade, you are attacking comrade Stalin.' The worship even spread to Lenin. At one stage some branches had 'little Lenin corners' in their meeting-rooms, like secular shrines.

We were all shocked when the executions of old revolutionaries started to take place in Russia. They happened very quietly at first, and we were given to understand that these men had been working with the Nazis. The *Communist International* was our bible as far as the international situation was concerned and we all read it.

When the Nazis took power in Germany the *Communist International* argued that they would only last a few months, and we believed that. We were amazed that they had taken power at all. We didn't realise that the 'social fascist' policy of the Communist Party was largely responsible. The German Communists were behaving just as we were in Britain: calling the other workers' parties 'fascists' and not co-operating with them at all, even against the real fascists. The Nazis took over while three socialist parties - the Communist Party, the German Social-Democrats, and the Independent Socialists - held three separate demonstrations.

The German Communist Party was the biggest in the world outside Russia, and we couldn't believe that they had been defeated. As before the first world war, our hopes of spreading the revolution had been pinned on Germany. Thaelmann, the German communist leader, went to the police after the Reichstag fire to explain that the Communist Party had nothing to do with it. He never got out again. I remember saying that I had never heard anything so bloody stupid as going to the police and handing yourself over. Some of the German CP managed to escape to Russia but later on, when Russia and Germany were allies, some were executed and some were handed back; if we knew the full story of what happened to the German communists in Russia I think it would be seen as the biggest act of treachery in human history.

Before Hitler's victory the communists had formed 'the Red Fronts' and marched in military formation in their thousands: the clenched fist salute was their answer to the Nazis. Therefore, at first, people like us assumed that Hitler couldn't last and that the communists would come to power in six or ten months. We actually debated about how many months it would be! After a year, and growing Nazi repression, it became obvious that the CP's military solution had been no substitute for a united front of all workers' parties against Hitler; and the 'social fascist' policy began to be challenged.

In 1935 the Communist Party in Britain produced a policy pamphlet called *For a Soviet Britain*. At the same time, the 7th World Congress of the Communist International - the *last* Congress of the Communist International - completely reversed its previous policy. Dimitrov and Togliatti spoke and led the way to a new policy of a popular front of all classes against fascism. They never said that the previous policy had been wrong, but now there was a swing from describing everybody on the right as a 'social fascist' to working with anybody at any price. It wasn't just a 'united front' policy on important issues, but a complete subordination of the Communist Party to 'popular' policies.

Once the line had changed, nobody ever mentioned the old policy. It was never explained. To quietly forget it was an unprincipled thing to do, but that became typical of many decisions made inside the Communist Party over a long number of years. The average party members weren't affected very much by the change in policy because they hadn't changed as much as the leadership in favour of the policy of 'social fascism'. I, for example, had happily described the Labour Party as 'the third capitalist party' because I always thought it was; but I had always worked with individual members of both the ILP and the Labour Party. That was true for many of our members; but, unfortunately, the 'social fascist' policy had lost us a lot of support at a time when workers were becoming fed up with those organisations.

The new 'popular front' policy did give more scope for the Communist Party to work on trades councils and with the Labour Party. Some CP members had been thrown out of the Glasgow Trades Council, and our position was very weak in the early thirties. In 1934 the TUC had issued 'The Black Circular' in an attempt to ban Communist Party members from being delegates. But after the change in our policy, it was possible for quite a number of CP members to be active on the Glasgow Trades Council. They were led by Joe MacMillan of the NUR; he was an outstanding debater and a very good comrade, and would always put forward any proposal the Glasgow NUWM wanted him to make. One of our aims in the thirties was to link up the unemployed with the employed workers, but because of the demoralisation and disorganisation in the trade unions we were unable to do so.

In the NUWM we didn't always work according to the party line, and Hannington and I were on the carpet a number of times. We got away with being unorthodox because the NUWM was the only mass organisation the party had, and Wal Hannington had great personal standing in the party. In 1929 when Tom Bell, Johnny Campbell and others were put off the executive because of their previous opposition to the 'social fascist' policy, Hannington fought the executive recommendation and stayed on. He said that he was no right-winger, and had always fought a class-against-class line because he worked in the mass movement of the unemployed.

Although I also had some standing in the party, I was never put on the executive. The only time that it was proposed I should be, Abe Moffat moved against it on the Scottish Committee. It was well-known that I was a 'heretic' on some issues. On one occasion someone remarked how strange it was that the comrades who did mass work were always being awkward on the party's leading committees. The reference was to Wal Hannington, Arthur Horner and myself, and it was true - we were all heretics.

In many ways one of the tragedies was that so many able communists were removed from mass work. Gallacher was an industrial leader who became a national official and suffered because of it. Gallacher had good instinct and fought for anything he believed in. From the outbreak of the war to the General Strike he was in prison four times; he could take punishment and come out without any signs of being affected by it.

In 1935, as in 1931, all the forces of the Scottish Communist Party were thrown into the fight in Fife where Gallacher was standing. The leading communists of the Miners' Union, Abe Moffat and others, were determined that Gallacher should win the seat. But when he *did* win, the only communist to do so, it was to everyone's surprise. The last man in the world who would fit into parliament was Gallacher - to picture him discussing legislation in the House of Commons was fantastic! He never was a parliamentarian and stuck to his old working-class habits; the party actually had to try to groom him a bit. When he was first elected it was discovered that he had promised so much of his MP's salary to different causes that he would have nothing left at all. The party had to sort it all out for him. He would have given his entire salary to the party - he was never a selfish man.

Gallacher's election in 1935 was looked upon as a beginning. There had been Walton Newbold and Saklatvala before him, but Gallacher was hailed as the greatest MP ever. Which was nonsense - he was at his best as an industrial leader, and could hold an audience of many hundreds. He was not an MP of the kind they made him out to be; he never lacked courage, but he was totally committed to party policy and always carried out the instructions he was given.

However, he made some outstanding speeches in parliament. The 1935 election had, of course, returned a Tory Government, and in 1936 J.H.Thomas was forced to resign from the cabinet because of 'leaking' budget secrets to two of his friends. Gallacher got up in the house and put the responsibility for Thomas's actions squarely on the establishment, who had made him the man he was.

The 'popular front' line led to the NUWM being encouraged to work with the Labour Party, and on the 1936 Hunger March we actually got a great deal of Labour support and had Labour speakers on the same platform in Hyde Park. On this, we co-operated much more with the Labour Party than with the ILP. In Scotland the march set off from Edinburgh at the time of the Labour Party Conference which was discussing the Communist Party's application for affiliation (it was, of course, turned down).

A march down the East Coast from Edinburgh to England was entirely new, and I was sent across to lead the East Coast contingent. Peter Kerrigan took the West Coast march down to London on the established route. I had marchers from Dundee and Aberdeen and the miners from Fife, whilst Kerrigan took the Glasgow and Lanarkshire sections.

We left Edinburgh at the beginning of October and went through Galashiels and Hawick to Langholm. At Langholm we had a day I shall never forget. We were met by the whole town; they brought long tables out to the streets and spread them with food they had prepared. It was a tremendous surprise - I had never known it happen before. There was a great atmosphere among all the people and all the marchers.

As on the West Coast, accommodation was difficult in the small towns on both sides of the border. At Alston we went to the church hall to sleep, but the minister was completely against it and came down to prevent us staying there. He and I had a row and our shoemender on the march, a man called Noble, threatened to punch the minister on the nose: he retreated, and we spent the night in the church hall.

We had a similar argument with a minister at Middleton on Teesdale, and finally stayed in the Salvation Army hall. That evening, when we held our meeting in the town I referred to this minister's refusal to give us accommodation, and after the meeting the minister arrived with the police superintendent to demand an apology. He said it was his wife who had refused the hall, not him. His wife was with him, and she was prepared to take responsibility. I said: 'Of course. *I* always blame the woman!' and I told the police superintendent the matter had nothing to do with him - he seemed quite shocked. The next morning I held another meeting in the town and repeated everything I had said the previous night.

The man we sent ahead met with problems because none of the people he was dealing with had seen a hunger march before. However, the towns became larger and accommodation was easier, and we got a great deal of help from local Labour Parties. I also had the assistance of Abe Moffat's brother Alec. I wasn't very happy about it at first, remembering what had happened in Edinburgh in 1933; I wanted an undertaking that there would be no trouble on the 1936 march, and the party saw Alec and it was agreed. Actually he and I got on very well on the road down to London. He was a more tolerant character than his brother. Abe Moffat was leader of the United Mineworkers of Scotland by this time, and although Alec wasn't so prominent he was a councillor and was able to do a lot of speaking on the march.

In Leeds Sid Elias came out and met us and gave us a great reception. He had been the chairman of the NUWM and had gone to jail in 1932; we had released him at the request of the Communist Party to become its organiser in Leeds.

We met Ellen Wilkinson on our road as she was going to join the Jarrow marchers who were going to London at the same time as we were. Ellen Wilkinson was the MP for Jarrow, and she and the Labour councillors of the town had organised that march to protest against the specially terrible conditions of unemployment in Jarrow where all the shipyards had closed. There was no rivalry between our march and hers. She led the Jarrow march and led it well, and when our march met her we exchanged speeches of support.

We went through Chesterfield, which I knew well after my stay in

England in the twenties. I knew that Saturday night was market night in the town; our march needed money and publicity, and I led the marchers straight to the market place. A solid wall of policemen stood in our way. I went up to them and charged them with trying to cause a riot. They were quite taken aback; I said that we were determined to go to the market place, and in the end they cleared out of the way and we went and held our meeting. It was always the same story on the hunger marches. If you showed the slightest sign of hesitation you were for it from the police, but if you were determined to go through you made them think twice.

At the end of October, as we drew nearer London, our cook died. His name was Patrick Halpin, and to this day I can picture him stirring a big pot of porridge every morning. He was a clean cook, but I never saw a man with a face so dirty - it used to get black from the smoke of the fire. Our previous cook on the West Coast marches was Skilling, who had been jailed over an unemployed demonstration in Kilmarnock. Halpin wasn't a member of the Communist Party, and didn't seem to have any political background at all: he was just one of the unemployed. We got a clergyman and buried him ourselves in a small English village.

There had been deaths in other contingents on other hunger marches, but they had been hushed up; there seemed to be a feeling that such deaths shouldn't be talked about. I felt differently. We had a banner draped with a black border and we carried it at the head of our contingent. It said:

> The East Coast Scottish Contingent is marching one man short. Patrick Halpin died on the road on October 28th. He gave his life to end the Means Test and poverty.

We carried that banner to the end. When the East Coast Scottish Congingent marched into Hyde Park, the thousands there to meet us took off their hats as the banner passed.

In London we tried to get the Prime Minister to meet a deputation, but failed. We held a massive demonstration and had great meetings with Labour MPs and Communist Party members speaking from the same platforms: Attlee and Aneurin Bevan both spoke with us in Hyde Park. We also formed a march council which was supposed to carry on the work after the marchers had gone home. It included Tom Mann, Harry Pollitt, James Maxton, Aneurin Bevan, Jennie Lee, Ellen Wilkinson, as well as Wal Hannington and myself.

The Communist Party had decided that this march council would carry the struggle of the unemployed forward. The 1936 Hunger March had, for the first time, actually made a surplus - a thousand pounds. Hannington and I wanted it to be given to the NUWM, but the party decided it must go to the march council to further their agitation (which Hannington and I thought would mean *no* agitation). We went to the council meeting tied by the party line, but Ellen Wilkinson moved that the surplus be given to the NUWM and Jennie Lee supported her - Wal and I got the money we hadn't been allowed to ask for! We used it to put full-time NUWM organisers into the field at £2 a week each.

Shortly after the marchers had gone home, Wal Hannington was called in to see Harry Pollitt. Pollitt showed him a photostat copy of a letter written by Sid Elias to the Economic League, offering to work for them while remaining a member of the Communist Party. Apparently, just before our arrival in Leeds, the Economic League had put out a leaflet referring to this letter. Someone sent the leaflet to the Communist Party headquarters in London. The party made enquiries and the Economic League supplied a photostat of the letter. Hannington identified the writing as that of Sid Elias, and we had to report back to the NAC of the NUWM that our ex-chairman was no longer trustworthy.

The Communist Party was very anxious to continue the initiative of the march council and get united work with the Labour Party. Pat Devine, who had been on the London Reception Committee for the 1936 march, was put on the NAC of the NUWM by the Communist Party in order to carry out this new policy. The Party now wanted to use our reputation among the unemployed to create 'united front' work with the TUC - even to the extent of liquidating the NUWM! We were required to call a conference of the unemployed in order to form one national body incorporating ourselves, the TUC's unemployed organisation, and whatever the ILP and the Labour Party had. We didn't get very far with the idea, and Idris Cox came to the party members on the NAC and said the party was dissatisfied with our progress towards unity in the unemployed movement.

We had always been in favour of bringing together employed and unemployed workers in the NUWM, and before the change in the party line in 1929 Hannington had actually sat on an advisory committee to the TUC on unemployment. I therefore proposed to Cox that we write to the TUC asking them to call a conference of the

H

existing unemployed organisations with a view to forming one body as an *integral* part of the TUC. Cox agreed, and the next day the NAC of the NUWM also agreed.

I returned to Glasgow but, to my surprise, Aitken Ferguson came up from London a fortnight later and told me that I was travelling back to London with him that night. He didn't tell me what for, just that it was a party instruction. We travelled down by sleeper; when I arrived I found Wal Hannington waiting and he didn't know what it was all about either. Suddenly Harry Pollitt arrived, with five or six others. He looked at us and said: 'This won't take five minutes.' Then he repeated my formula word for word except that he substituted the word 'subordinate' for the word 'integral'. I said we had agreed the phrase 'integral part of the TUC', but eventually we accepted 'subordinate' and I was put on the train back to Glagow.

It made all the difference because the TUC never did anything about the proposal, and we were still trying to get the conference when the war broke out! The change meant that the party, when it reported to Moscow, could say it had instructed the NUWM to carry out such a policy.

The Communist Party decided that instead of continuing to organise the NUWM we should use it to set up 'broad committees' of the unemployed. We were not in favour of this. We had always had a distinct dues-paying membership of the NUWM, and only they had the right to vote, but we had never excluded any unemployed person from participating in our activities. To our mind the NUWM was already a 'broad' movement, but the party insisted that we call for the setting-up of these committees. They said that a broad committee of the unemployed had been organised in 1905 in St. Petersburg, and that was to be our model. They even published a pamphlet on it.

Then Wal Hannington was sent to Moscow. The intention was to get him to speak on broad committees of the unemployed. The party always did this: it got people who were opposed to the line in a position where they had to speak for it. But when Wal got up and spoke he spent two whole hours on the great achievements of the Soviet Union, especially the fantastic output of steel! As he came off the platform, Pollitt grabbed him and said: 'You bastard - you insulted the Communist International!' One of the Russians, Manuilsky, later said that Hannington had made a remarkable speech about everything except that which he was supposed to.

Shortly after Hannington returned, the party called a conference in London that he, I and others had to attend. Pollitt sent me a note during the conference saying that I had to speak after lunch - when I asked what my subject was, he said I could speak about anything I liked. I spoke about all kinds of political problems, but after half-an-hour Pollitt stopped me. 'You have been speaking for half an hour and you haven't yet referred to the organisation of the unemployed', he said. Everyone laughed; I told him I was coming to it, and he said that I had better come to it now!

I dealt with the question in very general terms. When I got back to my seat Hannington showed me a note from Pollitt which read: 'On a memorable occasion you gave your famous Cast Iron speech and now your sparring partner is not doing so bad. He has dealt with everything except unemployment.' But despite all their efforts, none of us did anything about their proposals. As far as we were concerned we *were* the broad committee, and the work we did in the NUWM precluded any such change in policy.

I actually did speak at the STUC at the end of the thirties. I had gone there to try to address them on behalf of the unemployed. At first I was refused, but after I drafted another letter (which Middleton had been against) the executive reversed its decision. I got a very fine reception from the delegates. In my speech I argued for the NUWM demands which included the raising of unemployment benefit, the reduction of working hours to absorb the unemployed, and for the whole trade-union movement to co-operate with the unemployed struggle.

Although I disagreed with some parts of party policy, it never occurred to me to challenge the authority of the party. During the entire unemployed agitation, one of the arguments we used was that while capitalism was collapsing socialism was being created in Russia and there was no unemployment over there. Of course, instead of unemployment they had massive labour camps; but at that time we didn't believe it. Even the capitalist press shared our view to some extent. A cartoon in the *Manchester Guardian* showed two Russians looking over a circular wall with the capitalist world in havoc inside; the Russians were smiling as if to say that they had solved all these problems.

Also, by the end of 1936 the Spanish Civil War had begun and the fight against the advancement of fascism in Spain. The Republicans were fighting for their lives, and many young comrades from Glasgow went out there to join them. Such was the sympathy for the deposed Spanish Government that a considerable number of the unemployed went too. In Glasgow George Middleton was in charge of organising them. I myself wanted to go to Spain but Kerrigan was against it. I was about forty years of age by this time, and there were reports that men of this age were breaking down.

The Spanish Civil War campaign was probably the best thing the Communist Party did in that period. In various areas some comrades were mobilised against British fascism - as in the East End of London — but the Spanish campaign involved the entire party. We all raised money to equip the men who were fighting. I remember vividly one great meeting in the Albert Hall. It was when the struggle was just beginning. Isabel Brown was given the job of taking the collection: she did it brilliantly and collected over £2,000, which was a remarkable sum in those days.

A large number of fine communists died in Spain. I remember one of them, James Rutherford (Harold Fry) of Edinburgh, particularly well. He was taken prisoner in Spain and was sentenced to death with four others. That afternoon they went out and played a game of football. Finally they were reprieved and sent home; some of those who were released denied that they were members of the Communist Party, and actually came to the party congress to be excused for this. Pollitt agreed that it wasn't a good idea to admit being communists to fascists!

James Rutherford returned to Scotland. He and I toured the whole of Ayrshire with a loudspeaker van holding meetings and raising money for the Spanish struggle. Our biggest meetings were at Kilmarnock and Irving, but we went to Saltcoats and Stevenson and all the mining villages. There was already a big campaign in Glasgow, and we attempted to spread it further. Although the Ayrshire villages had a big Orange element, they never showed themselves at these meetings. I could see that young Rutherford was very discontented; he desperately wanted to go back to Spain, and eventually he did. He used a different name, but when the fascists captured him he was identified and shot.

The campaign was very important in Scotland because of the strength of the Catholic Church. They were active in Glasgow, speaking up for the Spanish fascists. The *Catholic Times* came out strongly in Franco's support. Arnold Lunn, an English catholic and a champion skier became famous for his speeches in defence of the Spanish fascists. Fortunately the average catholic didn't accept the

line of the *Catholic Times*. As one of the CP members who had
grown up in the rules of debate, I had four debates with H.W.
Henderson; he was the brother of the communist Arnold Henderson, but the editor of *Common Cause*. Our debates were in defence
of Russia and also on the Spanish struggle and one of them took
place in the McLellan Galleries and attracted a large audience.

We were also engaged in an argument with the ILP. As well as
communists, there were other socialists and anarchists fighting in
Spain. The ILP supported the POUM in Spain and kept up a
continuous barrage of criticism against the Communist Party. We
got the impression that they were fighting for the interests of their
party instead of the interests of the Spanish people. I read all their
reports in their paper and paid attention to their criticism, but I had
the feeling that they were mostly used on guard duty in Barcelona.

We thought that, whereas the POUM, the CNT and others were
fighting for the restoration of the Spanish parliamentary democracy, *we* were fighting for something beyond that. In Spain itself
the communists looked upon everyone who was not supporting them
as a deadly enemy. Bob Smillie, the miners' leader's nephew, went to
Spain through the ILP and was actually imprisoned by the communists and died in prison. It was later argued that he died a natural
death - but, of course, he shouldn't have been in prison in the first
place.

There were many bad incidents in Spain. It became obvious that
the communists were labelling the anarchists and other socialists as
'Trotskyists', and shooting some of them. André Marty was in
charge of the International Brigade - he had made his reputation in
the Black Sea mutiny at the end of the first world war - and
presumably was following orders. Many party members actually
disagreed with the policy in Spain: Wally Tapsell came home with
two others after such a disagreement. We never learned what it was
about. I sometimes think it was fortunate that I didn't go to Spain; I
would have disagreed, and would probably have ended up in their
bad books.

The ILP circulated all these stories, of course, but we dismissed
them as ILP propaganda. When McCartney was shot in the arm by
Peter Kerrigan in Spain the ILP claimed it was deliberate, and John
McGovern repeated the story everywhere. Kerrigan said that
McCartney's gun was jammed, he had taken it to sort out and it had
gone off. Knowing Kerrigan, that was perfectly believable.

One of the problems we had was understanding the Russians' relationship to the Spanish struggle. There were no Russian troops there, only Russian advisers, and we had no idea whether they were sending as much help to the Republicans as Italy and Germany were to Franco. Tito was involved in the Spanish Civil War, but he spent most of his time in France getting men across the border. All the European countries, and America, sent men to the International Brigade.

When the Republic was finally defeated after more than two years of struggle, the only explanation from Russia was that Hitler and Mussolini had helped Franco and the 'so-called democracies' of Europe and America hadn't rescued the Spanish democracy. Years later I realised that the Russian policy had helped bring about the defeat. They were not fighting for a proletarian revolution and appealing to the other classes to follow the proletariat; they were fighting for a unity of all the classes in defence of the 'democratic' government. At the same time, they were also fighting the people nearest to them, the anarchists and the socialists.

In Britain, one of the communists who came back from Spain with a bad reputation was Bill Rust. He was a very strict disciplinarian and swore to every dot and comma of the party line. Before he went to Spain he was known for his criticisms of the party leadership, and a lot of us admired him for a period because we were looking for some kind of change. But Rust's objection to the leadership was that it didn't follow orders enough. He constantly spoke against people who 'wobbled' on the line; really he was attacking Pollitt and seemed to want Pollitt's job.

Bill Rust was the man who built up the *Daily Worker*, and that made his reputation in the party. In Spain, any anarchist and any socialist were the enemy to him, and he was prepared to shoot anybody who didn't carry out instructions. We knew about it, but we were in the middle of a struggle and there was nothing we could do. There were many in the party who were prepared to stand by Rust no matter what he did.

The development of the idea of a Popular Front led to a change in the communist position towards Scotland. Once it was accepted that communists should work for the unity of all classes, the next step was to start arguing for self-government for the Scottish people.

Further support for this came from the fact that the personnel of the party was changing - during the Popular Front period many more intellectuals and middle-class elements came to the fore.

The Scottish poet Hugh MacDiarmid joined the Communist Party and wrote his 'Hymn to Lenin'. He was a member for a good number of years, but in 1937 he and Gallacher fell out. McDiarmid disagreed with an article of Gallacher's which Kerrigan then defended. MacDiarmid made an awful onslaught on Gallacher and Kerrigan and was expelled from the party. We on the Scottish Committee recommended his expulsion, and it was endorsed by the National Executive.

Hugh MacDiarmid then appealed to the Communist International - really he was appealing to Moscow: it was quite a common practice. Moscow remitted his expulsion back to the British Communist Party, and the whole issue came up at the Party Congress. At that congress the voting was by delegation - Welsh, Scottish, Northeast etc. - instead of individual delegates. The Scottish delegation was the only one that voted in favour of MacDiarmid's expulsion; all the other delegations voted against it. We were (all except two) of the opinion that MacDiarmid had never done anything for the party, and that he was as much a Scottish Nationalist as he was a communist.

Before long the line on Scottish Nationalism itself changed. The Labour Party had always supported the idea of self-government; Keir Hardie had moved a resolution in favour of it before the first world war, and the ILP MPs had moved one afterwards. Radical Liberals like R.E.Muirhead were both supporters of Home Rule and supporters of the ILP and *Forward*. John McCormick, the founder of the Scottish National Party, was originally an ILP member. But the Communist Party attitude to Scottish Nationalism had remained unchanged since they derided John Maclean for 'socialism in kilts'.

However, in 1937 and 1938 this was completely reversed. MacDiarmid had continually raised the question of Scottish self-government inside the party, though he wasn't on the Scottish Committee. Helen Crawfurd wrote an article in *Labour Monthly* and repeated Engels's argument that Britain should be a federation of the four states of England, Ireland, Scotland and Wales. It was a common idea among radical Liberals in the 19th century that Britain should adopt the American model with a centralised government as well.

Aitken Ferguson, who had been in touch with Muirhead and McCormick, prepared a draft statement for the Scottish Committee, dealing with various Scottish problems and giving support to the idea of a Scottish Parliament. At the Scottish Committee this statement got one vote - his own! - but it was then endorsed by the National Executive in London. As this over-rode all previous policy and the executive had to get the endorsement of the Scottish membership, they called an 'extended' Scottish Committee as a substitute for a full Scottish Conference. The extended committee had forty or fifty people instead of the normal fourteen to twenty. A lot of the people invited to the extended committee were the literary elements of the party, and when the vote was taken on the statement there were only two against: myself and Jimmy Barke, the novelist and playwright.

The committee then instructed Aitken Ferguson and me to open discussions with the Scottish Nationalists. I had always liked R.E. Muirhead, who was a very honest old man with a small business and had devoted a lot of his money to radical causes, including the founding of *Forward*. Everyone had a great deal of respect for him. But I was suspicious of John McCormick; he had been involved in the Free Speech Fight in 1931, and I discovered then that he wasn't to be relied on. He was very keen on reviving the romantic side of Scottish Nationalism; it had become something of a cult, with people going around wearing kilts.

Finally it was agreed between us that we should arrange a Scottish Convention, and Aitken Ferguson was put into the office to organise it full-time. However, though Aitken was one of the most capable men in Scotland theoretically, he was no organiser. The convention was still being organised by the time of the outbreak of war, when it was called off.

Despite our disagreement on this matter, Aitken and I got on very well. He had got a good marxist background in the SLP, and for a time he had been attached to the Western Bureau of the Communist International and was stationed in Germany with Dimitroff and others. He had toured India disguised as a clergyman. He worked as a full-timer for the party in Britain for a long time, and he was one of the few members in Scotland that I grew really attached to. He was a very flamboyant character; when he wanted to make his point, in the Scottish Committee or elsewhere, he would jump up on top of his seat and speak from there!

There were some outstanding men, and others who were less so, on the Scottish Committee. Fred Douglas was an exceptionally good propagandist from Edinburgh. Andy Auld was also a good propagandist, but he became demoralised and left the party. Donald Renton of Edinburgh and Bob Cooney, Aberdeen, both fought in Spain. Bob Cooney was very vocal and, like Kerrigan, followed the line of the Comintern; Fred Douglas and others had a lot of doubts. The best-known people on the committee were probably Peter Kerrigan, George Middleton, Adam Haimes, Aitken Ferguson and myself.

The Scottish Executive was an important body. We even used to choose the secretary of the United Mineworkers of Scotland - it was formed in the late twenties when the left won the ballot vote and the old leadership refused to hand over. Willie Allan was the first secretary, and when he left Scotland to become chairman of the Northumberland miners we appointed David Proudfoot as the nominee for secretaryship. He got the job but hadn't the stamina for it, and that was when the party selected Abe Moffat. Abe did a good job and really built up the United Mineworkers; eventually it became the Scottish area of the NUM. Its members gave Willie Gallacher his base in Fife.

18. The CP in and after the Second World War

By the winter of 1938-39 the situation of the unemployed was desperate. The powers of the 1934 Act were being used to the full in some areas. Both the Unemployment Assistance Board, for those out of benefit, and the labour exchange, for those in benefit, could require that an unemployed applicant attend a Ministry of Labour Instructional Centre. These centres were in fact residential camps, using unemployed workers for heavy labouring jobs such as road-making and laying drains. From 1935 to 1938 nearly ninety thousand unemployed workers went to those centres. Wal Hannington and I toured some of the camps and the conditions were terrible.

One of the camps we visited was the Glen Finnart camp where thousands of fir trees were being planted. The men at the camp were very discontented - the nearest town, Dunoon, was miles away. Wal Hannington had an old car and we had to use that in order to even reach this camp, and the other camps in Argyllshire. In many cases it was difficult to reach them even by car. The conditions are described by Wal in his book *Ten Lean Years* but it was hard to describe the inadequate food, the lack of company, the misery of a camp where men were parted from their wives and children. That was all that capitalism would offer the unemployed! Many people in Scotland look at the trees planted by these men without knowing the misery behind that planting.

Then, in the 1938-39 winter, those who were receiving relief came under a severe attack. From the early twenties the principle had been established that extra relief should be paid in the winter to cover the extra cost of fuel etc. The unemployed movement had mounted campaigns to get increases in the winter relief. But now the extra relief was not to be given to all claimants: only to those with a special need. Obviously, that winter a very small number of claimants got extra payments.

The NAC of the NUWM did not plan a hunger march in 1938.

Instead, attention was drawn to the desperate situation by holding a 'funeral' parade in London. Hundreds of unemployed marched behind the 'coffin' and when we got to Trafalgar Square it was uncovered and showed the words: 'he did not get winter relief.' A huge crowd followed the coffin through the West End of London. A few days later the NUWM delivered it to 10 Downing Street - and it nearly got in!

All over the country there were massive protests against the denial of winter relief, and nearly every NUWM District had its own coffin. We used it to demonstrate through the streets of Glasgow and gradually, as elsewhere, we found the authorities were beginning to review cases which had previously been denied winter relief! It was a vast publicity campaign, and we thought up all kinds of stunts and put huge banners in the most impossible places in order to draw attention to the unemployed.

By the end of the winter we were heartily sick of hauling the coffin around. We had to get rid of it. We decided to use it one more time, to get publicity for a meeting of Wal Hannington's in Glasgow. We fixed it to a hoarding in the Gorbals, with a poster which read

It's not very often I leave my coffin
But I've got an excuse today;
Wal Hannington speaks in Kingston Town Hall —
How the heck can I stay away?

The police came to remove it, and thought that all they had to do was lift the coffin off the hoarding. They made a mistake. There were a lot of unemployed engineering and shipyard workers in Glasgow, and we had fixed big iron brackets and bolted the coffin down. The police had to get either side of the coffin and wrench it off bit by bit, bit by bit. I just happened to wander by, and one of them looked at me. 'I wish I knew the bastard who did this!' he said. The hoarding faced a long row of tenements, and in every window there was a woman laughing and enjoying the show. We did tons of things like that in Glasgow - our movement was much livelier then.

While we kept up the fight for the unemployed throughout 1939, it became increasingly obvious that war would be declared soon. The Communist Party had an ambivalent attitude to the issue. Prior to Hitler getting power in 1933 the communist attack was always against the 'imperialist' powers, America and Great Britain. Those countries were seen as the greatest threat to Russia, despite Hitler's victories. Though the Communist Party was reluctant to see the real effect of Hitler getting power, it was the CP members who were the greatest fighters against fascism, both in East London and in Spain. Therefore, although we argued for peace, we were also in favour of fighting fascism.

The whole situation was very confused. A writer in a paper called the *Sunday Referee* had argued that there should be an alliance between Russia and the western powers against Hitler. Gallacher, through Walter Holmes, replied in the *Daily Worker* that this was Hyndmanism - that British Imperialism and the Soviet Union could not possibly be allies. The Communist Party in Britain were in favour of Russia staying out of an imperialist war; but many, including Harry Pollitt, advocated that Britain should fight fascism.

Shortly before war was declared came the news of the Nazi-Soviet Pact of 23 August 1939. It was an agreement signed in Moscow by Ribbentrop and Molotov in which Russia promised to stay neutral if Germany was involved in war. It ran completely against the previous Russian policy of arguing for a peace campaign of 'collective security' by all the 'democratic' nations against fascism, as well as the previous French-Soviet pact. It was an absolute surprise to all the members of the Communist Party.

Aitken Ferguson and I discussed the Nazi-Soviet Pact, and both of us had grave doubts about it. At Aitken's suggestion I raised the matter with Peter Kerrigan, but all Kerrigan would say was that it was the new line. When it came up before the Scottish Committee, Aitken and I were attacked for our attitude. I pointed out that there wasn't even a saving clause in the pact that permitted Russia to break with Hitler if circumstances changed. McIlhone spoke very sarcastically: 'It's a pity that comrade Stalin didn't think of a saving clause!' That was that.

It was said in the party that the pact was a move for peace, to prevent the Soviet Union being attacked. The party remained in favour of Britain declaring war on Germany - especially Harry Pollitt. I was in London on the night Chamberlain was supposed to speak on Germany's invasion of Poland, which Britain had promised to defend. We were having a meeting of the NAC in order to wind up the NUWM in the event of war - obviously there would be no more unemployed in wartime. That Friday while I was there the blackout started.

Wal Hannington and I went for a drink in the Euston Tavern before I got my train. To our surprise, we found thirty of the leading party members sitting at the large semi-circular bar. They were just as surprised to see us. Then Pollitt swept in, saying: 'I have been sitting in the gallery of the House of Commons, and that old bastard Chamberlain refuses to declare war!'

Then Pollitt called all the others out of the bar and they went off for a secret meeting. Walter Holmes told me about it later. Pollitt explained that Chamberlain had said nothing that night - it was 2 September - despite Hitler's troops having gone into Poland. The whole House had been expecting a declaration of war. Willie Gallacher, our only MP, had called for war to be declared. Pollitt proposed to the party meeting that the Communist Party should fight for a declaration of war against Germany, that a National Government should be formed, and that a 'man of the people' should be in the government. Walter added that he had the impression that the 'man of the people' should be someone like Harry Pollitt.

Our declaration in favour of war led to even more confusion in the Communist Party. There was a tremendous hatred of fascism; but there was also the old anti-war attitude, and a fear of repetition of 1914 when the entire socialist movement collapsed. War was declared on 3 September. The Communist Party was in favour of it - but we still didn't understand Russian policy.

Despite the Nazi-Soviet Pact, I argued in Glasgow that as the Germans had marched into Western Poland the Soviet Union would march into the Eastern section. Russia had always claimed this part as belonging to her; the people were of a different religion from the rest of Poland and were oppressed by the Polish government; I thought it was obvious that the Red army would go in and take them over. When I said this on Friday night, Colin Currie told Peter Kerrigan who immediately phoned Harry Pollitt. Pollitt promised that he would write an article for Monday's *Daily Worker* denouncing such ideas, and would send Kerrigan his notes in a letter by train to use at a public meeting on Sunday night. I was oblivious to all this: when, in the usual Saturday meeting of the Scottish Secretariat, Bob Cooney denounced comrades who were 'wobbling' on the Soviet Union, I didn't realise that he was referring to me! Aitken Ferguson had to explain it all to me. The next morning the Russians marched into Eastern Poland. Harry Pollitt's article never appeared, and Peter Kerrigan said nothing.

That was on 17 September. I was in jail very shortly afterwards. I had been arrested at the beginning of August over an eviction in Barrhead, but the trial didn't take place until 22 September. There had been a whole spate of eviction cases, and on this occasion someone had phoned the party offices for help. Colin Currie had gone straight there, and I followed him up. We stopped everyone getting into the house and finally the sheriff-officer came with an army of policemen and arrested me, Colin, John Dolan and several others. Three of us were sent to prison: Colin was sent down for two months because he was there first, I got six weeks because I was there second, and John Dolan a month because he was there third! At the trial we were defended by John McCormick of the SNP because at this time we were still working with him on a Scottish Convention.

On our way to prison Colin asked me to join the Church of Scotland so that we could meet on Sundays at the services. I agreed because I was worried about how he would take prison - it's always difficult for people the first time. The first week, the warder looked at me and said: 'We don't sing the Internationale in here.'

While we were in prison a complete about-turn occurred in the Communist Party's policy and leadership. A warder came in and told me that Pollitt and Campbell had been removed. I refused to believe him, and he said he would prove it by bringing in a copy of the *Daily Worker*. He brought it and made me read it while he stood there - he wanted to take it back immediately for fear anyone should see me or him with it. What he had told me was true. Pollitt and Campbell had been removed from the leadership of the party, and the paper was now arguing that this was an imperialist war between capitalist powers: Britain and France were the 'aggressors' who had rejected peace moves! The new policy was based on a statement from the Communist International - which hadn't met.

Harry Pollitt went back to Manchester as a full-time organiser, and Campbell came to Glasgow. Palme Dutt became the new secretary of the party. I was quite pleased to have Campbell back in Glasgow, because I was able to get some support from him against some of the bureaucrats on the Scottish Secretariat. When I demanded money for the Glasgow District from a big collection we had taken at a meeting, he was prepared to back me up. Palme Dutt wasn't a very good secretary, and after a while Pollitt and Campbell were reinstated.

Gallacher was also a victim of the switch in the party line on the outbreak of war. When Chamberlain was in power, it was he who made the speeches in the House of Commons calling for the declaration of war. Then he had to change reluctantly, very reluctantly, to opposing the war (in 1941 of course he had to switch to supporting the war again and calling for the opening of the Second Front). Gallacher had a great admiration for Harry Pollitt, and his attitude to those who had removed him never altered - he thought they were a bunch of bastards.

In March 1941, there was a by-election in Dunbartonshire, and in order to pursue the anti-war line we ran Malcolm McEwen as a peace candidate. I spent a month on the campaign; we covered the whole of the Vale of Leven and held hundreds of meetings. Pollitt came up and spoke against the war, and he was tireless; as he finished speaking at one meeting he went on to the next. Of course when it came to the vote we were nowhere, and our relationship with the Labour Party became very vicious during the campaign.

The NUWM had closed down, and I was working on the *Daily Worker*. At that time we began producing a Scottish edition, and had a team of four or five comrades working on it in Glasgow. We used to spend all night getting the paper out, then get out the next morning to collect the stories! We had it printed at Kirkwood's, and it had a circulation of five to six thousand. The circulation rose steadily, and it appeared that our anti-war line was spreading.

In my contributions I concentrated on the inadequacy of Glasgow's Labour Council. In particular, I attacked the provisions for bomb shelters: the council had put struts in the various tenements and called these 'shelters'! Dollan, who was now the lord provost, had gone to London for the day and said they were better than any shelters they had seen in London. I attacked him further in the *Daily Worker*, he replied to me in the corporation, and it got quite lively.

I used to go to the city chambers every day to watch what they were up to, and I was even there the day Churchill arrived. Willie Elger, of the Scottish TUC, stopped me and said: 'You have just walked up the passage that was meant for Churchill.' We both had a laugh, then Churchill arrived and for an awful moment I thought that he was trying to shake hands with me. Fortunately it was the woman next to me - she was the only one who had cheered him.

My job with the *Daily Worker* didn't last very long. In January 1941 the paper was suppressed. Really, its stand wasn't an anti-war stand. The chief argument it carried was that Britain and France were the aggressors because Hitler had talked about making peace, and its policies were almost pro-German. When the *Altmark* was sunk off Norway the *Daily Worker* strongly attacked Britain. George Middleton objected to this article and others like it, and the party hacks got very angry with him because they found it difficult to reply. It was the beginning of the end of George Middleton's support for the Communist Party.

After invading Poland the Soviet Union took control of the other Baltic states - Latvia, Estonia, Lithuania - with their 'agreement', and then went on to invade Finland. The *Daily Worker* promptly argued that Finland's borders were too near Leningrad, and Russia was taking this action to defend herself. Their line on the war was not at all similar to the socialist anti-war stand we had taken in 1914-18, against *all* belligerent nations.

With the closing of the *Daily Worker* I was out of a job. The party was quite apologetic about it, but I never cared whether I was a full-timer or not. It would be difficult for me not to be taken on somewhere, because I was a skilled engineer and in wartime every job needed men. The labour exchange sent me to Stephen's shipyard, but when I got there the manager and the foremen kept avoiding me! In the end I found the men working in the engine room of the ship and simply joined them, and that was how I got my start. Most of the men there were forty or fifty years of age, and there were several members of the Communist Party working on the boat. Our wages were £4 to £5 a week, although during the thirties they had sunk as low as £2.13s.

A few months later, in June 1941, Hitler declared war on Russia. No one had expected it. Russia was supplying Germany with war materials, and this seemed to be the last thing Germany would want to do. The Communist Party had to change round completely once more. We began to agitate for Britain and France, previously the 'aggressors', to open a Second Front against Germany to divide the German forces and help Russia. To this end we started to support the British war effort. Instead of arguing for increased wages, we now argued for increased production.

With the change in party policy the Glasgow Secretary disappeared. Archie Hunter frequently disappeared for a week or so, but this time he didn't return for a year; when he did, he was in uniform. I was asked to replace him, at half the wages that I was getting in Stephen's. When I took over, the Communist Party had three or four hundred members in Glasgow, but with the new policy we attracted many more. By the end of the war we had several thousand.

The situation enabled us to build factory branches as well as district ones. Rolls-Royce was the biggest factory branch, but we had them in a number of engineering workshops and a lot of prominent shop stewards were members of the Communist Party. Money came rolling in; we were in a very strong position. We were able to take offices in Princes Square, which was unusual for a working-class party. There were 12 geographical branches in Glasgow besides a lot of factory branches, and we frequently held aggregates of four to five hundred people.

In this period we were able to get prominent Labour people to speak on platforms with the Communist Party. There was a lot of feeling that we were right in arguing that the Soviet Union was making all the sacrifices in the fight against fascism. There appeared to be very little resistance in France. This was the time of the worst bombing of Britain, and the argument that opening a Second Front would bring a speedy end to the war won a lot of enthusiastic support.

We were able to hold enormous meetings and demonstrations for the Second Front. Several thousands attended one I organised at Glasgow Green. I was very angry when three of the Young Communist League got up and started making speeches in support of Russia - they hadn't consulted anybody about it at all.

Our attitude to the war made the Communist Party extremely popular. Russia was looked upon as that brave country fighting on alone, and Stalin became a national hero. A lot of new members were recruited, but they had no education in marxism and the whole character of the party changed. For the first time we had a predominantly paper membership. Hundreds of people filled in membership forms during the huge Second Front meetings - Harry Pollitt could fill any hall in Glasgow; but only about a third of them ever turned up to branch meetings.

The older party members didn't take supporting the war to its extremes, except for attacking the Trotskyists when they were on strike. But the new members did: I remember being on a demonstration where members of the Communist Party were carrying Union Jacks! An old ILPer came up to me - I wasn't carrying one myself - and said *he* would never march with that flag. Leaders of the party got carried away with this new-found popularity, and some members of the Young Communist League became intellectuals overnight and were laying down the law to everybody else. The present membership of the Communist Party is largely made up of these people who joined when it was very easy to do so - during the second world war and afterwards.

We didn't do a lot of outside educational work in the Communist Party. Only members were educated, and only along the current party line. During the war we emphasised that the whole future of socialism was at stake, and gave them a lot of figures on increased industrial production in Russia. This was all background to the struggle to open the Second Front.

From July 1941 the CP entirely supported war production. It was the first time ever that the Communist Party had come out in favour of increasing capitalist production. Because of this they didn't support strikes, and that gave the Trotskyists the chance to develop an organisation in Glasgow. Roy Tearse was brought up to Glasgow as their organiser; they obtained support in the Albion Motor Works, Singer's, John Brown's engineering works, and Barr and Stroud's. They made some attempts to extend strikes for increased wages, but were defeated by our opposition. Communist Party members inside the factories spoke up against the Trotskyists as saboteurs of the war effort - because Russia, the only socialist country, was in danger. It wasn't difficult for us to hold them off. We were better organised than they were, and they were conducting an unpopular fight; we were able to use the war atmosphere against them.

I was the secretary of the Communist Party in Glasgow for over a year, and then the ban on the *Daily Worker* was lifted. Obviously, now that we were pro-war a lot of people, including the employers and the government, were very pleased with us. The party sent someone up from London to run the Glasgow office of the *Daily Worker*, but he only lasted six months and then Bill Rust came up to ask me to go back on the paper. I had a suspicion that Johnny Gollan wanted me out of the Glasgow secretaryship and for a long time I refused; eventually I went back, and McIlhone became the new secretary. He was a bureaucrat, but completely devoted to the Communist Party. He had been in Russia for long periods and spent two years at the Lenin school.

We set up the Scottish office, and I used to travel down to London to take part in the discussions of the *Daily Worker*. In London it was clear that Bill Rust completely dominated the paper. He attended every meeting about everything. The other men were superior to him as journalists and technical workers, and he and Johnny Campbell were both on the executive and on the *Daily Worker*, but it was Rust who set the line.

The best contributions at the *Daily Worker* meetings came from Allen Hutt. He was a likeable person and a competent newspaper-man, and would have made a much better leader than either Rust or Campbell. Johnny Campbell relied on Pollitt for his understanding of mass work, and the fight between Rust and him was really the fight between Rust and Pollitt. For years Rust was after Harry Pollitt's job inside the Communist Party, and the struggle was only resolved when Rust died of a heart attack at an executive committee meeting later on. He was the man who wanted every little thing done just as Moscow said; Pollitt was a different character.

Whereas Rust had come into the movement through the Young Communist League, Harry Pollitt was in the movement earlier, as I was. He had obviously read widely in the free-thought literature; he and I discussed Haeckel's *Riddle of the Universe*. I got the impression that this was part of his background. He was in the BSP during the first world war, and had come to prominence over stopping the *Jolly George* taking armaments to the anti-Soviet forces. Throughout the Communist Party it was thought that it was Pollitt in the photograph of the incident, though some argued that it wasn't; but he was undoubtedly involved, and he was very active in the Minority Movement during the twenties.

Except when I was involved in a fight inside the party, I found Harry Pollitt a very likeable decent human being. He was not a political thinker, but he occasionally told me he was disgusted with some of the things he was asked by Moscow to do. They would demand that a certain person be given a job and he had to agree. He was a dedicated communist, although he often found himself arguing for a line which he didn't necessarily completely understand.

I stayed on the *Daily Worker* until I left the party in 1953. During the war I concentrated on finding out about the Polish army in Scotland. It was, undoubtedly, a fascist army. In its ranks there was a hatred of Russia and everything progressive. A Pole who had fought in the Spanish Civil War joined them, and he was terribly badly beaten up - I managed to get him to London and arrange for interviews to expose what had happened. On another occasion I found out that twelve NCOs had been imprisoned and were being kept in chains! I arranged for someone unknown to attend a press conference there, and read out a list of twelve names and demanded to see these men; some of the men were produced, and the newspapers got hold of the story.

By the end of the war the Communist Party was completely tied up in supporting the Coalition Government's policies. So much so, that in the debate over a general election in 1945 the CP demanded the continuation of a National Government including 'progressive' Tories like Churchill and Eden but with a Labour and socialist majority. It was an amazing suggestion. Churchill had always been the villain of the socialist movement: he had supported the Ulster Unionists, ordered gunboats into the Mersey in 1911, and had been prepared to shoot the anarchists in Sydney Street. The Communist Party seemed to have no idea of the real feeling of the British working class, and it never occurred to them that the Labour Party would win the election by a landslide.

During the election the Tories made vicious attacks on the Labour Party, especially in Lord Beaverbrook's newspapers. Churchill even described a socialist government under Labour as not being very different from Gestapo rule. During the election he toured the country as the man who had won the war. when he came to Glasgow Bob Horne and I organised a series of demonstrations against him. When he was passing along George Street we produced two donkeys, wearing placards saying 'I am a Daily Express man' and 'I am a Churchill man'. Churchill came along with his two fingers held up in the 'victory' salute, and then saw the donkeys; his hand stayed down a good while after that.

After the war there was a permanent shift in Communist Party policy towards British capitalism. We had been in favour of increased war production in order to win the war against fascism.

We had quoted figures to prove the increased output of production in Russia and to show that the socialist state of the Soviet Union was becoming stronger. We argued that Russian production was in the workers' interests. But it had never occurred to us that we should even think about planning capitalist production in Britain. Yet immediately after the war the Communist Party produced a pamphlet called *Looking Ahead* which was on just that.

Looking Ahead was a programme for 'rebuilding Britain'. It was drawn up by nine people in the party office in London but, of course, Harry Pollitt's name was put on it. Harry had been a war strategist - knowing just how it should be won! - and after the war he became a planner - knowing just how to get Britain back on its feet again. The pamphlet called for increasing production, and increasing exports in particular.

Inside the party it was said that the pamphlet would sell a million copies like Blatchford's *Merrie England*, but after a few months it was withdrawn. The whole programme was so much in contrast to what the Communist Party had always stood for that the membership couldn't accept it. But that didn't mean the policies were withdrawn. Almost all our propaganda at this time was about the need to plan a new Britain, apart from our attacks on the Nazis as war criminals.

Feeling against the Nazis ran very high in the Communist Party, and the party became very anxious that none of them should be allowed to get away. Goering managed to commit suicide the night before his execution, and I remember several members being indignant that the prison conditions were so slack as to let him do this. Another Nazi made a speech on the scaffold, attacking Russia and warning the Allies that they would be hanged by the Bolsheviks. Members were again indignant, about him being allowed to speak and the harm done to peaceful relations between Russia and the West. It was very strange - the old attack on capitalism seemed to disappear for a while.

In Scotland we were once more calling a Scottish Convention. There had been a revival of Scottish Nationalism, but the elements attracted to it were far from radical. When the convention was at last held, it lasted for two days and made an open declaration in favour of a Scottish administration that would have powers over the affairs of Scotland. An enormous number of people attended including Lord Macleod, and representatives of the universities and the legal profession. During the preparatory work one of the lawyers, Campbell, phoned me and told me that a thousand people were praying for me; I said I knew something had been wrong all day!

Campbell was one of the executive that was to guide the affairs of the Scottish Convention when the meeting was over. A whole bunch of middle-class people had emerged to take hold of this executive. They weren't completely unknown to the press, but they were unknown as far as any work in the movement was concerned. Byrne of the Dockers' Union went on it, Lord Cameron the judge, Campbell, John McCormick, of course, and Bob Horne from the Communist Party. At one of the executive meetings, with Bob Horne sitting there, Lord Cameron said that communists should be put up against a wall and shot! Bob told me about it, and I wrote it up for the *Daily Worker*, but the Communist Party still kept hanging on. The last thing these people wanted to be involved with was a revolution.

Even the radical wing of the Scottish National Party was nowhere near revolutionary. Oliver Brown was one of their main propagandists, and he was an uncompromising and courageous pacifist; but some of his ideas were quite reactionary. When the Knoydart crofters took hold of their land in November 1948, I met him and some of the others in the *Daily Worker* offices to discuss it. To my surprise and disgust I found that none of the SNPers wanted the crofters to use modern farming methods, although they were supporting their seizure of the land; they thought they should continue the old primitive methods with no tractors but hand ploughs. Oliver and I had a terrible row.

Johnny Gollan had come up to Scotland during the war and in 1948 he wrote a book called *The Scottish Prospect* for our use. It was a plan for Scotland; it included nationalisation, and as far as most of the party were concerned that made it socialism. Despite the disagreements with the *Looking Ahead* programme, the whole notion of planning for capitalism had become acceptable within the Communist Party. Russia was a successful socialist country, it was argued, because of the Five Year Plans. Everyone became a planner, and they didn't realise that they were planning capitalism. It became the curse of the movement after the second world war. Everywhere you turned there was a plan to solve the problems of Britain by increasing the output of this and that.

Another pamphlet was brought out under Harry Pollitt's name

called *Plan for Prosperity*. I remember Pollitt speaking on it in North Frederick Street, and saying that if only 'we' could get forty million tons of coal exports Britain would be back on its feet! It was a complete departure from all the marxist fundamentals, the concept of the exploitation of the working class by the capitalist class. It was a complete departure from the idea of the class struggle, of all workers against all bosses. It was a plan for British bosses and British workers together.

All these shifts in Party policy drove the older members out. But also, some members saw no point now in working inside the Communist Party when the party was no longer distinguishable from the Labour movement; they might as well be in the trade union as officials, or inside the Labour Party. Many communist 'sympathisers' who became Labour MPs in 1945 soon drifted away. In Glasgow George Middleton became secretary of the trades council and then secretary of the Scottish TUC, dropping his Communist Party affiliations altogether.

George was one of the most competent men in the Scottish Communist Party. However, when he was with the trades council he had several disagreements with party members there. Eventually it was he who arranged that there should be only one speaker at the May Day Parade, which was going to Queens Park because he had clashed with the joint committee that was organising the march to Glasgow Green. I objected strongly to the idea that one speaker, especially one from the Labour Party, could speak for the whole movement; although I had been one of those who had encouraged George to take the job of Glasgow Trades Council Secretary.

To become secretary of the Scottish TUC he had to break with the party, since Communist Party members were banned from holding office with the STUC. He did that quite openly in 1948. Lauchlan and Kerrigan spoke to him and told me that he had agreed to think it over, but George told me he had only agreed to keep it quiet. Later the story came out in the *Sunday Express*; there was very bad feeling about it, and the connection was completely severed.

19. Leaving the Communist Party

Being on the staff of the *Daily Worker* kept me exceptionally busy. I travelled up and down Scotland covering the conferences of the Scottish TUC and the individual trade unions, and collecting information from workers inside the factories. One of the questions I paid most attention to was housing, and over this issue the members of the Glasgow Town Council and I clashed many times.

Even before the end of the war I was concentrating on a housing campaign. There had been no building during the war; there were shortages previously; and it was obvious that there would be an acute shortage of dwellings. Tom Johnston, who became Secretary of State for Scotland, said that the target should be 100,000 homes in 10 years in Scotland. I argued that as Glasgow had a fifth of the population of Scotland it should get a fifth of the houses - 20,000.

I also argued for temporary housing until permanent houses could be built. On the town council Jean Roberts said she had seen temporary houses, and she would wait for permanent ones. I pointed out that she would do her waiting in Mosspark, where she was well housed. I demanded 10,000 temporary houses, and to my surprise the Tories also took it up. The Glasgow Corporation finally did erect 2,500 of them in ten years. The rent was fixed to recover the cost of building them, in those 10 years; but some of the houses lasted 25 years and the rent was still charged, although the cost had been covered more than twice over.

I spent a lot of time in the city chambers arguing with the housing committee, and after the war I wrote four pamphlets on housing. I had researched all the facts about Glasgow housing and the pamphlets were very popular - each one sold about 10,000 copies round the doors. Housing was always an issue which interested the people in Glasgow. It was the issue on which the Labour group on the Corporation had gained support, and big demonstrations could be held over it. When the Corporation proposed to sell the council houses at Merrylee in 1952, workers even came out on strike to join the demonstration. The Scottish Tenants' Association and the Communist Party organised it, and Communist Party members found they could get the factories to stop work. Jock Sheriff brought out Weir's.

I was also a member of the Scottish Committee, the only one who was active in a local party branch. We were still having weekly propaganda meetings in the Gorbals. However, by the end of the 1940s clashes between me and others on the Glasgow Committee led to interference with the Gorbals branch.

I had been unhappy about the plans for increasing production in order to 'save Britain', but that was not the source of my major argument with the Communist Party. After the war that policy was actually reversed for a few months. Pollitt stated that the road forward was the seizure of power by the workers, and took full responsibility as party secretary for the position held in *Looking Ahead* and the other pamphlets.

My disagreements came to a head over the 'peace' agreements that dominated Russian foreign policy from 1944 onwards. In 1943 Stalin had met Churchill, Roosevelt and Chiang Kai-shek in Teheran to discuss how to win the war in Europe. In 1945 they met at Potsdam to finish dividing up Europe. There was a spate of diplomatic agreements at the time. It was hailed as a tremendous achievement that the great 'statesmen' of the capitalist and socialist worlds had come together ... then the entire Communist Party became enthusiastic about the United Nations!

The idea at the end of the war was that there should be a peace agreement between the statesmen of Britain, France, America, China and Russia. At first the statesmen were Churchill, Chiang Kai-shek, etc., but as they lost power other names took their places. The Communist Party thought it was progressive that Stalin was meeting the other world statesmen, even though they were the ones who had agreed to drop the atom bomb on Japan. Truman told Churchill and Stalin about the 'big bomb' America had, and they agreed to its being used. They must have known more about the atom bomb than just that it was big, but that was the Communist Party's defence.

The proposal for a 'peace pact' between the Five Powers was

supported by the collection of signatures for a petition. In 1950 a peace conference in Britain was suggested, and the party wanted us to drop all other work and concentrate on collecting the signatures for a Five-Power Peace Pact.

I wouldn't agree. I argued that the whole conception was anti-Leninist, that it was a policy concerned with diplomacy rather than mobilising the masses. I had always rejected the idea that negotiations between diplomats could replace the self-activity of the working class. I refused to stop holding our weekly propaganda meetings in Gorbals, and I refused to collect any signatures.

Two girls in the Gorbals branch wanted to take out the petition, and they did so regularly; but the rest of us did nothing. Immediately, the leadership of the branch was attacked for not carrying out the decisions of the party. That led to enormous bickering; the Glasgow Committee became nothing but wrangles between those of us who didn't like the bureaucrats and the bureaucrats who didn't like us.

Then the Communist Party pushed the demand for a Five-Power Peace Pact in the Glasgow Trades Council. It was carried in the trades council and sent not to the Scottish TUC, where all resolutions are supposed to go, but to the five governments concerned. The Scottish TUC used the issue to disaffiliate the Glasgow Trades Council, on technical grounds: the trades council has no right to communicate with anybody except on the policy of the STUC.

The Communist Party members fought the disaffiliation in the courts for over six months, but finally the Glasgow Trades Council was disaffiliated; it had to be reorganised, and John Johnstone became the new secretary. At the STUC George Middleton, now secretary, Davie McGibbon, another ex-communist, and John Johnstone made bitter attacks on the CP.

One of the most confusing things about this period was that although the Communist Party were in favour of making agreements with capitalist statesmen, they were violently hostile to Tito. In 1949 Derek Karton produced a book called *Tito's Plot against Europe*, and then in 1951 Klugmann produced one *From Trotsky to Tito* - you know what they thought about Trotsky! Pollitt held a meeting in Glasgow to explain the disagreement with Tito, but it was the first time I had ever seen him completely at a loss; he couldn't reply to criticisms, and it was obvious that he knew no more than the rest of us. He just used all his authority - Pollitt was worshipped in the party - and his usual phrase when someone questioned party policy: 'Comrade, you are attacking Comrade Stalin.'

In 1951 the Communist Party's drift towards planning and diplomatic agreements was crystallised in the discovery of a new road to revolution: parliament! *The British Road to Socialism* was published, and overnight we all became democratic and amazingly interested in Acts of Parliament. It was argued that in Britain even a Tory government would find itself constrained by the will of the people, and we could have a quiet, peaceful road to socialism.

Pollitt said this new policy had been put to Moscow by the British Communist Party, and Stalin had proclaimed it a creative act of marxism. However, in 1963 in East Berlin when Khrushchev spoke on British policy, he said that Stalin had told the Communist Party in Britain that this was to be their new position. Some of us guessed then, anyway. The British Communist Party leaders were so confused that they even floated the idea of liquidating their own party!

John Gollan was in Scotland at the time, and he came back from the executive in London with the suggestion that we should dissolve the party but keep the *Daily Worker* going. The members could enter the Labour movement and strengthen the left wing, but we would keep the paper going as a voice and guide to the left. I was completely against it, and said if there was any attempt to form another party after the Communist Party went out of existence I would support that. There was a pause, nobody answered, and the whole thing was dropped.

A week later Gollan asked me out for a cup of coffee, which was strange in itself. He told me Pollitt had said that, just as Churchill wouldn't preside over the liquidation of the British Empire, he wouldn't preside over the liquidation of the Communist Party! I suspect that they were trying out the idea in Scotland, and decided against it.

It was obvious that Stalin was using the weakest Communist Party in Europe, the British, to overturn policy throughout the European communist movement. Britain was the first country where the Communist Party announced a parliamentary road to socialism. It was complete nonsense. Working-class power can't be won through a capitalist parliament, workers' power is about workers controlling their own lives through their own organisations. It is a completely different state which the workers run themselves.

With the shift to parliamentary work and elections, the work of the factory branches became secondary. There were full-timers all over the country working for the Industrial Department, organising workers at the point of production; but the idea was floated that this department should disappear and be replaced by a Labour Movement Department. But the new department didn't seem to function. There was a big protest from Peter Zinken, the Scottish industrial organiser, and from myself and others.

The idea was that, whereas the old Industrial Department was concerned with industrial action, the Labour Movement Department would influence the Labour Party and the trade unions and change the character of those bodies. The argument was that following the second world war there was a whole new situation and the Communist Party had to respond by broadening out. Nowadays the party has an Industrial Department again, as well as its factory branches, but it doesn't operate as it formerly did.

Any criticism of Stalin was intolerable to the party leadership. If a new change in line needed to be justified or a point needed to be proved, all that was necessary was to find a quotation from the works of Stalin and that was that.

I was never a Stalin-worshipper. I had been in Canada when Trotsky was deported from Russia, and I remember feeling very angry about it; we had always placed Lenin and Trotsky together as the leaders of the Russian Revolution. I was very disturbed by the executions during the thirties, but when the old Bolsheviks 'confessed' at their trials I had to believe the accusations. We couldn't believe that the Moscow Trials were a complete fake. But still I wouldn't join in the adulation of Stalin. I once spoke at a workers' open forum on Stalin's early background as a socialist, and surprised a lot of the audience by saying I was against praising him to the skies.

Because of my long involvement with the labour movement I knew its history, and when Stalin's *History of the Communist Party in the Soviet Union* came out I knew there was something wrong. In his book, everything worthwhile in the Russian Revolution was done by Stalin and everything that was treacherous was done by Trotsky. It simply wasn't true: Trotsky was the organiser of the Red Army which saved the Russian Revolution. But the Communist Party actually ran education classes based on this book! They asked all the branches to run the same classes, but I made sure that the Gorbals branch never did. Apart from the history that was all lies, the chapter on dialectical materialism was bloody terrible.

The very last book Stalin wrote was the *Economic Problems of Socialism in the USSR*. In it, he said that the law of value operated in Russia. In Marx's economics, the law of value is bound up with the expropriation of surplus-value from the working class, and the exploitation of that class by the capitalist class. To say that the law of value existed in Russia was damning. It meant that Russia wasn't socialist but capitalist: that there was commodity production, with labour-power sold as a commodity.

Finlay Hart, a plumber by trade and a member of the Boiler-makers, and one time Scottish secretary of the party, supported everything. When I criticised the book at the Scottish Committee he jumped to his feet and said that *this* was the turn that the party had been waiting for. He always said that, no matter what the turn was; and the other sycophants followed.

One of Stalin's last acts was to accuse his doctors of treason and conspiracy. No sooner were they arrested - not even sent for trial - than the *Daily Worker* came out with the most savage indictment of these men. It found them guilty almost before knowing their names. It was scandalous, and sickened a lot of party members. Fortunately for the doctors Stalin died, and they were reprieved.

The worship of Stalin affected all levels of life inside the party. Because decisions were taken in Moscow and the party leaders merely had to justify the line, the party became dominated by men with no independence: mere bureaucrats. Harry Pollitt had done mass work, but the other leaders were people trained inside the Communist Party. John Gollan gained his reputation during the 'social fascist' period, when he made his famous appeal to the troops. But he had no real experience of the movement - yet Pollitt was determined that he would be the next general secretary. Gollan was walking along the road in front of us one day when Pollitt said to me: 'There is your next general secretary.' I wasn't very happy about it, and among the mass of the membership there wasn't much enthusiasm either.

The new members on the Glasgow Committee didn't have much background in the movement. They had come in during the second world war, not understanding marxist politics; they followed every latest shift in the party line, and the meetings became a battle-ground. Some of the new members seemed to be obsessed with the petition for the Five-Power Peace Pact. No matter what was under discussion, my branch was always being criticised by the Glasgow Committee for its attitude to that damned pact.

Whatever the Gorbals branch said or proposed was turned into an attack on us for not carrying out the policy of the party. Eventually a committee of investigation was set up with McIlhone, the Glasgow secretary, and Jim Hill on it. Jim Hill was a probation officer, and the investigation was more like a police enquiry. I respected McIlhone because he had always made great personal sacrifices for the party, but he was also very bitter against anyone else who didn't hold the same views as he did. Then they tried to set up a three-way meeting of the Gorbals branch, the Glasgow Committee and the Scottish Committee.

It was obvious that the party wanted me removed from the leadership of the Gorbals branch. The day of the meeting I phoned Lauchlan and advised him not to propose it or he would be defeated; but I said that I would leave privately. He said that such a proposal was the last thing he would dream of. At the meeting however, he seconded McIlhone's motion that I leave Gorbals branch. I was furious, and went to town. Their proposal didn't get a single vote, and then the whole thing had to go to a Glasgow aggregate.

At that aggregate I fought against the whole Scottish leadership, and I was amazed by the support that I got. Over four hundred came to the meeting in the McLellan Galleries, and a large number took part in the discussion. The members seemed to be pleased that at last someone was raising their voice at an open meeting of the party. The Glasgow Committee were afraid to take the vote, and adjourned the aggregate for another week.

Such an adjournment was very unusual. During the week they kept interviewing me and finally, on the day of the meeting, Kerrigan was brought up from London to talk to me. He wanted to know what I was going to say at the meeting. I honestly didn't know. All I could tell him was that whatever I said I wouldn't split the party.

That night I was the most popular communist in Scotland. Everyone wanted to shake my hand. I had saved the party and was therefore a hero. I was completely wrong: but I still thought that the Communist party was necessary for the development of the working-class movement.

It didn't last long. The situation between me and the Glasgow Committee became impossible. For two years before I left I wasn't invited to speak at any propaganda meetings apart from our outdoor ones in Gorbals. Each quarter I filled in a form saying which dates I had vacant and gave it to the Glasgow Committee. Then I learned that branches were asking for me and being told I was fully booked up. I stopped filling in the forms, and the committee even had a row about that.

My final break came a year after the aggregate at the McLellan Galleries. It was over an incident at the Scottish Congress of the party, at Woodside Halls. At the beginning of the congress there was a standing ovation for the secretary, Lauchlan. At the end there was another ovation for his closing speech, which was a load of tripe. I was outside the hall at the time, phoning the story of the congress to London. A lot of the younger members wouldn't stand up. Two of them, Les Foster and Eddie Donaldson, were on the Glasgow Committee, and they and two others were pulled up before the Scottish Secretariat. I was asked to agree that something must be done to discipline them. I refused; the whole thing was absurd. To my surprise, two of them were suspended from membership for three months.

Of course the real reason for the suspensions was that they had been opposed to the Five-Power Peace Pact and *The British Road to Socialism*. Eddie was from the Maryhill branch, and he had been supporting the Gorbals branch on the Glasgow Committee. As I refused to agree with their suspension, a motion was proposed that my position on the *Daily Worker* should be examined and that I should be removed from the Scottish Secretariat. Lauchlan opposed the motion and it only got two votes. When he went to Hungary the secretariat met and discussed the issue again.

By now the fight had become very personal and bitter. Instead of being a political battle, it dissolved into one of personalities. The party attacked me for lack of discipline and for attacking the Scottish leadership. They said I had been a member of the Scottish Committee for twenty-three years, had stood countless times as a parliamentary and municipal candidate for the party, and all I was doing now was disrupting the party. In return I made jibes about police methods and the bureaucracy that had developed.

While Lauchlan was in Hungary Gordon McLellan, the present general secretary of the Communist Party who was then the assistant secretary in Scotland, asked me to go and see him. He had all the correspondence spread round him and he said: 'They want you to change your attitude or else.' 'Or else' was obviously expulsion from the party. Rumours were circulating about my disagreement with the CP, which both they and I kept denying. The *Daily Express* offered me £500 for the exclusive story, and the *Daily Record* wanted a series of articles at £50 each. I loathed those papers, and wouldn't hear of it.

The Friday of that week I received a letter from the Communist Party outlining my alternatives - either withdraw my attitude or face expulsion. In reply I wrote a letter to the Scottish Secretariat and went to the Scottish Committee. While I was there I was called away to open up the *Daily Worker* offices. Thinking about it, I realised there was no point in going back. I sat down in the office and wrote two letters of resignation: one from the *Daily Worker*, and one from the Communist Party.

It was obvious that the newspapers would print versions of what had happened, and to prevent this I decided to give the story to the *News Chronicle*. But I had forgotten that the other papers would see the Tuesday edition on Monday night. That night I was trying to hold off a dozen reporters at the door.

After the story broke in the *News Chronicle* I had a meeting with Matthews of the *Daily Worker* and John Gollan. They kept asking me what the attitude of my friends in the Labour Party would be, what my friends in the Catholic Church would say. It was all news to me. I didn't know that I had any friends in either, specially the Catholic Church. I told them I intended to go back to engineering. Gollan told me that idea was hopeless but perhaps Jock Anderson, a Communist Party member with a small engineering business, might be able to fix me up.

Before we parted I promised to meet them at nine the next morning. But that night Harry Pollitt was interviewed on the radio; he said he was sure that I would regret my resignation and the publicity I had given to it. The next morning I met Gollan and Matthews for two minutes and told them that I was finished. I wrote my own version of the whole business and I gave it to *Reynolds' News*, the Co-operative paper, for the NUJ fee of 15 guineas.

Only a handful left the Communist Party when I did. Eddie

Donaldson, Les Foster, Alec Bernstein, Bill Gunn, Bill McCulloch, Hugh Savage, Matt McGinn, all came out. We were expecting more to join us. A whole number of people used to come to the office and tell me their grievances, but they all stayed in.

If I had persisted against the Scottish leadership the previous year I would have got half the audience at the aggregate meeting, the Glasgow Committee would have been divided and it would have been a political battle. Members were worried because of the growing reformism. But I doubt if I could have split the party even then. In 1951 Eric Heffer had tried to raise a vote against the line at the Party Congress, but he didn't get anybody to support him. He quoted Lenin to attack Pollitt, and was expelled from the party; his branch, Welwyn Garden City, was reorganised, and he couldn't fight at all. I was better known and had a better base in Glasgow, but I am doubtful if we could have got a real fight.

To us the Communist Party still stood for the revolution. Despite everything it appeared to be the only marxist party and we were sure that outside the party we would be excluded from the fight for the revolution. Lukacs, the Hungarian communist, explained his own compromise in his writings by the fact that he thought he would not be able to play a part in the struggle against fascism in the thirties if he was excluded from the party. We felt the same.

The Communist Party spread the most fantastic rumours about me. To get away from all the newspapermen I went to Ireland for a few days; when I got back, I found that the reason I had gone was to be trained as a Catholic missionary. There were stories that I was going to join the Labour Party, or work for the *Daily Record*.

People started getting in touch with me from all over the country, and there was talk of forming another Communist Party. Gerry Healey the Trotskyist wanted me and the others to join with him. He came up and we had a meeting; but he was a very hard, aggressive character, and his organisation was even more bureaucratic than the Communist Party. If someone disagreed with him he used to say 'Send him to the dunghill - that's where he belongs', and throughout the organisation there was very little discussion. It created a bad impression.

Finally Eric Heffer came along with the idea of forming a federation of marxist groups in different cities. We called a meeting

I

in Glasgow which was attended by a couple of hundred people. Both Eric and I spoke. We gave out reprints of Lenin's last will and testament, in which he described Trotsky as 'the ablest man on the Central Committee' and said that Stalin should be removed. It caused a big stir. The ordinary Communist Party member had never even heard of the letter.

We followed this up by issuing a paper called *Revolt*. Matt McGinn was in favour of forming another Communist Party, but we only had twenty or so members and Eric and I stuck to the federation idea. We issued nine or ten numbers of *Revolt*, and printed about 2,000 copies each time. We sold it in the trades councils and whichever factories we were in; we never sold it in the Labour Party, and had very little to do with the Labour Party. It was printed in Glasgow, but the real headquarters of the federation was Liverpool, where Eric lived, and we held meetings there every two months or so. We were trying to revive the revolutionary trend inside the Communist Party, to revive the ideas of workers' councils and workers' power against the parliamentarism which had overtaken the CP.

The Glasgow group in the marxist federation met every Sunday night. We stuck it for a couple of years, but eventually we exhausted ourselves. The entire federation lasted only about eighteen months. Eric went back into the Labour Party and became Vice-Chairman of the Liverpool Trades Council and ultimately a Labour MP.

Instead of concentrating on the Communist Party we should have gone to the workers who weren't yet acquainted with marxism and won them to our ideas. The federation was really too small and too loose, but it was a tragedy that it broke up before a large number left the Communist Party in 1956. It is a mistake to think that people left over Hungary only: they streamed out all year. One of the crucial factors was Krushchev's speech at the 20th Party Congress. The speech was held in secret session but the papers got hold of it and it was reprinted in full. In the speech Krushchev denounced Stalin and admitted to the crimes of the labour camps; he also pointed out that the majority of the delegates to the 17th Party Congress, when Stalin had said that all the problem had been solved, were themselves executed.

But in Glasgow the Communist Party never referred to Khrushchev's speech except to repeat the phrase that he had used to explain the terrible crimes - 'the cult of the individual'. Only last year, in 1976, did John Gollan finally use lengthy quotes from the speech.

The day after Krushchev was removed from office *everything* he had ever written was removed from the shelves of the Communist Party bookshop in Glasgow.

Some of those who left had been wanting to get out anyway. They had joined the Communist Party during the second world war when it was popular, and were more Liberal than Communist. But many of those who left were sincere, devoted people who thought that, since so many had become disillusioned over Hungary, it would now be possible to set up a new workers' party.

Not very many left in Glasgow, because there didn't appear to be anywhere else to go. I understood this: when I left I simply didn't know what I was going to do. There was a strong local leadership in Glasgow, and a good working-class base, and these prevented people leaving. The middle-class element in the Glasgow Party was small, and they were already drifting out. Those who joined Gerry Healey's group didn't stay very long. Part of his policy was to work within the Labour Party, so that when people were disillusioned by his organisation they remained in the Labour Party and took positions in it.

I felt no temptation at all to join the Labour Party. I had spent so much time watching their manoeuvrings; I had left both the ILP and the Communist Party because of their reformist tendencies, and I wasn't going to join another reformist party. In some ways the ILP was better than the Communist Party. When Bernstein said to Kautsky 'It's not the goal that matters, it's the movement', that was a terrible thing for a socialist to say. But now, for the Communist Party, it is not even the movement but the party that matters. The party has become a clique in substitution for the mass movement, and the only socialism their eyes can see is that which is patterned on Russia. The old ILPers had a better picture than that - there was a dream of freedom in their socialism.

After the marxist federation collapsed I became a member of a new, small group of marxist humanists. They were an American group who kept writing to me about their ideas. Earlier, Eric Heffer would have nothing to do with them, and I was very wary because I thought they were trying to turn Marx into some kind of bourgeois democratic thinker. Finally I read a book called *Marxism and Freedom* written by one of their leading members, Raya Dunayevskaya, and I realised that what she was saying was of exceptional importance.

She dealt with Marx as a philosopher, as a student of Hegel, but did it in a way that ordinary people could read and understand. The book pointed to marxism as being more than economics, and I think that is true. What actuated Lenin, quite apart from the marxist scientific analysis, was a dream of a future society. The analysis is of no use unless it opens the possibilities of great human developments in a society free from oppression and exploitation. Raya pointed out this element in Marx's thought and linked it with his philosophical development.

Raya came over here twice and we organised some fairly good meetings. Of course the meetings were small, and some of those people have dropped out now, but we were able to publicise the book and push the ideas out. Our marxist humanist group in Glasgow used to distribute a small bulletin and it was useful while it lasted because many people in Glasgow didn't know that there could be another type of communism other than that of the CP. Really the Communist Party have no right to call themselves communists; state planning has nothing to do with workers' power and real communism.

We tried to explain communism as a system where the workers themselves make the revolution, and Raya's book showed that this was what Marx and Lenin thought as well. She also put forward the state-capitalist analysis of Russia. She argued that it was no longer a socialist country, and had the same type of development as a capitalist society except that everything was owned by the state. The International Socialists, who were very small then, had a very similar analysis, and their subsequent growth as the alternative to the Communist Party has proved that those possibilities were there.

After years of working in the Communist Party it was very hard to join a small group and find myself isolated from the mass of workers. My area of activity was always street meetings and demonstrations. I had to turn my energies in another direction, and became a delegate to the Glasgow Trades Council.

20. Back to Work

For eight months after I left the party and the *Daily Worker*, I couldn't get a job. While I was on the paper I had bought a room and kitchen in Glasgow for £250, and now I was having a struggle to pay it off. I tried for a number of jobs. One was at a place I had applied to before the first world war, when I was put on a short-list of six out of fifty applicants. They asked what school I went to: it was a catholic school, and of course I didn't get the job. In 1953 they took me round and showed me the engine and I was quite entranced with the job. Then they asked me where I had been employed before and I said the *Daily Worker* - and that was it for the second time.

I was over sixty and it wasn't easy to find work. Every week I had to sign on at the Kinning Park Labour Exchange. One week I met Jock Sheriff there; he had got the sack from Weir's but now had a job at Harland and Wolff's, and he asked me if I wanted one. Another CP member, a labourer in the shipyard called Johnny Gunn, spoke for me to the foreman. The foreman started me, even though as soon as he saw me and found who I was he realised there might be trouble.

I was sixty-two when I started in. I could have got a job outside of industry, but I liked working in engineering. Lay-offs came after I had been there a fortnight, but although the time-keeper was a catholic and everyone was expecting me to be laid off he kept me on. I worked there until I was sixty-nine, and even now I miss it.

I had a very interesting job. I was given the drawings for all the tanks and had to see that all the pieces of each tank were laid in place so that the fitter only had to put it together. I had four labourers with cranes to lift the various pieces, and I got them laid so that the fitters didn't have to consult any drawings at all.

This led me into a very embarrassing position when the foreman went on strike. The men were waiting for work, and I was worried that I might be doing part of the foreman's job. I consulted the head foreman. He wasn't on strike but he seemed sympathetic, and he said I shouldn't speak to any of the men or tell them where anything went - I should leave the pieces in position and let them make their own mistakes. I did this. The foremen were out for three months and won their increase, and I was pleased - the foremen in Harland's were decent people although, of course, it was associated with the Belfast yard and therefore most of them were protestants. But they did not discriminate against people who held other opinions.

We had some big disputes in Harland's. There was a time when five boilermakers stopped the whole yard. It was a typical boiler-makers' dispute. The men's shop-stewards brought them out without consulting the other unions through the shop-stewards' committee; they were asking for more money to maintain the differential between them and the shopfitters. We didn't mind them trying to get more, but we did object to them ignoring the rest of us. In our union branch we condemned their action for breaking the unity of the workers in the yard, and the sectarian attitude to their own craft interest.

I re-joined the AUEW as soon as I got my job in Harland's. Because I was now over-age I had to join as a Class 5 member instead of Class 1. I had been a life-long Class 1 member, but when I went to work on the *Daily Worker* I joined the NUJ and was a member of that for 14 years. I was made chairman of my AUEW branch and I am still the Chairman even though I am retired.

From my AUEW branch I was elected to the trades council. When the Scottish TUC reorganised the Glasgow Trades Council after its disaffiliation John Johnstone became the new secretary. David McGibbon was the chairman - an ex-communist and now bitterly anti-party. After him Tony Hart became the chairman and he did not have fights with anyone. He was an excellent chairman; he held the meetings in order and allowed plenty of scope for discussion.

I did a lot of work for the trades council while they were in charge. John Johnstone was a Labour man and far from revolutionary, but he was a very honest fellow and did much more effective work of a mass character than the Communist Party members who have more recently been in charge. He kept a tight hold on the organisation of the trades council, specially on finance - every last penny was accounted for. He worked very hard despite the fact that at that time the secretaryship was still a voluntary unpaid position, and he worked very hard also as a councillor.

When the hundredth anniversary of Glasgow Trades Council came in 1958, I mentioned it to Tony Hart and was given the job of doing the research on the history of the trades council for a booklet. It was thought that the minutes-books had been lost in a fire before the first world war, but I discovered them and took them to the Mitchell Library. I used them for my booklet and travelled round looking up old records of the trade-union movement. It was all published as a centenary pamphlet.

After this someone drew my attention to the Carlton weavers who were shot down at Molendinar Bridge in Townhead, in 1787. I discovered that six weavers had been shot, not three as had been believed. The leader, James Grainger, was tried and whipped through the streets before he was deported for seven years. The Dragoons who shot the weavers down were given a present of boots and stockings by the magistrates!

In 1820 Scottish working men tried to form an army and march to Stirling. They were caught, arrested and beheaded. Two are buried in the Site Hill cemetery, and every year a gathering to commemorate their rising is held there. I often attend and speak. It is the only working-class event that the SNP attend.

After I was retired from Harland and Wolff's in 1960 I was able to give my time to working on campaigns on behalf of the trades council. One of the best was a demonstration against the American nuclear submarine base at Holy Loch. The first demonstration there was organised by CND in 1961; we organised the second with their support.

CND, the Campaign for Nuclear Disarmament, grew at the end of the 1950s and was one of the most encouraging developments after the second world war. Many of the people leading the campaign were ex-communists, and it seemed like a new start for the labour movement. In London Peter Cadogan became national secretary, and in Glasgow prominent members included Norrie Blythman, Roddy McFarquar and Neil Carmichael. The Communist Party itself came round only slowly and reluctantly to supporting CND, and then attempted to dominate it.

I helped organise the Holy Loch demonstration alongside John Johnstone. We visited trade-union branches, sent directives to them, and put out leaflets: the aim was for the demonstration to come from the trade-union movement as well as from CND. I was most insistent that we shouldn't carry anti-American slogans. The Communist Party's line was that Russian diplomats were looking for a way to peace and only American imperialism was threatening war. They took a really anti-American stance - nothing good came out of America; and as we were marching against an American base it was an easy position to win people to.

However, the International Socialists (IS, now the Socialist Workers' Party) came out with the slogan 'Neither Washington nor Moscow, but International Socialism'. I was delighted with that slogan. I made it my line, and we managed to curb the anti-Americanism on the demonstration and stopped them shouting their slogans in Dunoon.

To take this stand against anti-Americanism was very important, because we could then raise the issue of Russia - a 'socialist' country having nuclear weapons. The utter hypocrisy of the Communist Party was shown up in the Glasgow Trades Council during the Cuba crisis. Dan Kelly - the best communist speaker on the trades council at that time - got up on his feet to argue that Russia would not withdraw her missiles from Cuba unless America withdrew her bases from Greece. Nuclear war could easily have broken out within the hour, yet the communists were still prepared to play party politics. We had a terrible battle that night.

Shortly before John Johnstone ceased to be secretary of the trades council I was sent as a delegate to the Scottish TUC. When I spoke, I argued that the shipbuilding industry faced grave problems and that we were due for a decline in the whole industrial complex in Scotland because of its traditional dependence on the shipyards and marine engineering. I collected a great deal of information while I worked in Harland and Wolff's and used it to predict the growth of international competition, the decline in orders and the closure of the yards. Had I still been a member of the Communist Party my speech would have brought the house down. There was a large CP element in the Scottish TUC by then, and they weren't going to applaud an ex-member: the silence was stony!

After the STUC had met, the Glasgow Trades Council called a conference on shipbuilding. I re-stated my figures, and said the future was terrible. John Chalmers, the secretary of the Boilermakers then argued that the future was rosy. Finlay Hart came in to speak and said neither of us was correct, and a middle ground between our views existed. What has happened since then can hardly be described as a middle ground. When I was a boy there were 23 yards on the Clyde; now there are six.

The fight at Upper Clyde Shipbuilders was supposed to save jobs through the 'work-in' - but it didn't. Instead of sitting in, holding the ships they were working on, and extending the fight - they finished the ships for the receiver! Over two-and-a-half thousand jobs were lost at UCS. Jimmy Reid and the Communist Party led that policy; now he has left the Communist Party.

After Johnstone left the trades council it was taken over by the Communist Party. None of the chairmen was a CPer, but the party took and has kept control through the secretary's full-time post. First Hugh Wyper was appointed secretary, then he decided he needed an assistant secretary; this was John Reidford, who was once an official in the Firemen's Union and is now the secretary of the trades council. The lifting of the ban on Communist Party members enabled Hugh Wyper to get a job as an official of the Transport and General Workers' Union, although he had only held a union card for a couple of years.

With Wyper as Secretary, the CP began to dominate the trades council and the form that its discussion could take. This is their attitude to international solidarity and 'peace' conferences. The international delegations sent abroad by the trades council are usually to Leningrad and back! On one of the return delegations, one of the Russian representatives was a member of the government as well as a trade-unionist. I took the opportunity to raise the question of the mass executions in Russia. I pointed out that it wasn't only Stalin who supported this policy but the whole party: Khrushchev himself had called for executions at a mass meeting in Red Square. The atmosphere was very hostile, and the delegate said that Khrushchev was speaking not for the party but as a party worker! I have had similar arguments over bodies like the European Security Council which the CP was very keen to support.

Since the communists took over I have not been asked to do anything for the trades council. In fact, apart from supporting one or two demonstrations, they haven't led any struggles; even their proposals to the Glasgow District Committee about housing and education are very vague. The reason why they have been able to dominate is that the trades council nowadays has no life. The delegates are sent from trade-union branches, not shop-stewards' committees. Often they don't represent anybody - they are simply asked by the branch secretaries to attend. The vitality of the labour movement is now on the shop floor.

The Scottish TUC likewise is no longer a powerful body. Once there were a number of Scottish trade unions - the Scottish painters, the Scottish miners, the Scottish joiners, the Scottish bakers - that could make their own policy decisions. Unlike the British TUC, the trades councils in Scotland still send delegates to the STUC - in fact the Scottish TUC was founded because the TUC stopped all trades councils delegations at the end of the last century. Recently the Scottish TUC also has attempted to do this, but the proposal was defeated. But in spite of having this direct representation, the STUC is not the lively body it once was. Its policy-making powers are completely curbed by the decisions of the big national unions and the TUC.

The biggest event the Scottish TUC was involved in during the seventies had nothing to do with industrial policies at all. It was the calling of the Scottish Assembly. Almost all the speakers there were in favour of Scottish nationalism and some kind of Scottish administration. Jimmy Reid, who was still in the Communist Party, made a stronger nationalist speech than any of the members of the SNP, and the SNP tried to get a standing ovation for him! However, Jimmy Jack, who was the secretary of the Scottish TUC, made a closing speech which attacked the SNP and the whole idea of separating Scottish and English workers.

There is a lot of confusion in the Labour Party, the Communist Party and the Scottish TUC over the whole nationalist debate. In the past the old radicals were in favour of a federated Britain; it was incorporated in the ILP's attitude. From the 19th century there was a Scottish Home Rule Association to which members of the ILP and the Labour Party were always sympathetic. And the Communist Party, having changed its position towards other organisations, worked with the SNP which was established in the thirties.

When the CP was a revolutionary movement in the twenties it opposed Scottish nationalism, but the Labour movement in Scotland has never been against it. Labour antagonism developed not on matters of principle but when the SNP grew as a rival political party;

but the Labour Party were correct in pointing out that the SNP wasn't a working-class party and had no social policy. The fact that all the SNP's other policies are Tory is disguised by its total identification with Scottish self-government. Their record in local government in the late sixties almost destroyed them, it was so bad - on housing particularly. The major attraction now is that they might be able to get more parliamentary seats and have promised the earth from 'Scottish oil'.

The Scottish nationalism of today is nothing like what was advocated by John Maclean, although some of the nationalists use his name. He drew his inspiration from the Irish national struggle, and was hoping for a speedier revolution of Scottish workers. He would have supported the present struggle in Northern Ireland against the Orange state and the British army. Although demonstrations have been organised in support of the Irish Civil Rights Association, and in sympathy with those massacred by the British army on 'Bloody Sunday', members of the SNP - or the Labour and Communist Parties - did not take part in them. None of them had the courage to offend the protestants in Glasgow. It proves that their nationalism is only a reflection of British nationalism and does not mean national liberation.

It is not surprising that Ireland erupted in 1968-69. I well remember 1912 when catholic shipyard workers were dumped in the river, and others murdered, to help ensure a monopoly of jobs for protestant workers. When the protestants actually became the majority government in 1921 the results were terrifying. Apart from the most open gerrymandering of boundaries to ensure that the catholics got no representation in local councils or in parliament, there was legalised anti-catholic violence. It was in effect a protestant dictatorship and the policemen wore guns in their holsters, with the most extreme powers of search and detention.

The Falls Road where the catholics lived in Belfast was a terrible district with bad housing and enormous unemployment. Many protestant districts were not much better - living conditions which wouldn't be tolerated elsewhere in Britain - but they have always been just that bit better than the catholics, and that keeps them supporting the Orange state. It was only right and proper that the catholic minority should make a fight of it and try to get the civil rights they had been denied all those years. No one who pretends to be a democrat can actually justify the denial of the right to a job, a house and a vote to the catholics of the North; the movement of 1968 was a popular one. Bernadette Devlin was elected to parliament, and the government made some slight concessions.

But as soon as the catholic population got even a little more aggressive and demanding, the state stepped in. Demonstrators were brutally beaten up by the police, and the whole situation erupted. Once the police had attacked them the catholics defended themselves from the Orangemen (who had all the arms) and the British government sent in troops. Now the government can see nothing beyond more and more troops and sending men to jail. Although the majority of people murdered in Northern Ireland have been catholics, it is seldom the protestants who are behind bars: nearly all the men in jail are catholics. With the British government backing the status quo and protestant bigotry, it is no surprise that the IRA was able to re-establish itself in 1969.

The more enlightened of the British working-class movement are organising for the withdrawal of troops and arguing that the problem is one for the *whole* people of Ireland to solve themselves. One of the problems of the Irish crisis since 1968 has been that the catholics in the North have not had the support of the South - if they had, it might have been possible to force the British government to re-unite Ireland. The Communist Party policy for more legislation to protect catholic 'rights' is no solution at all, and the Belfast Trades Council has played no part in the struggle. A 'peace' movement will not help the catholics either. While the entire state apparatus is founded on protestantism, what hope is there for the minority from the 'peace-keepers'?

It is harder than ever now to raise the Irish question in Glasgow, though I have spoken at the demonstrations which were organised. While the Labour Party and the communists have been completely unprincipled on the matter, the Catholic Church and others are making sure that the ordinary Irish don't get mixed up with revolutionaries. The only people who have supported the demonstrations have been IS, IMG and one or two other left groups. Whereas thousands should have marched, only hundreds have turned out.

Throughout my life my main revolutionary activity has been organising street meetings and mass demonstrations, and even now I feel isolated from the mass movement. Fortunately the growth of revolutionary groups and the revival of interest in marxist ideas has made it possible for me to address meetings both on current problems and on the history of our movement. I have spoken to many meetings and many bodies of people, but the first time in my life that I spoke in the Albert Hall was in 1976 when I was nearly eighty-five!

The meeting was organised by the Right to Work Campaign. This is a campaign against unemployment organised by members of the International Socialists. Although IS is the leading body, it isn't confined to IS members just as the NUWM was led by but not restricted to the Communist Party. In Glasgow IS have a number of delegates on the trades council and organised some good meetings - at some of which I spoke - on the right to work.

I was invited to speak in Manchester at the meeting which saw off the first Right to Work march to London, in March 1976. The hall was so packed that the doors had to be shut, leaving people outside. The atmosphere was electric. The marchers were sitting on the platform and in the front seats. John Deason, the secretary of the campaign, chaired the meeting and Paul Foot of *Socialist Worker* was one of the main speakers. I had known Paul from a long time back, when the Glasgow branch of IS held tiny meetings in the Horseshoe Bar in the early sixties. I always liked him. He is one of the great speakers of today's left. He is humorous and knows how to hold an audience, and he appeals to workers.

When I spoke I said that the labour movement was *our* movement and didn't belong to the trade-union leaders. The people below made the movement, not the people at the top: we had to let the likes of Jack Jones and Len Murray know that we had come to take possession of our movement. The Communist Party now argues that everything must be done officially, but it is the strength of the rank and file that counts. I pointed out that the General Strike had been official - and so had the betrayal. Those people who required the signatures of Len Murray and Jack Jones to provide a revolution in Britain were not to be trusted. That speech went down very well with the audience and with the marchers.

The next day I joined the procession to see them off from Manchester. There were four or five hundred of us, and it was obvious from the enthusiasm that the march was going to be a success. It did something we never did: the marchers went into factories and building sites and challenged the employed to support the unemployed. We were against overtime and wanted a shorter working week in the thirties, but the trade-union movement was very weak and all the employed workers were frightened of losing their jobs. Only once on a hunger march did we enter a factory: that was in 1932 and we really did it to get out of the rain - the manager was very surprised! Wal Hannington took part in some factory raids in the early twenties, but it was never made the purpose of a march.

At the end of the march a huge meeting was held at the Albert Hall. More than five thousand people were there, and a collection was taken of over £4,000. Ernie Roberts, the assistant secretary of the Engineers, was there. Most of the audience were actually employed workers, and that was one of the most encouraging things. The Right to Work Campaign has shown that it is possible to get a unity of employed and unemployed workers, because those in work are themselves prepared to fight. Workers now fight threatened redundancies by sit-ins, whereas in the old days they fought after they were made unemployed. The Right to Work Campaign doesn't talk of 'social fascism' but of the unity of the entire working-class movement. I believe that with that attitude we could have built an NUWM ten times the size it was.

The revolutionary socialist movement now is very different from the one I grew up in. All we knew of Marx was his economic writings. Now that we have his early work, the outlook of the movement has completely changed. Though the majority of people in the movement may not have read those writings they have still been influenced by them; that has changed the whole approach to propaganda and education. The understanding of socialism is extended far beyond the confines of the study of capitalism - although that cannot be ignored - and into the study of Marx's philosophy.

After I left the Communist Party I read widely. I probably read more marxist theory than at any other time of my life since the first world war. I came to the conclusion that the present-day movement has three lines to work on. First, we have to attach greater importance to the part played by man himself in changing history. Second, we mustn't separate Marx as a philosopher from Marx as an economist. Third, we must recognise that the abolition of private property is not enough to establish socialism: Russia is not socialist.

These three aspects can help us to form a marxist approach to the problems facing us, and identify what is really revolutionary marxism against those who merely claim to be marxists.

The Communist Party has always had a mechanical materialist view of the relationship between man and history. They do not appreciate man's part in changing the world; as far as they are concerned, history makes men. Yet Bukharin and Lenin went to great lengths to explain that man was not something pushed around by economic forces but was part of the dialectical process of human development in which human action was the most important contribution. Action is changed by ideas. The proletariat are workers, not just an economic force, who hold and discuss ideas.

When Lenin wrote his marginal notes on Hegel's *System of Logic*, he seemed to be surprised at the realisation that thought is not just a reflection of the real world but is also creative. Of course in marxism thought is not spirit, as in Hegel, but part of the activity of real human beings living in a material world. Lenin realised, and other marxists must realise, that the mechanical materialism of the past was all wrong. He broke with the assumption of the German Social-Democrats that socialism would *inevitably* be brought about by economic forces, and saw that it was the creative act of the working class to solve the economic crisis of capitalism. Because it is creative, it isn't inevitable; the capitalist system can end up as fascism, as in the thirties in Germany, rather than socialism.

Because Marx wasn't a mechanical materialist I don't believe that there is any break between his earlier works like the *Economic and Philosophical Manuscripts*, and the subsequent writing of *Capital*. Marx's philosophy is expressed all through *Capital*. It is entirely wrong to split the two as if there were a young philosophical Marx and an old economic Marx. This is the approach the Communist Party used - Stalin and his theoreticians constantly denied the 'philosophical' Marx and therefore denied the self-activity of the working class. But whereas the Stalinists used to say 'only look at the economics', the intellectuals now are only looking at the philosophy or the 'politics'. Both approaches are wrong: our job as revolutionaries is to see the economics in the philosophy as well as the philosophy in the economics. The intellectuals are writing for one another instead of for working-class people; they seem to think that workers can't read!

The existence of state-capitalist countries which are described as 'socialist' or 'communist' has led to a lot of confusion among working-class people. Socialism isn't about state planning, and the state controlling and exploiting the working class; it is about the working class owning the means of production and planning their lives for themselves. The existence of a Communist Party which is in favour of parliamentary politics, has abandoned Leninism, and does not organise rank-and-file industrial struggles, has also led to confusion over the term 'communist'. I was a member of that party for over thirty years, but I always had a dream of communism as something more than a nationalised industry. All of us who joined in the early twenties had a vision of Soviets and working-class power.

I think I am clearer now than I ever was about what socialism means for humanity. The careerism of various trade-union leaders, and the way the minds of many workers have been poisoned by racialism, do not conceal the fact that there are more struggles for freedom now than ever before. The future is ours. Attempts to use the working class to extricate capitalism from its difficulties will meet with only limited success. Our job is to fight off racialism and all forms of reaction and give *our* message to the workers and to all humanity. We know now how to fight unemployment and raise living standards, and that fight is inseparable from ending capitalism and bringing in the new society. I hope that my life has been of some use to that movement; but in the end it is the self-activity of the working class that counts.

In my life I have probably, almost inevitably, made mistakes. But though for many years I was misled, and misled myself, into believing in a society which wasn't socialist, I don't regret the time and energy and sometimes the hardship involved. The movement kept me alive. The movement owes me nothing; on the contrary, I owe it much. Life would have been empty without it.

Appendix

The book was written over a period of five years. The first two-and-a-half years were spent in weekly tape-recording sessions with Harry, which were then transcribed. The remaining two-and-a-half years consisted of various attempts to construct the transcripts into a coherent written form. Looking back, it might have been possible to cut the time taken by half, but certainly no less. It may therefore be of some use to others undertaking similar projects to outline the various stages of this one.

1. Initially I recorded two tapes in which Harry spoke without interruption about his life and what he considered to be the major events in it. Because Harry is a public speaker and has read widely in the working-class history of his own time, he spoke about many things he had not been particularly involved in at the time. I should have spent more time on this, allowing Harry a free rein in order to capture his summary of his own life and reading, before my questioning began. His story was itself a historical document in terms of the questions he had consistently been asked in the past.

2. We then embarked on a series of tape-recordings which more or less covered Harry's entire life-story. We met once a week; each time we dealt with a few years in rough chronological order, or a major event, or critical personalities in the story. The taping was not always chronological. Often a current event had sparked Harry's memory of previous issues, and after discussing the present situation we started to tape.

This stage took over a year, working on a weekly session lasting an hour to an hour and a half. The period could have been shortened by increasing the number of sessions each week. We were both tired and losing concentration at the end of a session, so it would not have been possible to lengthen them.

3. Having completed the first set of tapes, I began to re-record Harry's life starting at his early years in Glasgow and working

through those points which appeared to me to need elaborating or were missing. It often involved covering the same ground twice, but this in itself was useful. Harry would often add or omit details the second time. Also, because by now I understood the story, the questioning was more relevant and the answers sometimes quite surprising.

The tapes were being transcribed in London - a heartbreaking task undertaken by Vaila - while I was doing the re-taping. If transcripts were available I based my questioning on points raised in them. It was a mistake not to have had the first set of tapes fully transcribed as I made them: the second stage would have been much easier. At the beginning I had assumed that because I was only taping once a week I would be able to transcribe the tapes myself, but each one would have taken me at least two days. Any researcher or oral historian should arrange for continual transcribing facilities.

A book could have been produced on the basis of the first set of tapes alone, but it would have been skimpy and lacking a lot of the insights which emerged in that second round. By present publishing standards of 100 pages per book it would have been a book; but not this book.

4. The second set of tapes were transcribed as they were recorded. Each transcript was labelled and the information on each page noted, e.g. 01 p.1-6 Shop-Stewards' Movement, 01 p.7 Rent Strike. With this index in front of me I outlined the contents of each chapter, and by the side of each event listed the pages on which references to that event were to be found: e.g. South West District Committee of Unemployed 1922, Kp14, Zp1-7, Zp11-12, 16p12-13, 20p14-15, 21p16-21, 17p0-12, 24p1-4. These passages were then put together into a series of statements about the event, being as faithful as possible to Harry's original words and intentions. After several false starts, all the passages were worked together into a narrative structure with linking sentences and statements added. I decided against writing introductions to the chapters.

5. Eventually an entire draft was produced which was checked against local and socialist newspapers and books and pamphlets of the period. The most frequent references were to the files of the *Glasgow Herald* (which is indexed from 1909 to 1968), *Forward*, the *Weekly Worker* and the *Daily Worker*, but nearly all the major socialist papers were consulted at one stage or another. Information from them often resulted in a re-working of the first draft -

either disconnecting events which had appeared to be connected, or connecting others. In certain key years the narrative was completely re-worked, often due as much to my own initial lack of knowledge as to Harry's memory being faulty. This work produced an almost entirely new second draft.

6. I re-read all the transcripts with the second draft to see whether any statements had been misinterpreted by me initially or whether any information in the transcripts had been omitted. Any omissions were typed up and provisionally inserted in the second draft.

7. The whole manuscript with the insertions was read *with* Harry. This allowed him to clarify, add or re-write statements, and led to further taping on points he or I wanted to elaborate. We then scrutinised the whole manuscript: should this event be here, even though it happened then, in order to help the story?

8. The second draft, the insertions and the new recorded material were worked into a final third draft. It was checked and re-checked for accuracy before being read *with* Harry. This reading-over took more than a week each time, but was absolutely essential. Harry's final corrections were incorporated into the text, and the manuscript was then sent to the publishers and later edited by Robert Barltrop.

Looking back, I would advise anyone undertaking a similar project to keep a diary. It should have been an obvious thing to do - a diary of the research process is considered an essential in sociology; but because it was an oral history I was working on, another person's life story, it didn't occur to me until too late. I should have recorded the time, date and place of each interview and any major issue we had been discussing prior to tape-recording. Because both sets of tapes were typed up together, such a diary would have been the only record of the dates on which certain events were introduced by Harry into the narrative. The diary would also have been an extremely useful working document. It would have been possible to make extensive notes of the contents of the tapes while I was recording (playing back takes time), and also to take note of any questions or problems that should be raised at another session or at the end of the session. It might have been possible to identify crucial points that needed immediate re-checking, although that probably had to wait until the first draft was produced. Certainly it would have reduced the time taken to produce the book.

In the first draft I included lengthy introductions to edited extracts from the tape-recordings. But this form of presentation would have made Harry's life story inaccessible for the general reader. I therefore re-wrote the book as a narrative, adding in sentences and re-working parts of Harry's descriptions. Instead of adding notes on the people and organisations mentioned by him, information about them was inserted in the text. All these additions were not only approved by Harry, but often grew out of one or two remarks of his own. The book is therefore very much the product of a relationship between two people.

For those historians who would have wished to use this book as 'unadulterated' source material, this will be a disappointment. For them it would have been preferable to have my insertions indentifiable in some way, and Harry's mistakes left uncorrected except in footnotes. But they would be mistaken in thinking that, under those circumstances, the interviewer's influence on the final result would be limited. Another interviewer would have produced a different book; it might have given the appearance of presenting the 'pure' Harry McShane without in fact doing so. The very act of questioning makes the interview itself a joint production, and the book depends on who is asking the questions as well as who is answering. Harry had been given a tape-recording machine to record his life before I knew him - but that isn't how a book like this is written.

As E.H.Carr long ago pointed out in *What is History?*, it is impossible for the collection and organisation of the material not to impose a theoretical structure. The only difference in oral history is that *two* interpretations are at work. Harry is steeped in the history of the period, and so am I. I saw it as part of my job to select statements which were original to him and belonged to his experience, as against ones he had read and was not necessarily committed to. Whenever he discussed a particular event or organisation - such as the Clyde Workers' Committee - I always asked what *he* did, and weighted the amount of space in the book accordingly.

Equally, Harry saw his job as to tell me the things he thought it was important to know, and the lessons which could be drawn. He was teaching me, and through me another generation, what he had discovered. One example will make the point. In Chapter 5 Harry discusses why the most developed Shop-Stewards Committee he knew before the first world war was Weir's. Several answers are given to this question: that because work was steady in Weir's the ILP members there were not frightened of victimisation, that the modernised layout made it easier to organise the men, that the bonus system gave an added importance to the role of the shop-stewards collectively. These several answers to the same question were actually given over three different interviews. (I forget which answer came first.) All the reasons appeared to me potentially important, and therefore they are all written into the book. It was only when I began to get the same answers repeated that I stopped asking the question. This is because for *me* it was an important question.

There were dozens of similar incidents, which means that the questions that I considered important helped shape the book. Obviously it would have been possible to organise the questioning more objectively. I could have presented Harry with a series of questions culled from secondary sources. During the first set of tapes that is what I did do (in a rather unorganised way), but it didn't really get us far. I also used the interview schedule of the Essex project (see Paul Thompson, *The Edwardians*), as can be seen from the early chapters; and the questionnaire prepared by John Foster on the General Strike in Glasgow - I adapted questions to fit different periods in Harry's life. But in reality the book is most interesting where either Harry or I wanted to discuss an event from a different perspective. His own life and reading had led him to differ from many others, and my research often supported his interpretation or led to other ideas of my own.

Obviously it did matter to the book that Harry and I shared the same concerns and the same understanding of marxism as a theory of the self-activity of the working class and of workers' power (and *not* about state control). I think it is possible for someone from a marxist tradition to understand other forms of consciousness, but it would be impossible for a non-marxist to make sense of Harry's life. This means that in the last resort the truth of a book depends upon both the person himself and the researcher - there are no facts that cannot be reinterpreted from one class viewpoint or another, or from one party line to another. I think that both Harry and I have attempted to be scrupulously honest. My respect and affection for Harry and Harry's life and work would not allow me to distort his experience in order to write a 'party line' of my own, and for any future Harry McShane who may read this book it is important to tell the truth.

Harry's memory is fallible and I have attempted to check that, but whenever I have thought that his story illustrates this or that point that *I* wished to make I have omitted it, unless it was a point that he also saw. There is a handful of incidents I haven't been able to verify, and I have tried to indicate this in the text either by the words 'I think' or by some other formula. Everything else has been verified and re-written in the light of existing documents, apart from the whole period Harry was in the army (I was not able to check the *Police Gazette*).

I hope that the original tape-recordings will be made available in various libraries for others to use, and copies of the transcripts.

When I started taping Harry I was already working on a comparative study of working-class movements in Glasgow and Liverpool from 1906 to 1931, and therefore was familiar with the written primary sources for Glasgow in part of Harry's lifetime. The whole project of taping Harry, alongside my own research, proved to me the value of oral history as an added dimension of historical research. It is not a substitute; but, if used properly, it can give insights which other research cannot. The taping of people involved in the period is also a protection against the 'hindsight' of contemporary historians, or even of the autobiographies written in the 1930s.

At present it is impossible for me to tell how far Harry's attitudes and experiences can be generalised. He was, and is, a rare man. A catholic who becomes a skilled engineer before the first world war, who works with John Maclean, becomes the leader of the Scottish unemployed, and leaves the Communist Party at the age of sixty-two to remain a revolutionary socialist, is not a *typical* man. But a marxist understanding of society doesn't rely upon the typical. Harry McShane always was a member of an organisation who tried to change the world, tried to influence and lead a mass of men round him in the light of the strategy of that organisation - he was Gramsci's 'good sense thinker' *par excellence*: a leader who could translate marxism for the masses. His own understanding of the period is therefore very important, in terms of challenging the shibboleths of contemporary historians.

It is questionable whether there is any point in trying to identify *the* 'British Bolshevik party' before the early twenties. From Harry's narrative it is quite clear that none of the revolutionary sects of the time deserves the title. The British Socialist Party was committed to a 'political' battle, and even John Maclean's anti-war fight did not contain an industrial strategy (nor did he have the organisation to discipline other BSP members like Gallacher who were shop-stewards, to carry such a strategy through). The main contender, the Socialist Labour Party, had its chief support in Glasgow. The SLP had a disciplined organisation and an industrial strategy, but on the two major questions facing the working class - the war and Ireland - they were split. Their leading industrial theoretician, Johnny Muir, drew up the CWC dilution document which illustrates the limitation of the SLP strategy.

Harry's memoirs also raise the question of what is learned from pure experience without theory. Maclean did not learn the need for a disciplined organisation from the split of 1916; the SLP did not learn the need for a hard political position out of the war and Ireland; the BSP did not learn the need for an industrial strategy. There needed to be a theory of the party and of the revolutionary as a tribune of the people, as well as a theory of workers' power through soviets, before the British movement could re-make itself. Even if all the disparate sects of the British revolutionary movement had united themselves in 1920, without the influence of Russia, there is little evidence that their combined strategies would have spontaneously produced a practice superior to their previous efforts.

Given the above, it is possible to develop an understanding of the first Shop-Stewards Movement as a rank-and-file movement without a revolutionary party giving revolutionary leadership. It reacted to events rather than being able to impose its will upon them. Having fought a successful wages battle (the most unifying kind of fight) it was faced with something far more difficult, a plant-by-plant struggle over dilution with its own leadership split. One faction was represented by Muir and the SLP; the other held the possibility of an ILP alternative leadership.

The histories of the Clyde Workers' Committee and of the Rent Strike bring out the importance of organisations. Those who, because of the absence of a united revolutionary movement, have concentrated on the 'spontaneity' of the British movement have seen only one side of the picture. The leaders of the CWC were members of different revolutionary organisations. The leaders of the Rent Strike were members of a reformist organisation, the ILP, which had a strong housing policy dating back before the war. When the CWC split during the war, the division was between ILP influence and that of the BSP and SLP: between reformists and revolutionaries.

It is important also to separate the ideology of an organisation from the actual practice of its membership. It was not the SLP who formed the Weir's Shop-Stewards Committee before the first world war, but ILP members.

Harry's life stresses the most important element missing from the practice of any revolutionary party in Britain - support for the Irish struggle. It is no accident that both Hyndman and Blatchford, who ultimately became rabid nationalists, were always appalling in their attitude to Ireland. In the period before and after the first world war the question of Ireland is one of the acid tests. By that test revolutionaries can be found in the SLP and BSP and even potentially the ILP; and non-revolutionaries in them all.

Above all, I found that Harry's understanding of his experiences cured me of treating the working class of his lifctime as 1960s and 1970s engineers and dockers, only born a little earlier. His generation were *not* Victorian working men with their own specific skills, or lack of them, but neither were they men of a modern homogeneous working class. Harry's description of the Clyde Workers' Committee meeting - men in blue suits, bowler hats and carrying rolled umbrellas - was a sufficient corrective to my earlier view.

There are also much more specific insights. I had already noticed the references to barber shops in the autobiographies of some Scottish socialists. When Harry too stressed the number of meetings he had in barbers' shops with other socialists I began to understand how important these centres were. It was also clear that if shopkeepers like the Cater brothers (Hyndman supporters) were as prepared as John McAteer to hide guns in 1905, the attitude to violence must have been completely different in the movement then. Harry's memories of songs which were sung at periods of crisis are also important. It was an Irish audience that sang 'God Save Ireland' for John Maclean; it was a mass movement that sang 'My Ain Wee House' in 1919 and 'The Wells o' Werie' on the Hunger March.

It is instructive to note the two most important areas - as far as I am aware - missing from Harry's narrative. First, as a revolutionary socialist he was not particularly concerned with the fate of the trade union movement and the Labour Party. Neither Taff Vale nor Osborne was important to him; even though the former happened while he was very young, it did not become significant for him in retrospect. I suspect that while the official trade-union and Labour Party leaders and subsequent historians were greatly concerned with these issues, they were not crucial for the creation of revolutionary socialists. Socialists like Harry had little sympathy with either craft-trade unionism or the Labour Party, and certainly no coherent united political and industrial strategy. With their minds on propaganda, they had better issues to propagandise about.

Second, Harry has no consistent position with regard to the oppression of women, and it is clear that this was true of the entire socialist movement. The women who were active as leaders in it appear to have been widows and single women. That is hardly surprising - maintaining a family was hard, heavy labour in Glasgow as in other working-class homes. The iron ranges used for cooking and heating and the old wash-houses are proof enough of how little leisure women had. The women's contingents on the hunger marches were most successful from those regions which had a tradition of married women working, especially Lancashire, although Wales also sent women on its hunger march. The lack of a women's movement in those years is obviously a very serious lack, for much of the legislation aimed against the unemployed hit them hardest. The Anomalies Act prevented women workers claiming unemployment benefit, while the Household Means Test destroyed their home lives. It is obvious that our present-day movement has been transformed in this regard largely by the expectations of the women themselves.

Index

Date Due